IMAGES
*of America*

# EPPING

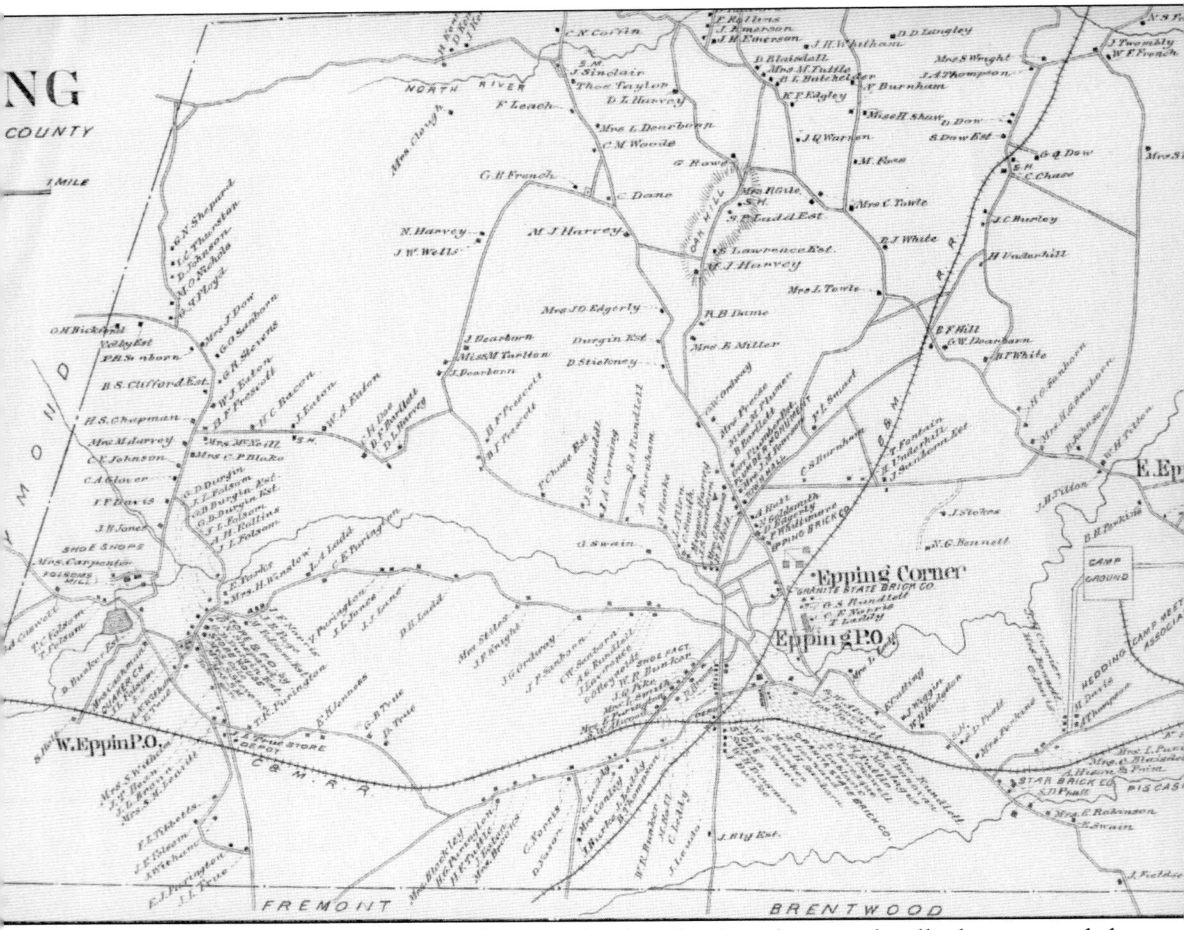


This 1892 map of Epping shows the many brickyards, shoe shops, and mills that powered the town's economic development in the 19th and 20th centuries. The crossing of the north-south running Boston & Maine Railway and the east-west running Concord & Montreal Railway can be seen at bottom center. A spur that ran from the Concord & Montreal Railway to the Methodist Camp Hedding can be seen at right. Prominent geographical features include the North River, Red Oak Hill, the Lamprey River, and the Piscasick (Piscassic) River. (Courtesy of the Epping Historical Society.)

**On the Cover:** The Folsom Saw Mill and Box Factory was established in 1876 by David and Thomas Folsom, next to the West Epping mill dam. Employees of the mill take time to pose for a picture. The wagon hitched to a pair of fine horses contains milled planks, and more stacks of planks can be seen in the background. Three boys have climbed a pile of boards to get into the picture. This bend in the Lamprey River supported mill operations beginning in 1746. (Courtesy of the Epping Historical Society.)

IMAGES
*of America*

# EPPING

Corey D. Blanchard

ARCADIA
PUBLISHING

ISBN 978-1-4671-2303-7

Published by Arcadia Publishing
Charleston, South Carolina

Printed in the United States of America

Library of Congress Control Number: 2014948297

For all general information, please contact Arcadia Publishing:
Telephone 843-853-2070
Fax 843-853-0044
E-mail sales@arcadiapublishing.com
For customer service and orders:
Toll-Free 1-888-313-2665

Visit us on the Internet at www.arcadiapublishing.com

*This book is dedicated to the men and women of the armed services and the public servants of the town of Epping.*

# Contents


| | | |
|---|---|---|
| Acknowledgments | | 6 |
| Introduction | | 7 |
| 1. | Main Streets and Back Roads | 9 |
| 2. | Places of Worship and Centers of Learning | 41 |
| 3. | Hedding | 51 |
| 4. | Farming | 61 |
| 5. | The Lamprey | 69 |
| 6. | Industry | 85 |
| 7. | Eppinites | 107 |
| Bibliography | | 127 |

# ACKNOWLEDGMENTS

This book would not have been possible without the help and support of the Epping Historical Society. Special thanks go to Joy True for throwing open the doors of the historical society for my many hours of research. Unless otherwise noted, the images in this book come from the collection of the Epping Historical Society.

Robert Goodrich generously donated images and information on Epping's brickmaking past. An important piece of Epping's culture would have been woefully missing if not for his help.

Donald Sanborn spent years clipping newspapers, taking notes, and preserving images of Epping's past. Everyone in the town of Epping, myself included, owes him a great debt.

This opportunity would not have been possible without Arcadia Publishing and the help of my editor, Caitrin Cunningham.

I would also like to thank those who have guided my career in the study of history. Epping teachers Susan McGeough, Michael O'Donnell, and Carol Bartlett helped foster a curiosity into a passion. University of New Hampshire professors Jeffrey Bolster, Eliga Gould, Jessica Lepler, and Cynthia Van Zandt have taught me more than I could have expected to learn about history and becoming a professional historian. Much of the credit for my undertaking this process goes to them.

Finally, my friends and family have given me more support than I could have expected. Special thanks go to my parents, Earl and Joyce Blanchard; my brothers, Jason and Todd Blanchard; Joicey McEdward; Norma Dodge; Irene Burhoe; and Jessica Anderson.

# INTRODUCTION

The land that is now Epping was left with rolling hills, winding rivers, deep forests, and even deeper deposits of clay after the retreat of the great ice sheets that covered the North American continent. Native Americans of the Squamscott subtribe of the Pennacok Nation hunted and gathered along the banks of the Lamprey River, atop Red Oak Hill, and in the forests. In fields, they planted the "three sisters": corn, beans, and squash. The tall, sturdy corn stalks acted as trellises to support the beans while the broad leaves of the squash plants guarded against water and wind erosion and prevented the growth of weeds. This Native American system of farming both increased crop yields per acre and reduced the amount of labor needed to support the field.

When Rev. John Wheelwright helped found Exeter, one of the four original towns of New Hampshire, in 1639, European settlers began drifting into the part of Exeter that would become Epping. For a time, European settlers and their Native American neighbors were able to live without incident. That changed with the start of King Philip's War, named after the Native American leader King Philip, in 1675. The war originated in Plymouth Colony due to tensions that arose from European encroachment on traditional Native American lands. The war soon spread throughout New England, bringing tremendous violence and destruction from both European soldiers and Native American warriors. Three garrison houses were constructed within Epping to help protect the western boundary of Exeter. Though King Philip's War largely subsided after the death of King Philip in 1676, the severity and cruelty of the war left bitter tensions between New Englanders and Native Americans for many years.

Thereafter, conflicts persisted between Europeans and Native Americans. During Queen Anne's War, which lasted from 1702 to 1713, Col. Winthrop Hilton, the highest-ranking New Hampshire officer, made himself notorious among the Native Americans for his part in the raid on Grand-Pré; the 1707 ambush and massacre of 18 Native Americans at Casco, Maine; and the siege of Port Royal. On June 23, 1710, while Colonel Hilton and 16 of his men were striping bark off trees felled for use as masts in Epping, a group of Native Americans ambushed and killed the colonel and two others. Colonel Hilton's body was reported at the time to have been found scalped with a hatchet stuck in the head and a lance through the heart.

As the years of turmoil slowly settled into an uneasy peace in Exeter, more and more settlers made their way into Epping. By 1741, it was decided by the residents of what would become Epping that the nine-mile trip to Exeter was too far to travel to attend town meetings and worship at the church. This was a common justification for the creation of new towns throughout New England at the time. Nine miles over hot and dusty roads in the summer, muddy and flooded roads in the spring and fall, and snow- and ice-covered roads in the winter could be dangerous or downright impossible to travel every Sunday to worship in the church that was most often supported by taxes. This led many parishes to apply to support their own church, which most often meant being established as their own towns. Epping's petition, signed by 56 members of the community, was accepted, and it became the first town to be incorporated by the first governor of the province of

New Hampshire, Benning Wentworth. Governor Wentworth, who had spent time in England, named the new town Epping for Epping in the county of Essex, England.

Now established as an independent town, Epping began to steadily grow in population and influence. In 1746, Joshua Folsom built the first mill in West Epping on the Lamprey River. Many more mills followed in the years to come as the winding Lamprey River proved to be a perfect source of hydropower. More farms sprang up in the fields and over the rolling hills as lumbering operations continued to supply masts and planks for New England shipbuilding and the construction of more homes, barns, warehouses, and all manner of businesses.

Epping continued to grow spiritually as well. In 1747, the Congregational Church hired Rev. Robert Cutler as its first pastor. The church grew in popularity under Rev. Josiah Stearns. Hired on in 1758, Reverend Stearns's sermons drew large crowds that filled the church to capacity. He would later be a strong supporter of seeking independence from Great Britain, giving both money and his sons to the struggle for independence. In 1772, Joshua Folsom began preaching to the Epping Society of Friends, better known as Quakers for the way that some would begin to tremble as they were touched by the inner light.

After the 1775 raid on Fort William and Mary in Portsmouth Harbor, 8 out of about 100 barrels of powder seized by New Hampshire patriots were stored in Epping. In 1775, Epping had a population of 1,569, and when the Committee of Safety of New Hampshire requested that the selectmen of each town have males over the age of 21 sign the Association Test in 1776, a total of 209 men signed the pledge, which read, "We the subscribers do hereby solemnly engage and promise that we will, do the utmost of our power, at the risk of our lives and fortunes, with arms oppose the hostile proceedings of the British fleets and armies against the United American Colonies." Of the 181 men of Epping who fought during the American Revolution, at least one was present at the Battles of Lexington, Bunker Hill, Trenton, and Saratoga, as well as the doomed March on Quebec and more. Col. Henry Dearborn, who spent most of his youth in Epping, distinguished himself at Bunker Hill, Ticonderoga, Freeman's Farm, Saratoga, and Monmoth and was present for General Cornwallis's surrender at Yorktown. He rose to the rank of major general and later served in the War of 1812.

After the struggles of the American Revolution and the War of 1812, Epping began to slowly grow again. More mills were established along the Lamprey River. In 1822, Levi Thompson established the first commercial brickyard in Epping, beginning the run of a long and prosperous enterprise for the town. The story of Epping throughout the 19th and 20th centuries is an interesting mix of industrialization and farming, town and country, political heavyweights and the average everyman.

# *One*

# Main Streets and Back Roads

As Epping's economy and population evolved, so did the town itself. A vibrant downtown that ran along Main Street sprang up. Shops in which Epping residents could buy anything from groceries to farm equipment to a new dress or suit created a self-sustaining efficiency that could support everyone in town. Farmers bought farm equipment downtown and then sold their produce to the grocers that lined Main Street. Businessmen and women could find fashionable and high-quality footwear in the shops that sold shoes made right in Epping's factories. Fires that occasionally swept through downtown, leveling houses and businesses alike, only led to newer and finer buildings on the main thoroughfare.

The crossroads of Main Street, which ran north-south; Pleasant Street, which ran west to Raymond; and Water Street, which ran east to Exeter, became the focal point of Epping. Both Pleasant Street and Water Street gave rise to more shops for goods and workshops of tradespeople. Churches and houses lined Main Street, Pleasant Street, and Water Street as they ran away from the bustling business district.

Following Pleasant Street to the west, one ended up in the village of West Epping. West Epping had its own post office, train depot, shops, factories, and mills that supported a smaller but still vibrant downtown area. While the town center was surely on Main Street, one could get along just fine in the bustle of West Epping village.

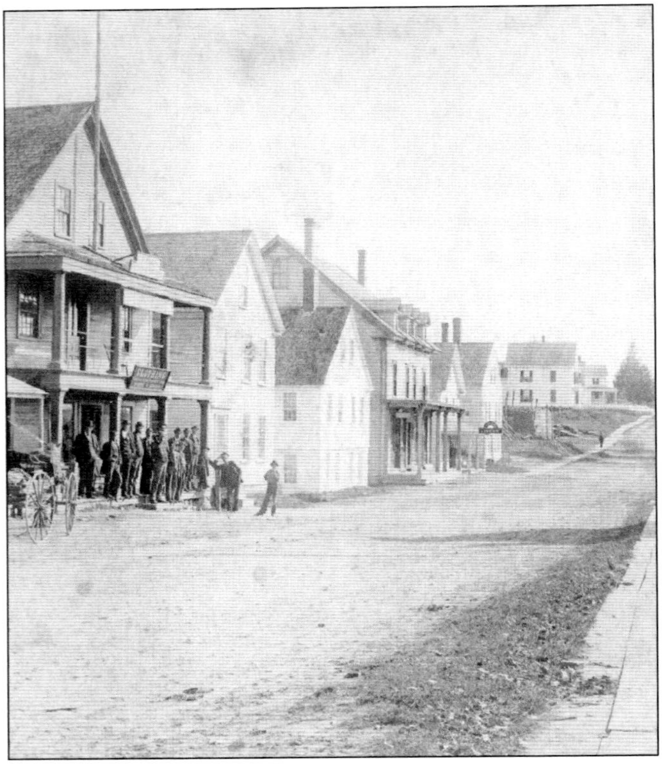

This image of Main Street was taken in 1890. Looking south, it shows a group of men posing in front of a clothing store advertising "Boots and Goods." Down the street is a sign hanging for Jenkins Livery, and past that, new construction is in process. At the lower left, the sidewalks, constructed of wooden planks, are shown. Fire destroyed many of these buildings in 1896.

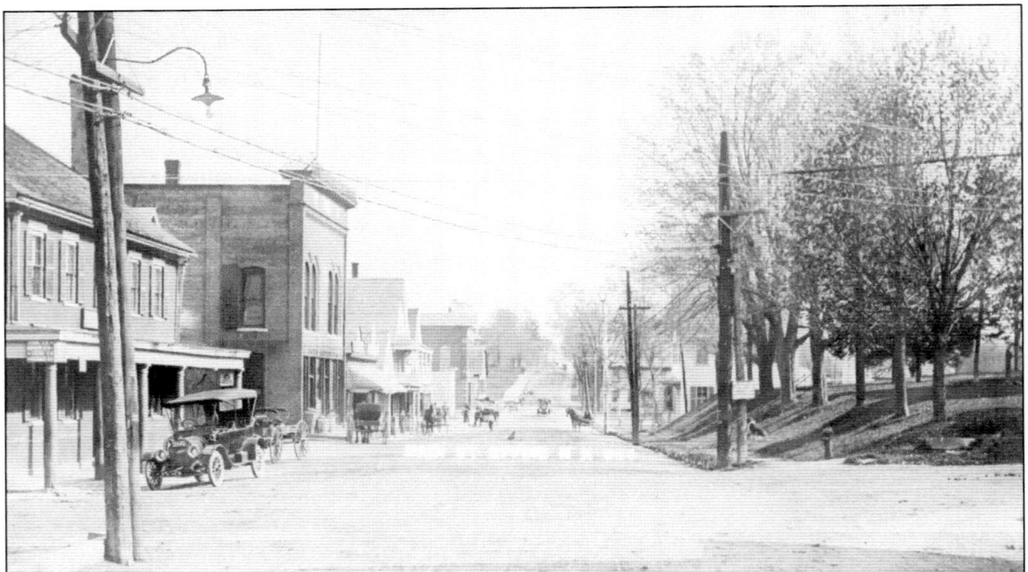

A later view of Main Street shows the development of downtown Epping. Wooden structures have been replaced by brick buildings. Brick buildings were both more resistant to the fires that occasionally took down structures and markers of pride for Epping's brickmaking industry that had begun in 1822. This image also captures an interesting crossover of time when automobiles were beginning to share the roads with horse-drawn carriages.

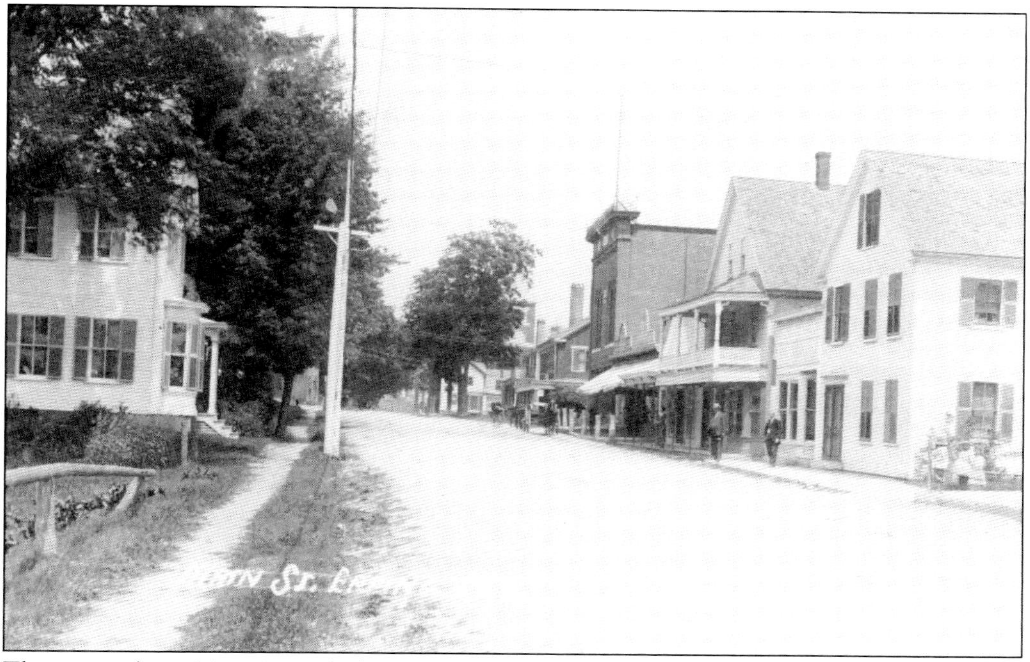

This image shows Main Street looking north. The tall brick building at center is the shop of John Leddy & Co. Here, Epping residents could buy their groceries and other goods. The sidewalks look well trod as two carriages wait for their owners to conclude their business downtown.

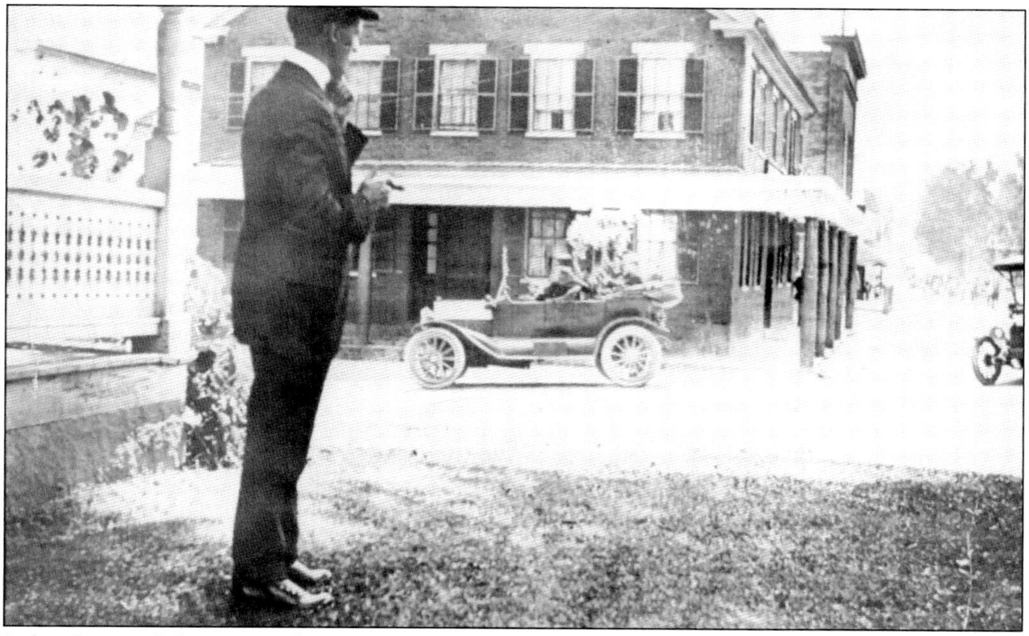

Judge George Gilmore stands on the corner of Main and Water Streets. Perkins Hotel can be seen across the street, as can the edifice of the store of John Leddy & Co. Judge Gilmore is watching the funeral procession of Joseph Proulx as it turns off Main Street and onto Water Street on its way to the Catholic Cemetery.

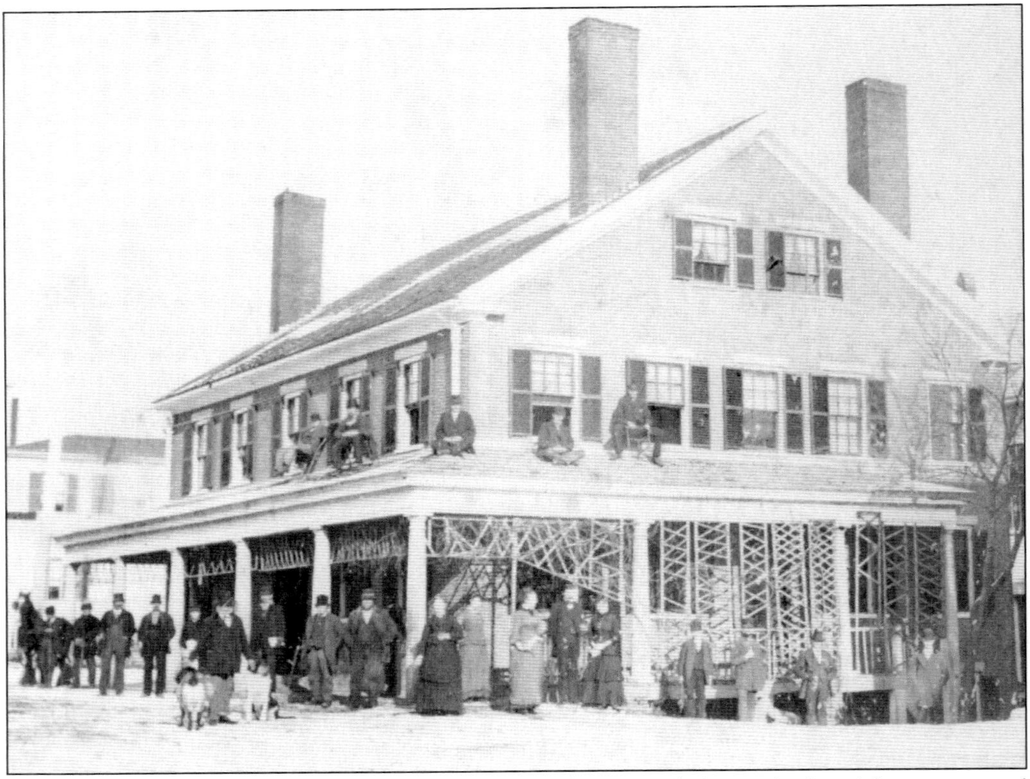

Shown in these images are two views of the large Perkins Hotel. A popular hotel for visitors and travelers to spend a night or two, the Perkins Hotel was operated by William Bunker from 1860 to 1884. The hotel passed hands a few times. G.E. Smith owned the hotel in 1888. In 1891, it was owned by M.D. Manville, and in 1906, it came into the possession of Moses Perkins. When the state of New Hampshire went dry, Moses Perkins decided that the hotel would not be able to survive without the sale of liquor. He closed the doors to the hotel, and it burned down after lying vacant for about a year.

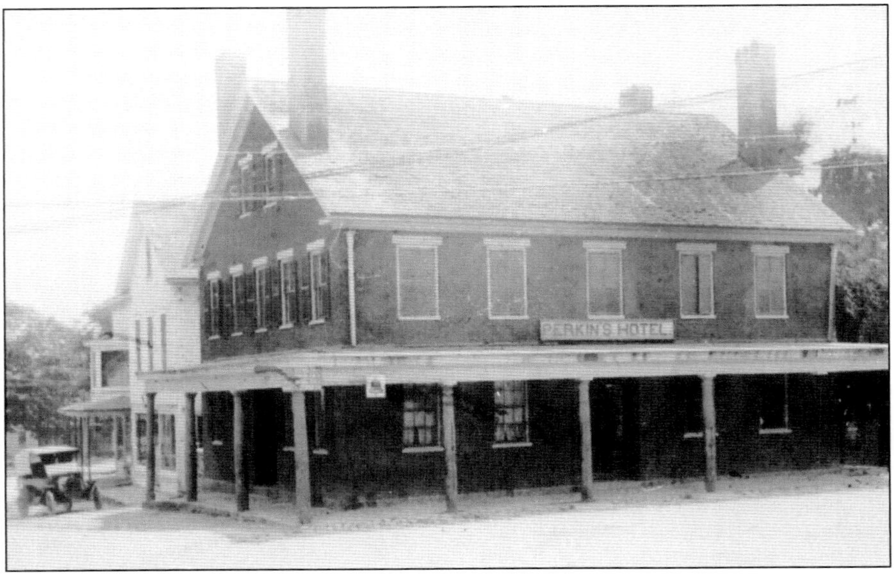

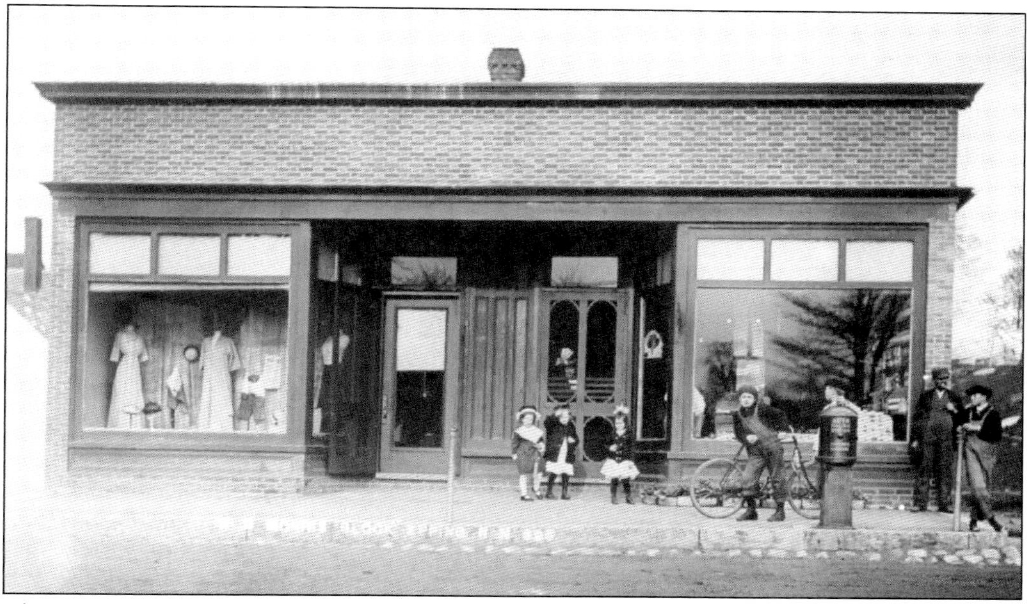

The W.R. Morris Block, owned by Bill Morris, is pictured here in 1914. By this time, the Main Street sidewalks were constructed of brick with granite facings. The shop window shows a sample of fine women's dresses and hats. Three little girls wait for their mother to finish her shopping. Meanwhile, a few boys crowd around an Auto Filling Station for Filtered Gasoline. Automobiles have not completely taken over. The boy to the far right rests on one of the two hitching posts for horses that remain outside the shop.

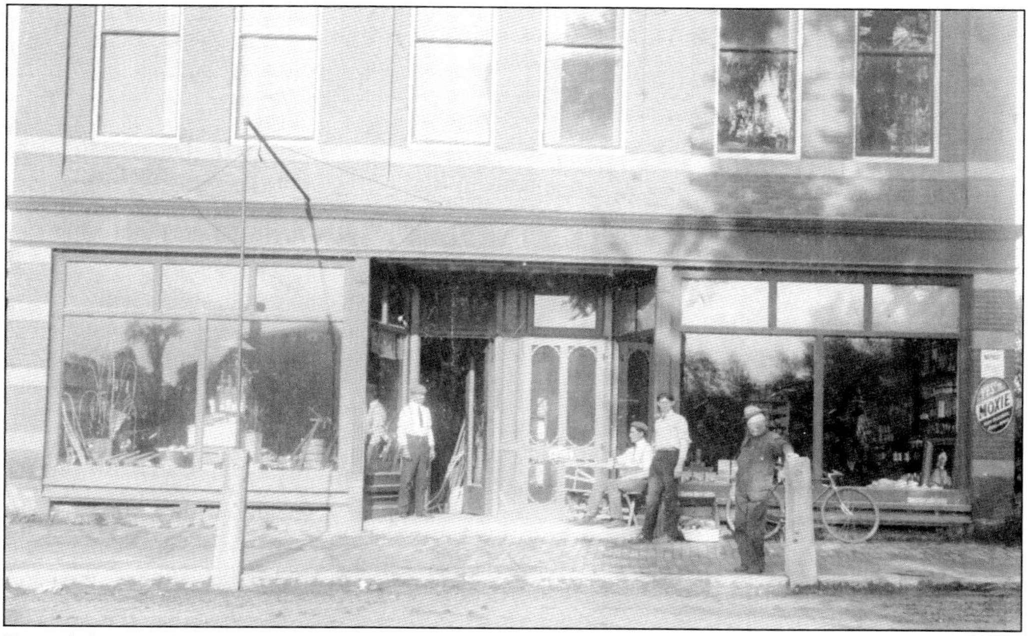

From left to right, N.R. Morris, Jay Thompson, Bum Knight, and Dick Abbot stand outside a shop in the Jordan Block on Main Street in 1900. In the shop window to the right can be seen all manner of dry foods, drink bottles, canned foods, and dishes. In the shop window to the left can be seen farm equipment, brooms, and lamps. There are two advertisements for Moxie, the larger of which reads, "YES! We sell MOXIE, very healthful, feeds the nerves."

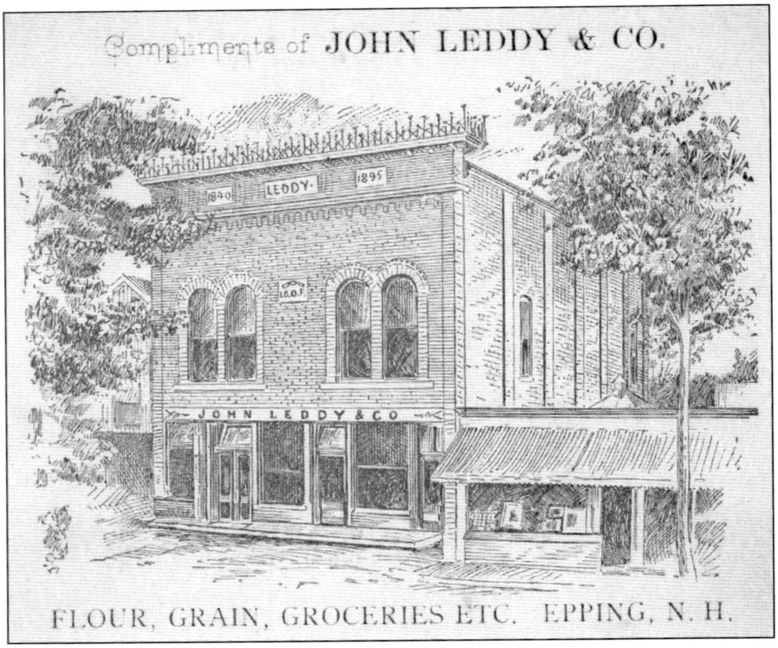


This is a promotional coaster for the store of John Leddy & Co. One of the largest stores in Epping, John Leddy & Co. provided goods to many of the farmers, millworkers, factory workers, and brickmakers in town. Promotions like these coasters could be easily distributed and diffused throughout town and were a good way to drum up business.

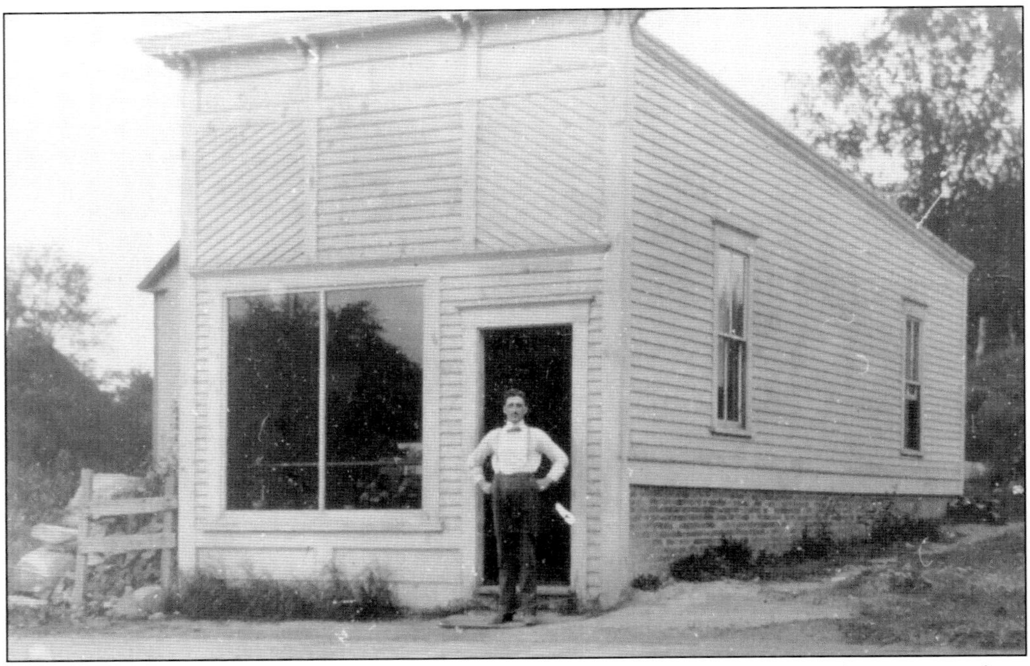

A saloonkeeper stands proudly outside his saloon on Main Street. Most saloonkeepers wore bow ties, as this one is, to avoid accidentally dipping a long tie into a drink. Saloons provided a welcome escape from the hard work of farming, milling, brickmaking, and factory work of Epping. They also provided a location to meet up with friends and swap stories and news.

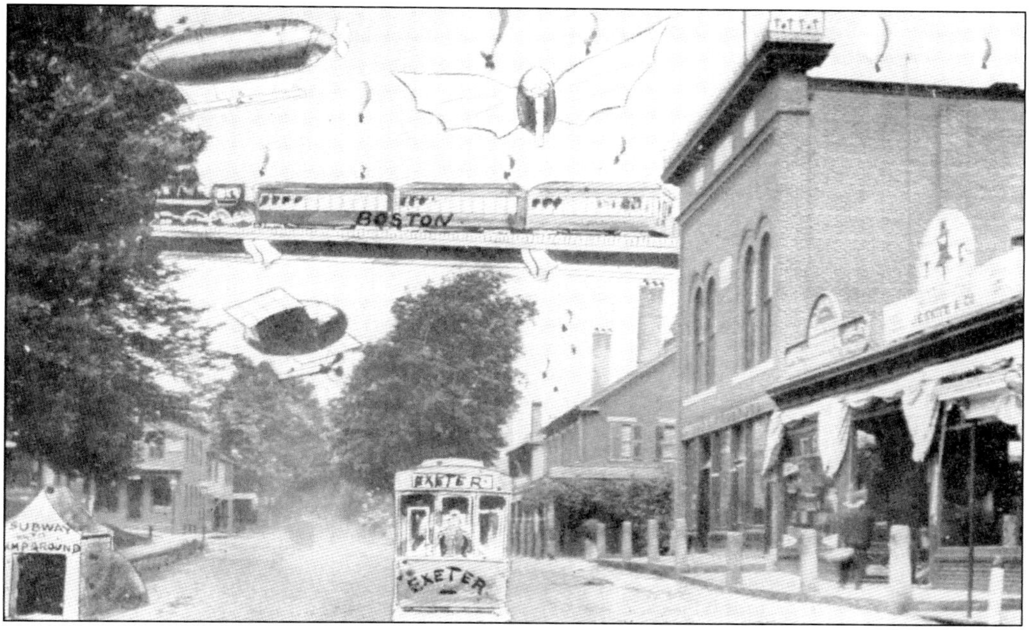


Someone drew this fanciful take on how the future of Epping might look in the early 1900s. A tram is heading down Main Street on its way to Exeter, there is a subway station to take someone to Hedding Campground, an elevated train is available for travel to Boston, and zeppelins and hot-air balloons crowd the sky headed in every direction. This probably did not seem as fanciful to the artist or those who saw it at the time.

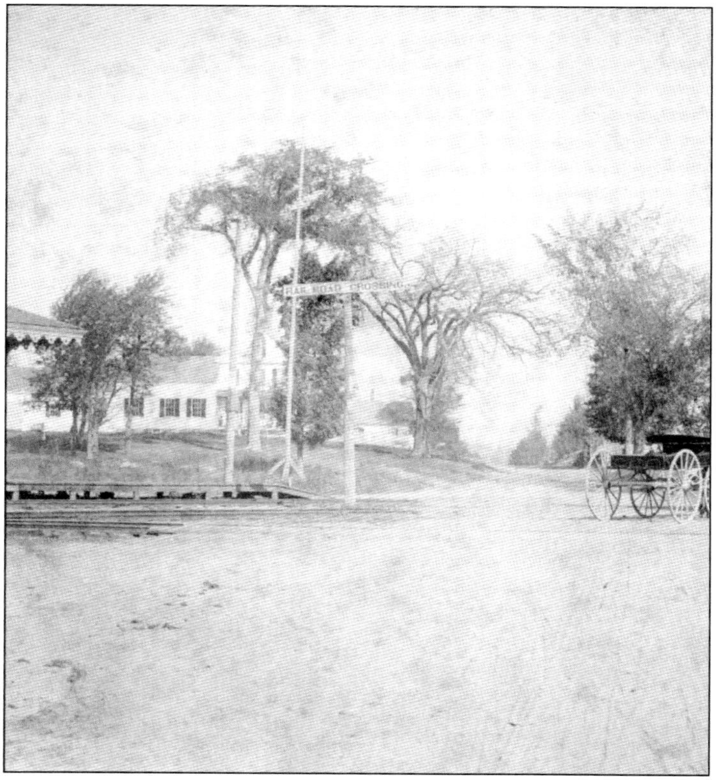

This image of Main Street looking north was taken about 1880. It shows the crossing of the Nashua & Rochester Railroad at the depot. The roof to the depot can be seen to the left. A fine carriage sits on the right, perhaps dropping off a passenger or picking up a returning traveler.

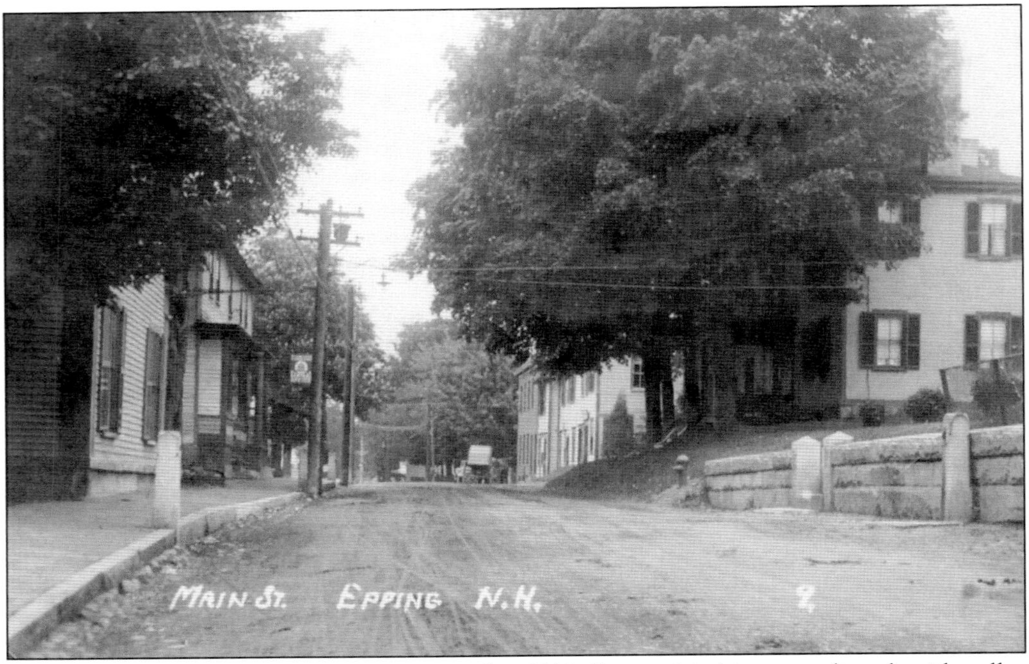

A section of Main Street is seen as it appeared in 1912. Granite hitching posts line the sidewalks. A fire hydrant can be seen at right. Epping had several major fires in the downtown area by 1912, and fire hydrants became necessary additions. Some carriages are hitched in the distance as their owners wander through the shops downtown.

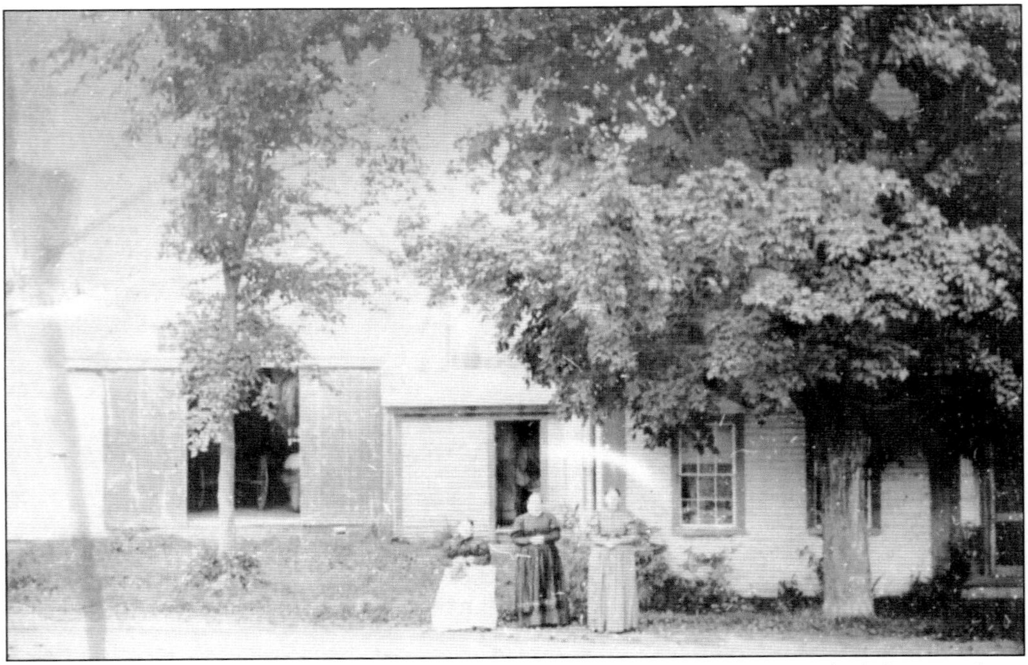
Three women, perhaps Levi Thompson's descendants, pose in a very matronly fashion in front of the Thompson house on Main Street. Levi Thompson founded the first commercial brickyard in Epping in 1822.

In 1892, the town of Epping voted to build a new town hall, and the building in this image was erected the next year. The town hall has a view over the Lamprey River next to the Main Street bridge, at the foot of Boar's Head Hill. Once home to the town offices and police station, complete with jail cells, the building is now solely the home of the town offices. The old iron bars still remain in the cell windows.

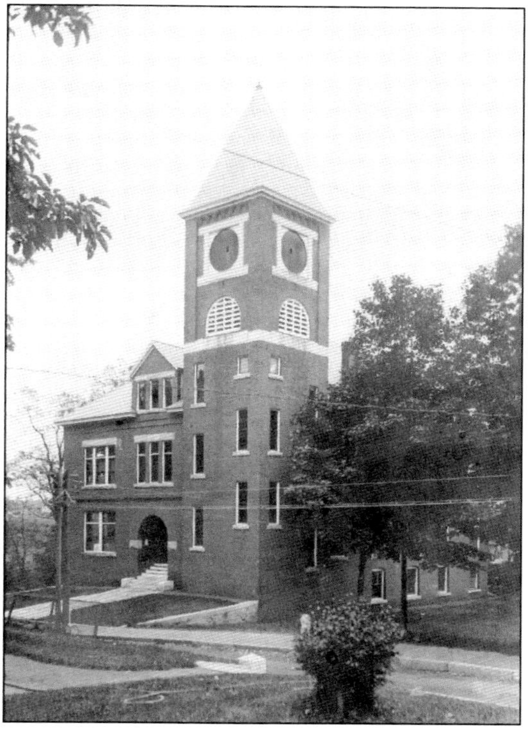

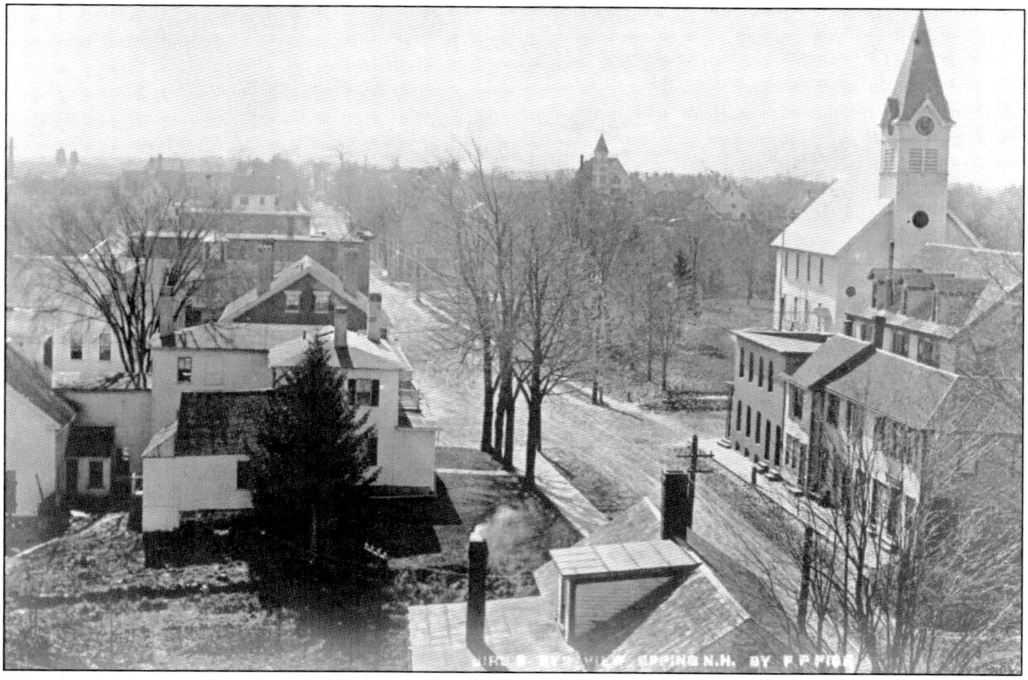


This bird's-eye view of downtown Epping looking south down Main Street was taken from the town hall clock tower in 1917. The bustling intersection of Main, Pleasant, and Water Streets is in the center. Main Street is a tree-lined avenue with houses and businesses alike. To the right is the Congregational Church with its clock tower that chimes the hour to this day. In the distance, at center, is Saint Joseph's Catholic Church.

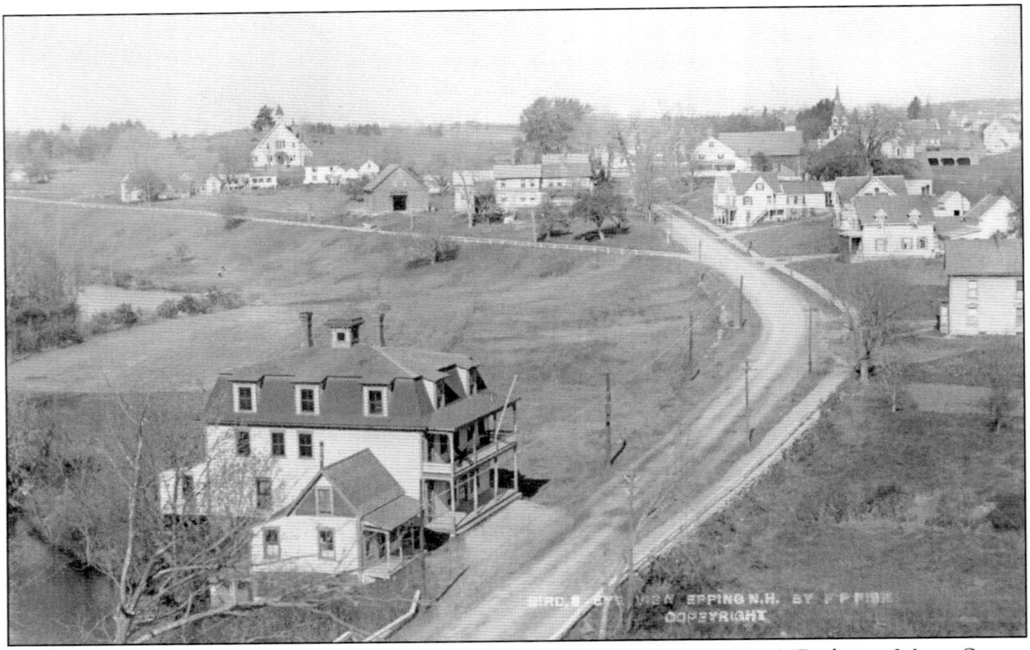


This bird's-eye view, again taken from the town hall clock tower in 1917, shows Main Street stretching north and winding up Boar's Head Hill. The large building at front is the Grange Hall that housed meetings and events for farmers. The smaller building in front of it was a print shop. Atop Boar's Head Hill at right can be seen the steeple of the Methodist church. To the left can be seen Watson Academy, Epping's high school.

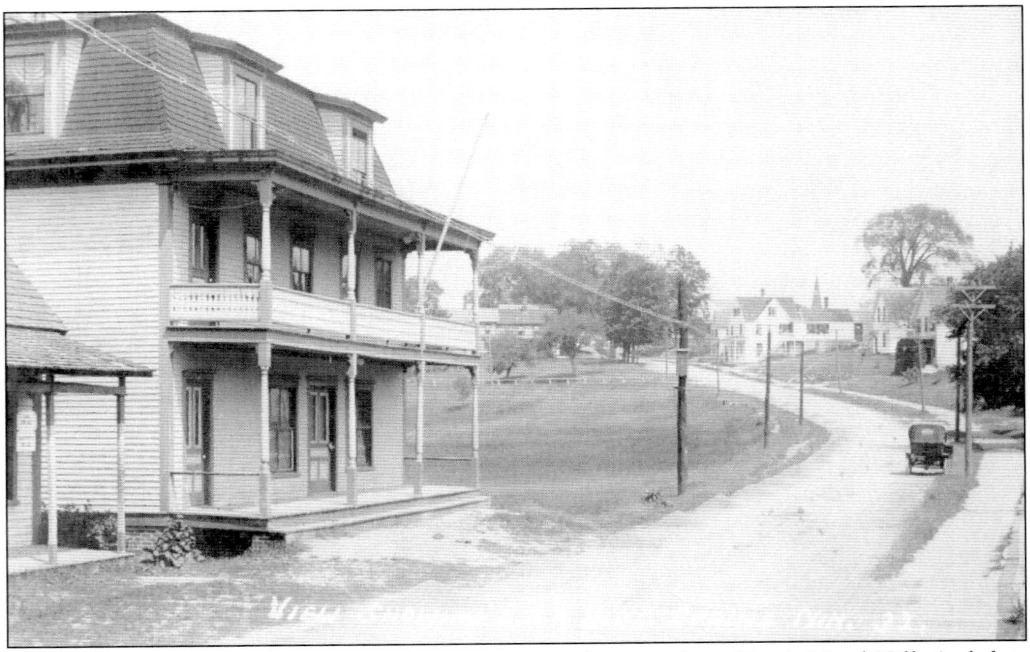

In this street view of Main Street, one can see it winding north up Boar's Head Hill. At left is the print shop next to the large, three-story Grange Hall. In the distance at right, the steeple of the Methodist church pokes up above the houses of Boar's Head Hill.

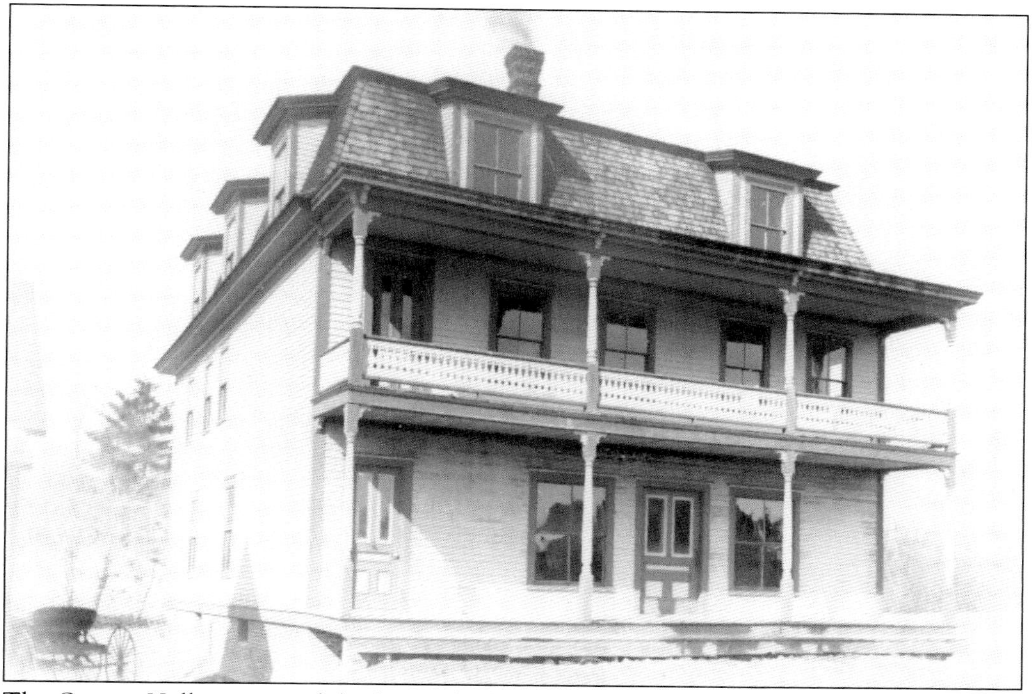

The Grange Hall was one of the largest buildings on this side of Main Street. It sits wedged between Main Street and the Lamprey River. Farmers held meetings to discuss crop rotation, irrigation, fertilizing, and new techniques. Dances and parties were also held to mark holidays, harvests, and other special events.

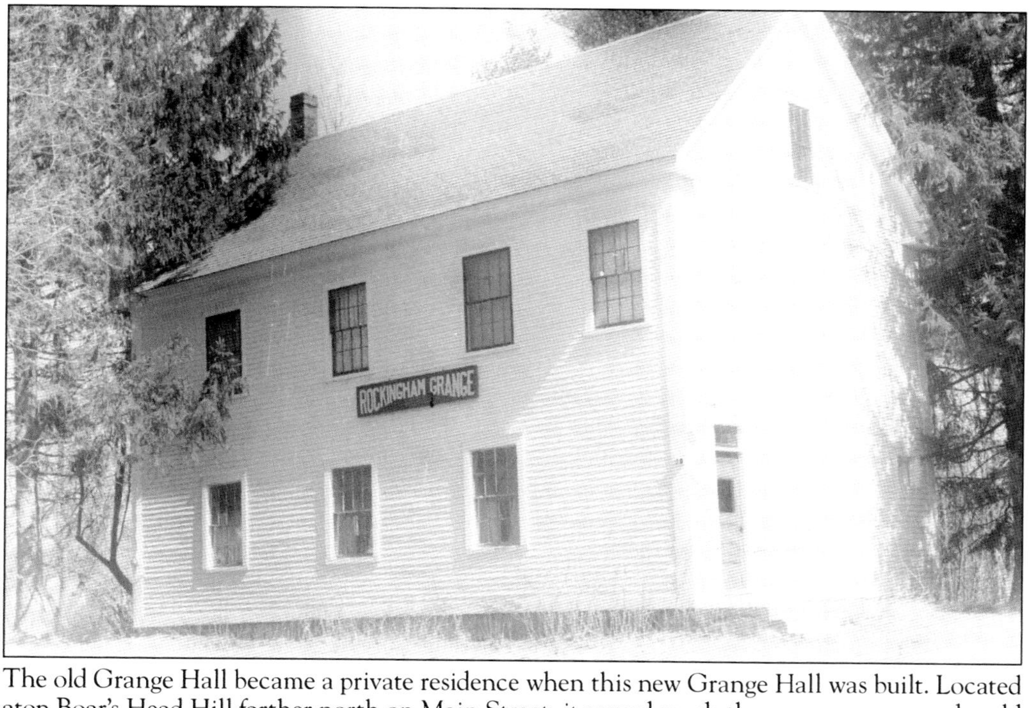


The old Grange Hall became a private residence when this new Grange Hall was built. Located atop Boar's Head Hill farther north on Main Street, it served much the same purpose as the old Grange Hall. This building still serves as the Grange for Epping's farmers.

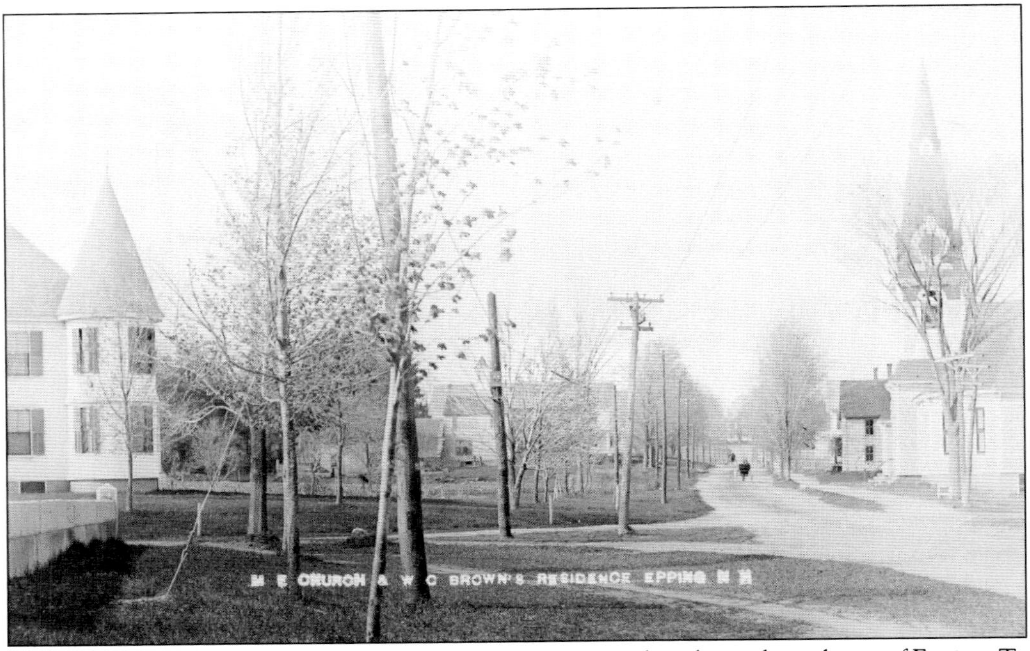

Main Street stretches north atop Boar's Head Hill. This is a largely residential area of Epping. To the right is the Methodist church. To the extreme left can be seen the granite wall of Epping's central cemetery. The fine home to the left was the residence of William C. Brown, a factory owner and successful businessman.

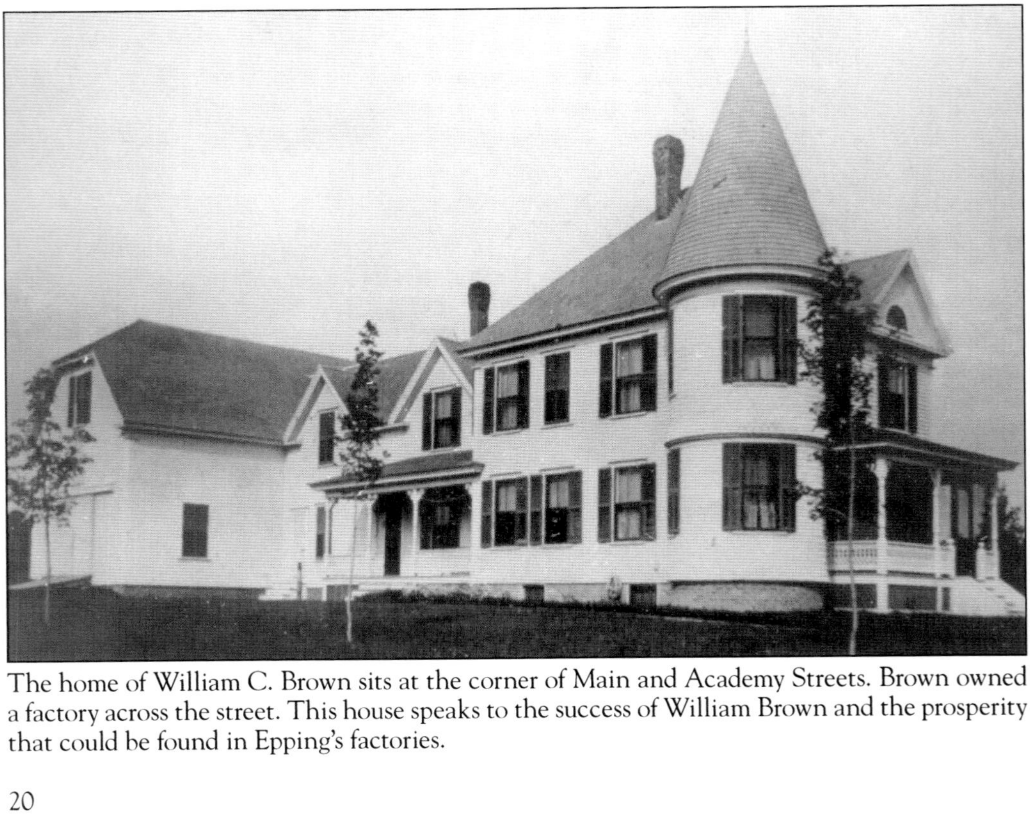
The home of William C. Brown sits at the corner of Main and Academy Streets. Brown owned a factory across the street. This house speaks to the success of William Brown and the prosperity that could be found in Epping's factories.

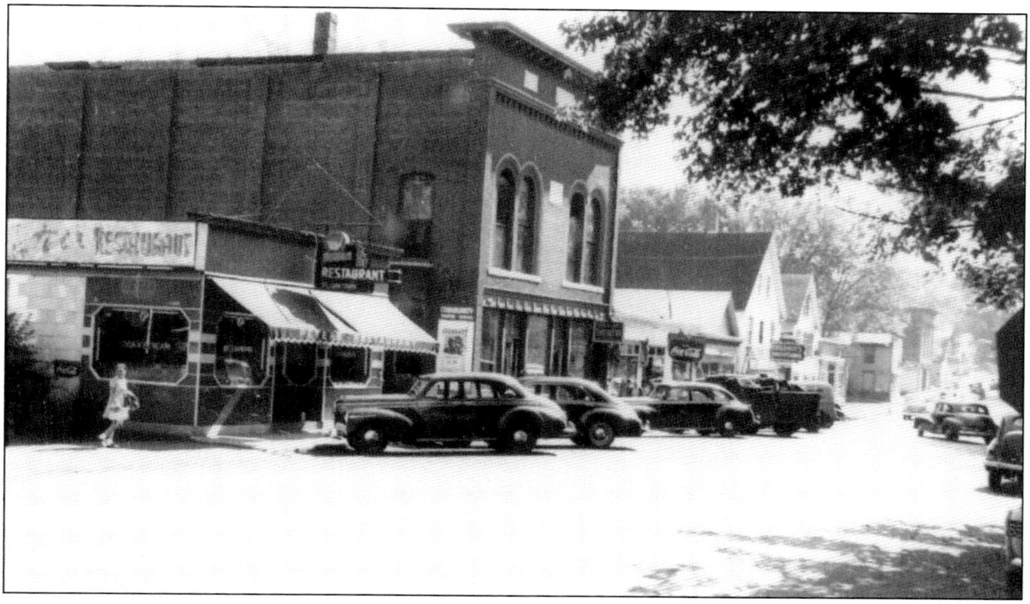


Two views of Main Street in the 1950s are shown in these images. The above image is taken from the Main, Pleasant, and Water Streets intersection looking south. A young girl looks to be crossing Main Street but might be heading into Peters Restaurant for a soda or ice cream. By this time, the John Leddy & Co. building had been converted into a community theater. The image below is taken down the street, looking north, by the W.R. Morris Block building that now houses Clover Farm Stores. The store advertises meats, groceries, and beer. Farther down Main Street is Caraway's Provisions. By the 1950s, Main Street remained the primary business district of Epping. Aside from modernized buildings, not much had changed besides the newer automobiles and the absence of carriages.

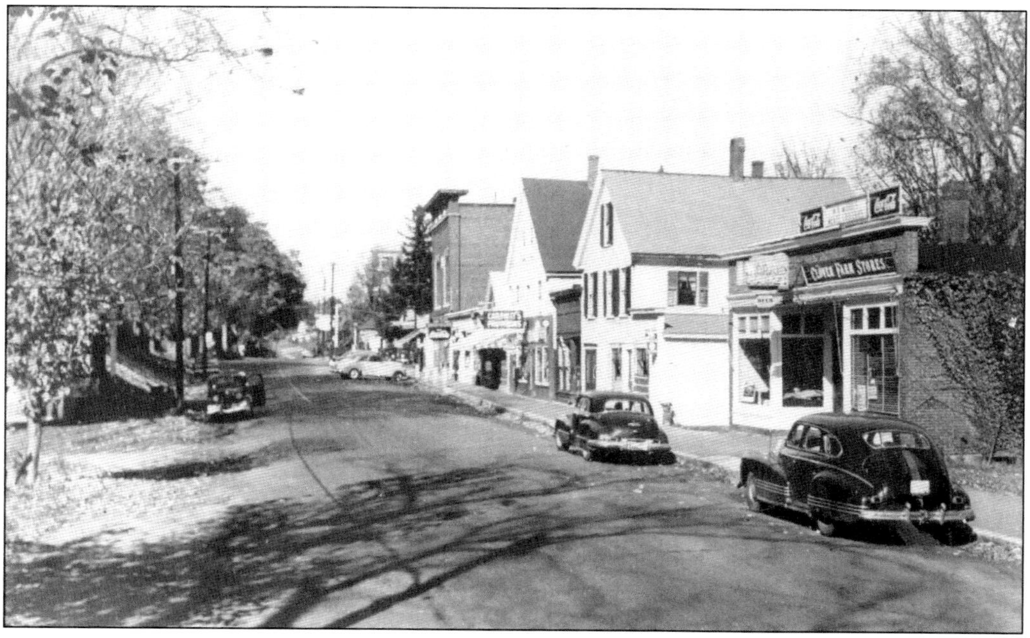

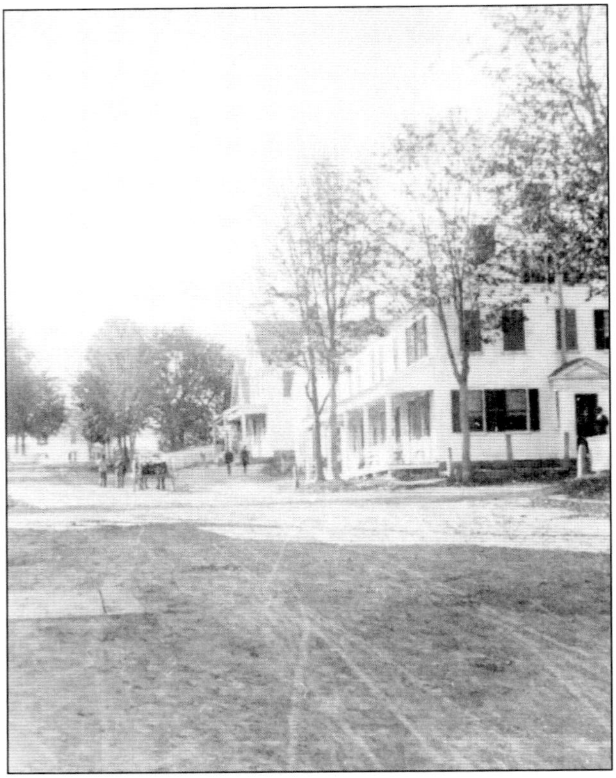

The house of James Rundlett was a large whitewashed Colonial with a porch that faced Pleasant Street. Taken looking west down Pleasant Street from the intersection with Main Street, which can be seen running perpendicular, this image shows people strolling down the broad avenue and a carriage, perhaps headed to West Epping or farther on to Raymond.

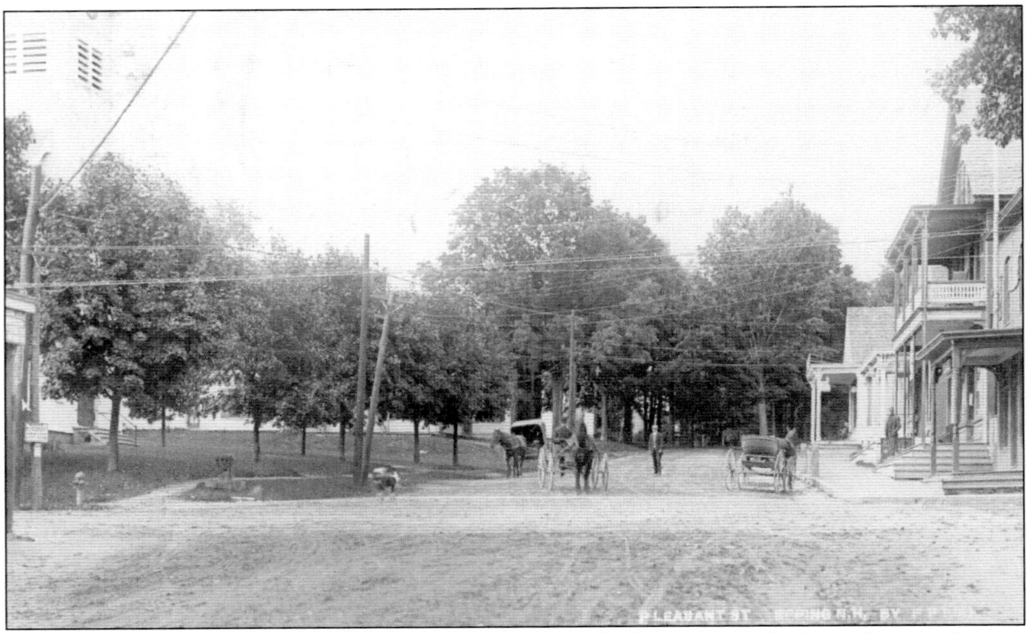

This photograph shows a later view of Pleasant Street looking west. The large house of James Rundlett is now gone, replaced in 1884 by the brick building to the extreme right. To the extreme left is a signpost marking the distances to Raymond and Exeter. Another sign posted on a telephone pole reads, "Notice. No Automobiles." The rest is not legible, but perhaps it warns against parking in front of the fire hydrant.

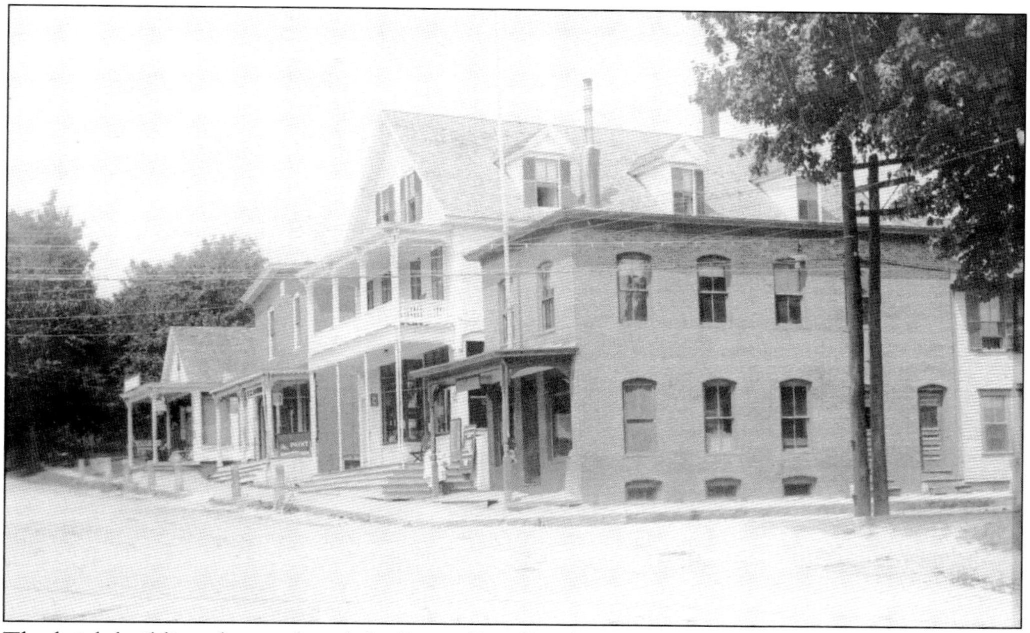

The brick building that replaced the James Rundlett house on the corner of Pleasant and Main Streets was Epping's new post office. The large white building next to the post office contained apartments for rent.

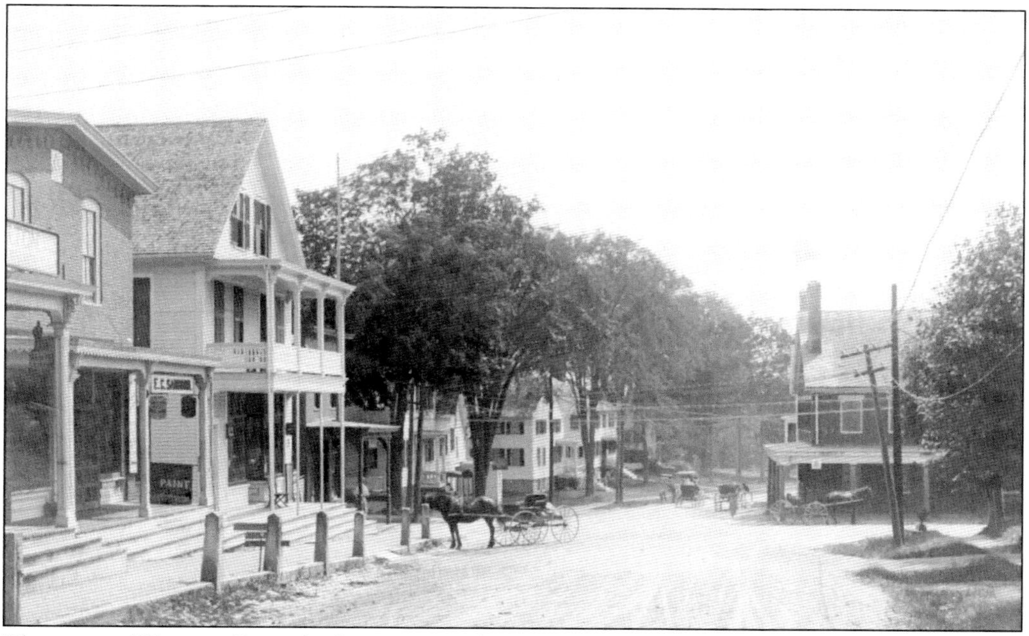


This view of Pleasant Street looks east toward Water Street. Main Street can be seen intersecting the two streets at center. A couple of carriages are hitched near the Perkins Hotel to the right while their owners rest at the tavern, visit with friends, or wander through the shops downtown. Another carriage is hitched outside the post office as its owner sends or receives some mail. The brick building to the left is the Masonic Hall that also housed the E.C. Sanborn paint shop.

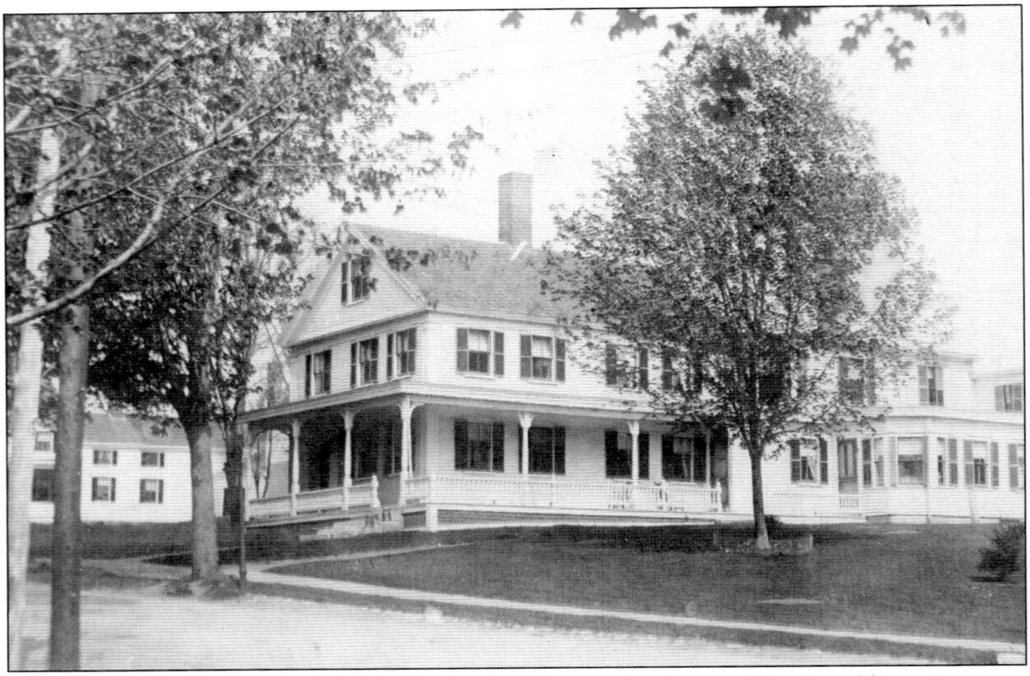

This house on Pleasant Street, built around 1860, was the home of Dr. Spaulding. Augustus D. Brown later purchased the home and ran a hardware store and undertaking parlor in the large house.

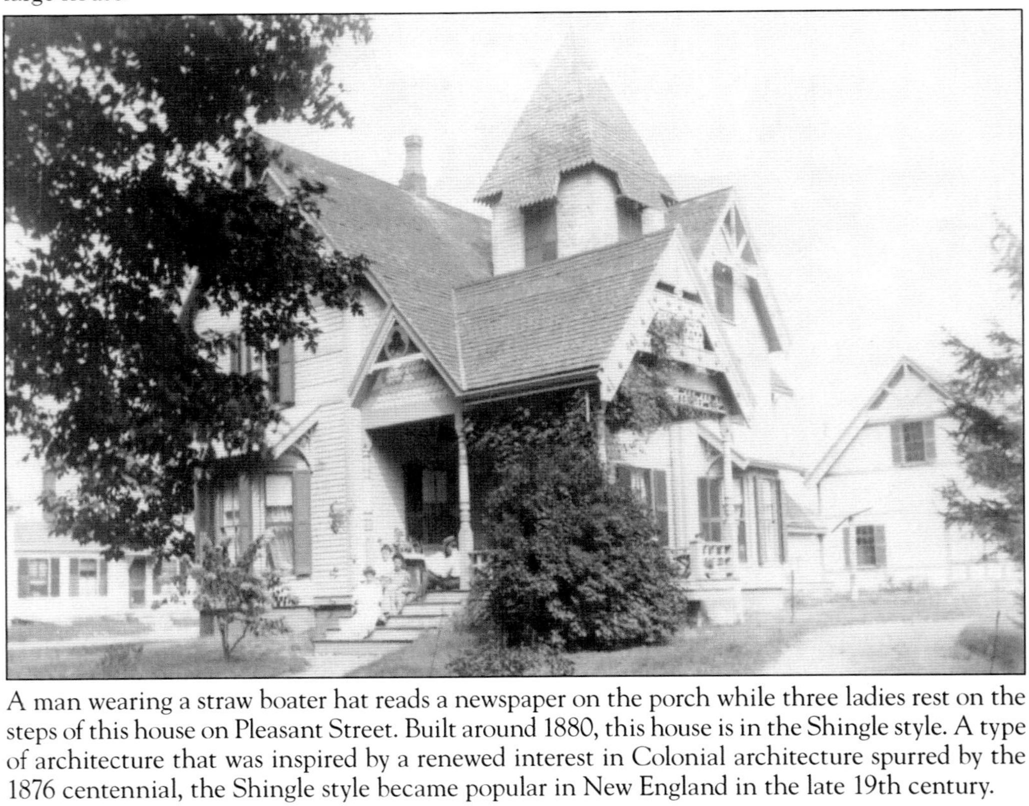

A man wearing a straw boater hat reads a newspaper on the porch while three ladies rest on the steps of this house on Pleasant Street. Built around 1880, this house is in the Shingle style. A type of architecture that was inspired by a renewed interest in Colonial architecture spurred by the 1876 centennial, the Shingle style became popular in New England in the late 19th century.

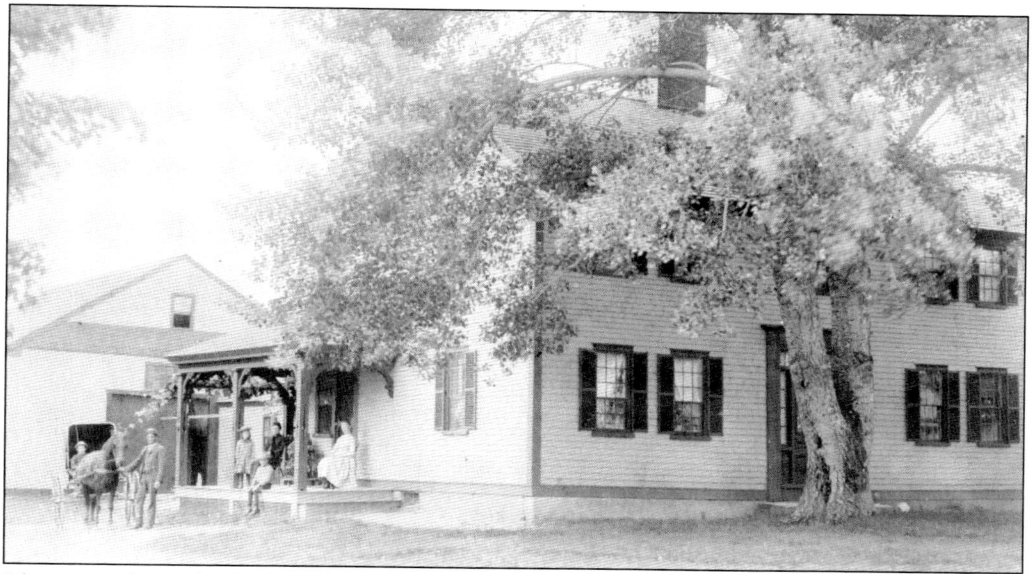

This image shows the Sanborn house on Pleasant Street as it appeared in 1886. Charles W. Sanborn stands holding the reigns while one of his sons sits in the carriage. The rest of his children sit patiently on the porch. The barn at rear shows some of the shingling of the Shingle style while the house is covered in more traditional clapboards.

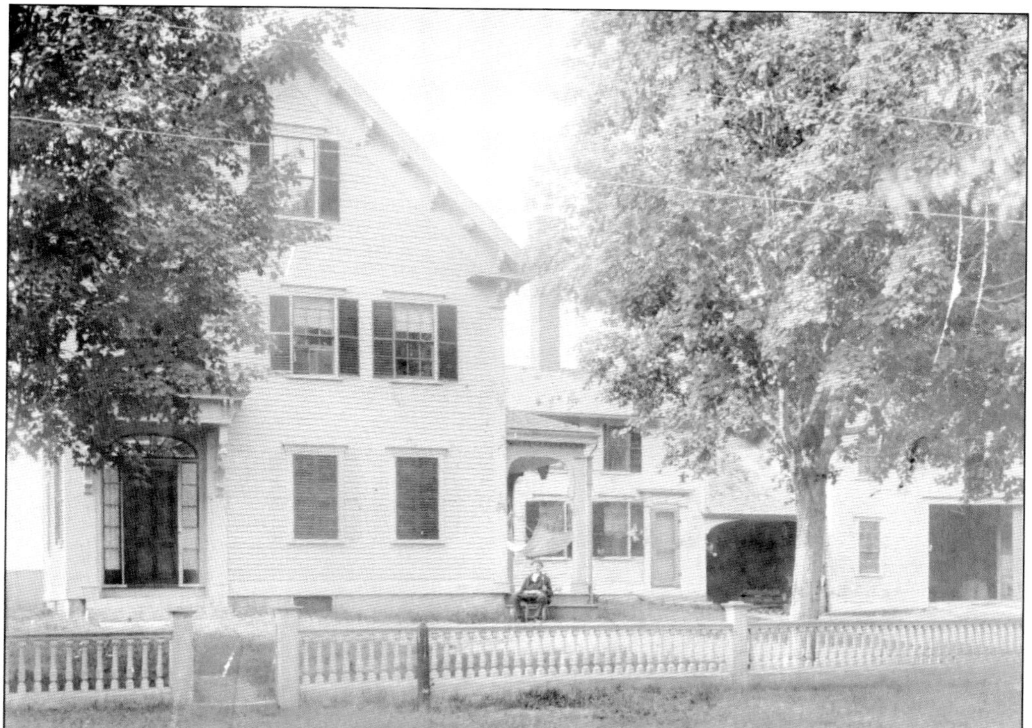

A man holding a book in his lap and a walking stick in his hand sits in front of this large house on Pleasant Street. A hammock hangs on the side porch while the yard is hemmed in by an ornate whitewashed fence with granite pillars. A brick walkway leads to the front door with sidelights and a beautiful transom.

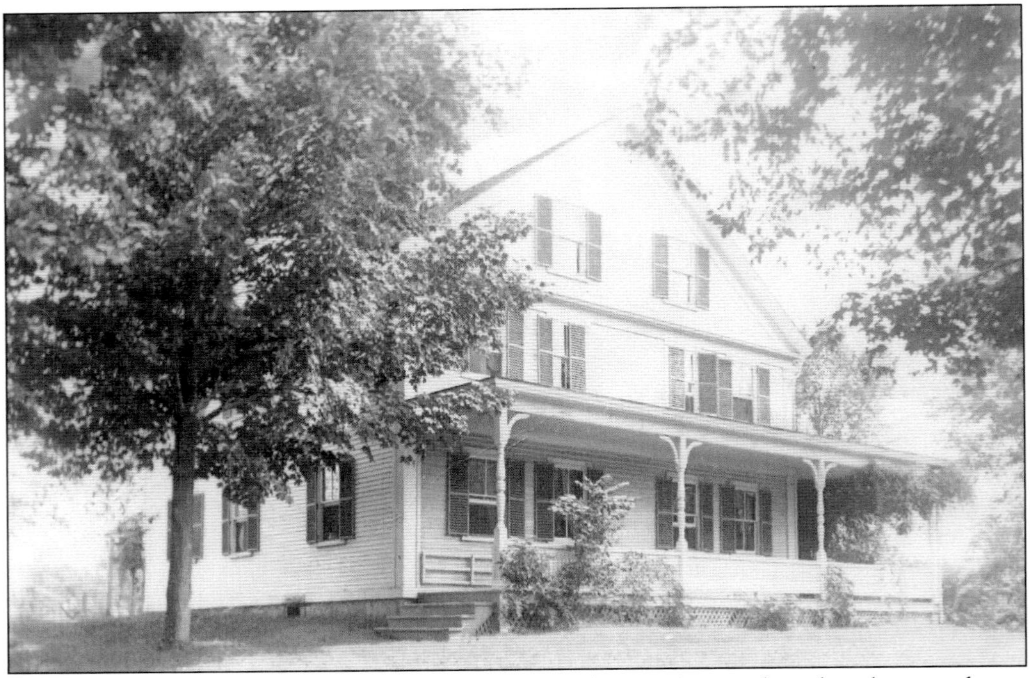

The home of Albert and Madge Pike was located on Pleasant Street when this photograph was taken in 1900. The home was likely built by the Pike family. A three-story home with a large front porch that faces Pleasant Street, it might have had a garden in the back. A trellis can be seen connected to the back of the house. This might have supported flowers or other vines, providing a peaceful shaded area to relax during the hotter months.

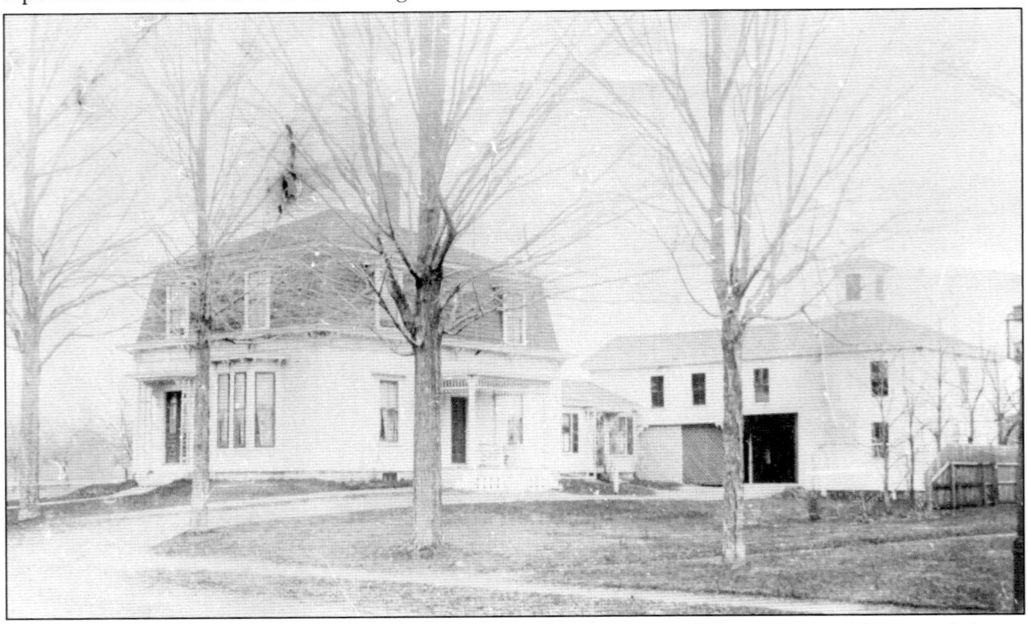

This home on Pleasant Street was built around 1873 in the Second Empire style. The raised slopes of the mansard roof, an architectural design of the Second Empire style, provided more room in the third floor for living space or attic space. It also became popular because it made a structure appear more impressive.

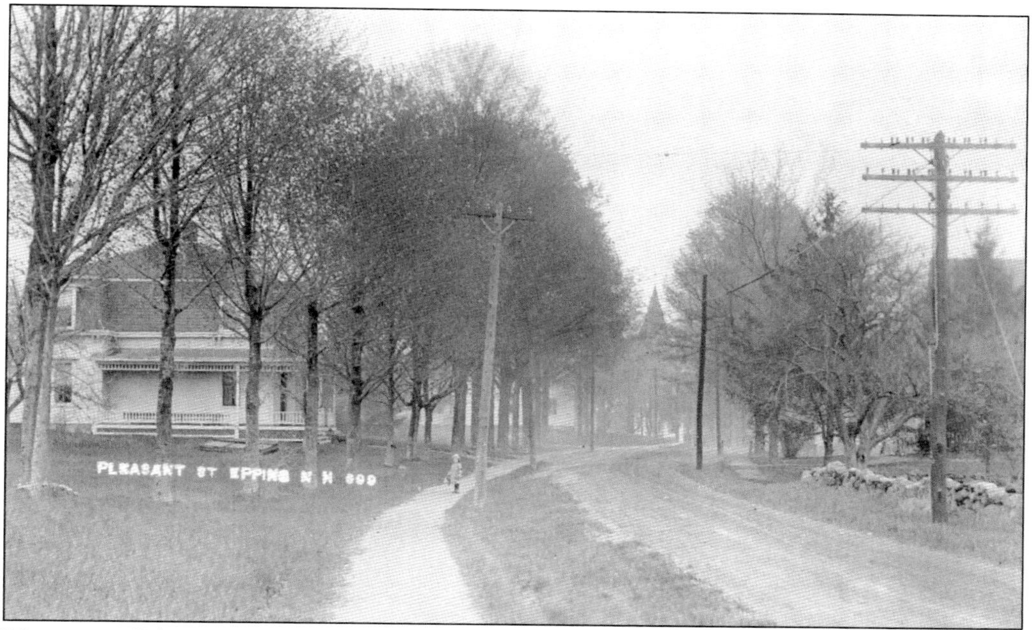

This view of Pleasant Street from up the road looking eastward shows how the lovely tree-lined avenue bends toward downtown. To the left is a home in the Second Empire style. A little girl waits patiently for the photographer to catch up. Down the road can be seen the steeple of the Congregational Church.

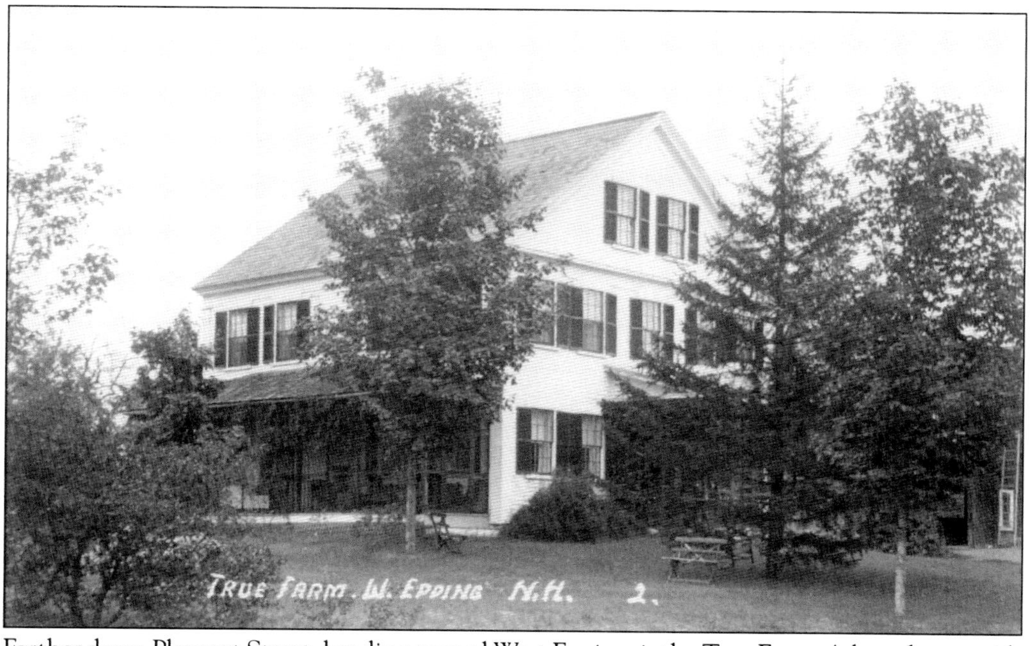

Farther down Pleasant Street, heading toward West Epping, is the True Farm. A large home with a screened-in porch on the side, this house sits a little bit back from the road. A rocking chair, a bench, and a lawn chair can be seen out front under the shade of an evergreen tree and a maple tree. A ladder leads up into the barn to the extreme right.

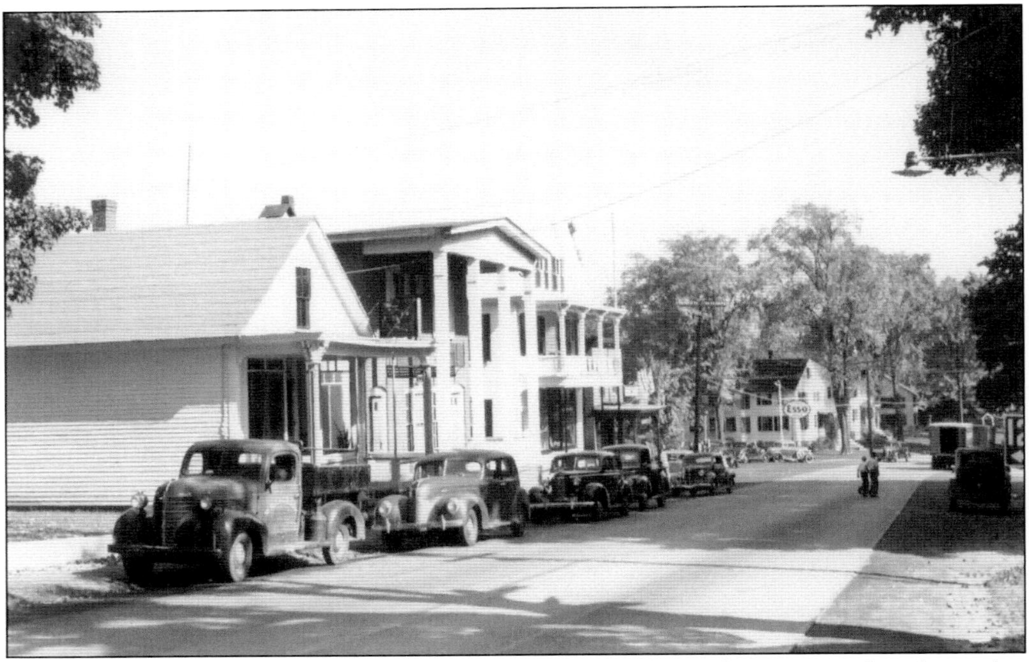

Shown is Pleasant Street as it appeared mid-20th century. The road is now paved, and a marker can be seen to the extreme right, indicating that Main Street is now also Route 125. The Masonic Lodge at center has been given more substantial columns in the front. The large whitewashed apartment building still stands, as does the post office.

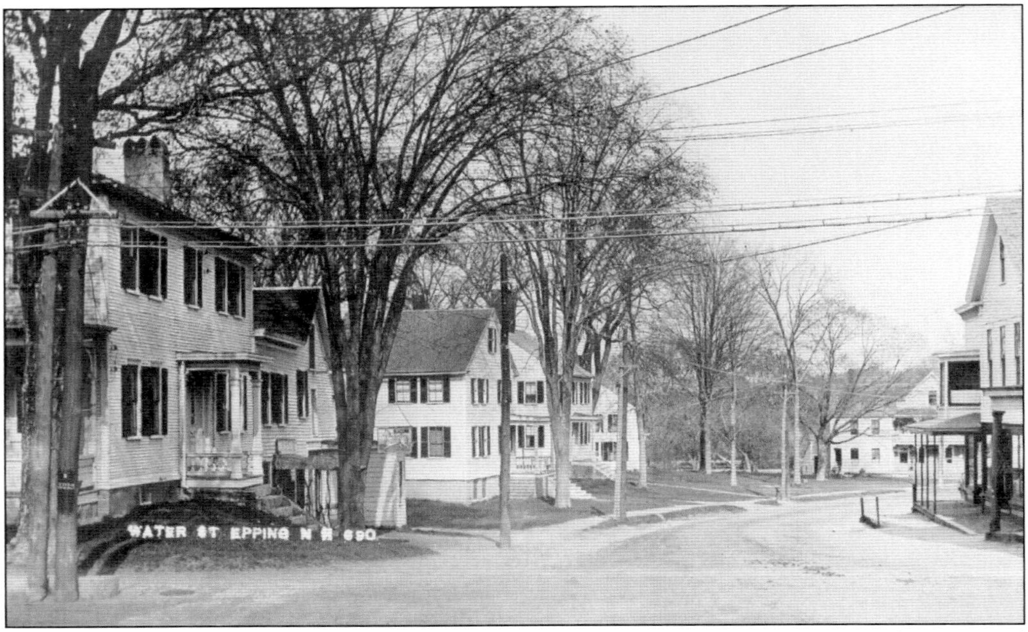


In this image, one can see how Water Street winds away from the intersection with Main and Pleasant Streets. The portion of Water Street shown here has a mix of homes and businesses. A sign hangs on the left side of the street with the picture of a horse and the words "Harness Maker." To the left of the tree, under the awning, a sample of harnesses can be seen, put out for purchase to any passerby who sees them.

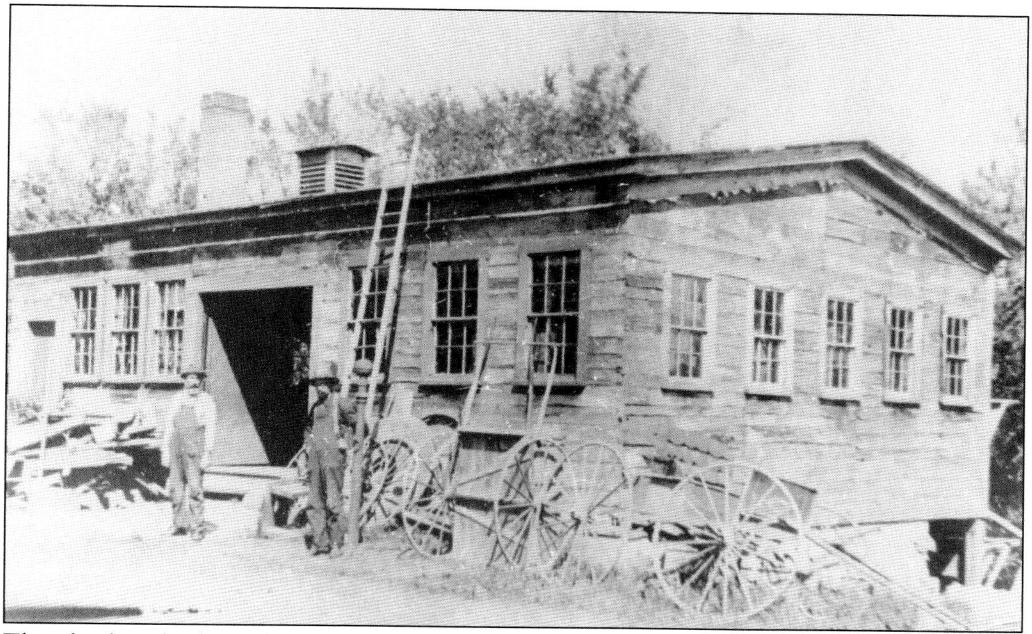

The wheelwright shop of Alvin Spencer was located on Water Street. This image, taken in 1900, shows two men, perhaps one of them is Alvin Spencer himself, standing proudly in front of a number of wheels crafted for carriages, carts, and wagons. To the left stands a scrap pile with what looks like the spare seat of a carriage thrown on top. The wide front door was needed in case something had to be wheeled directly into the shop.

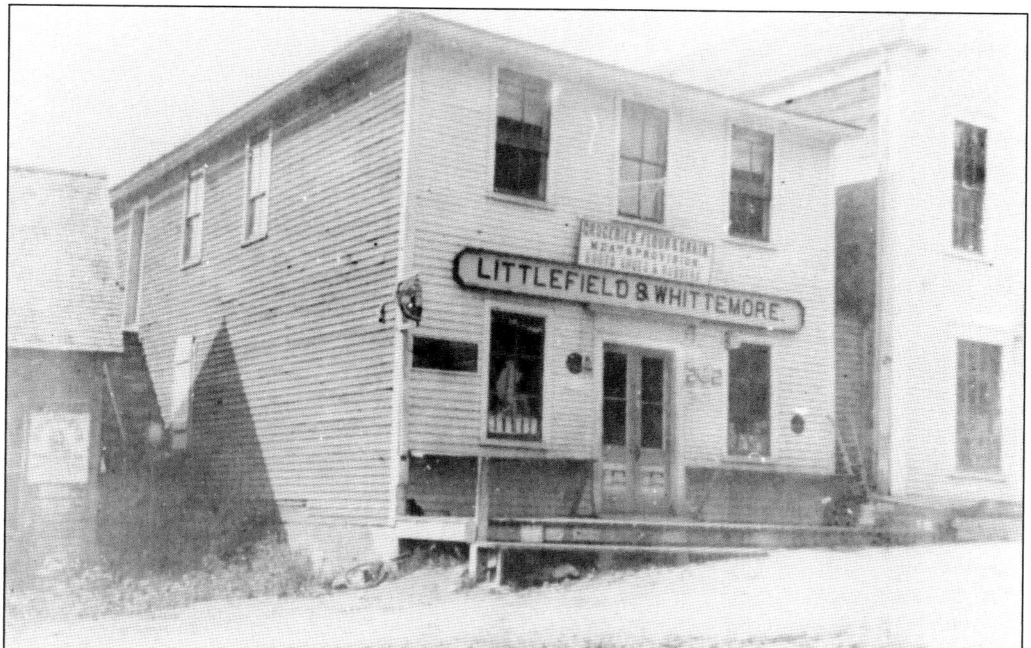


Littlefield and Whittemore set up their grocery, meat, boot, shoe, and dry goods store on Water Street after having saved their stock from ruin in the fire of 1896, which wiped out six buildings on Main Street. To the left of Littlefield and Whittemore's is a blacksmith shop, and to the right is Bunker's Hall. All of these buildings burned in the fire of 1919.

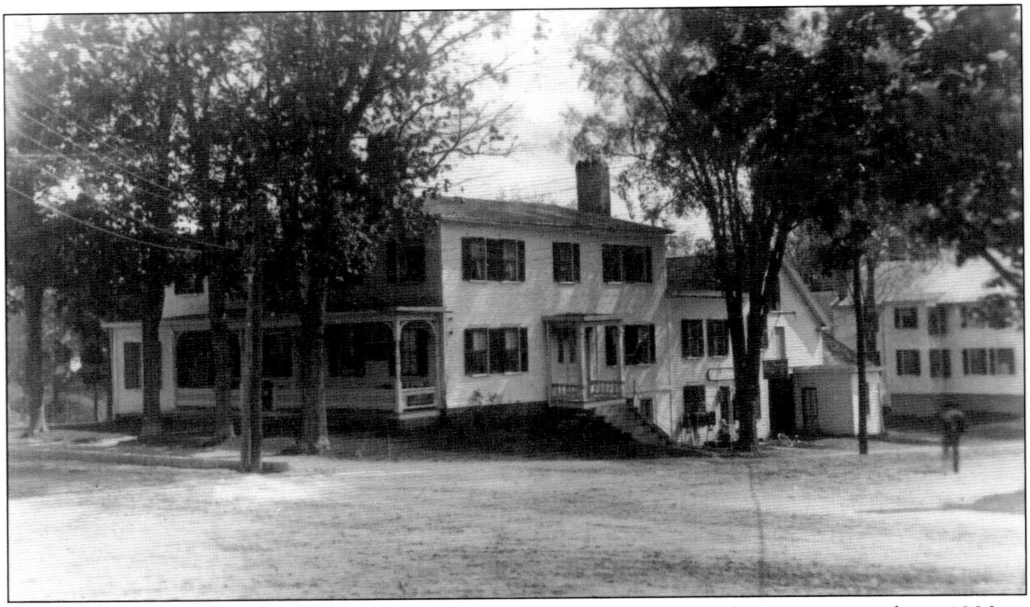

This Federal-style building sat on the northeast corner of Water and Main Streets from 1800 to 1935. This image shows the shop of the harness maker in the basement, with his wares out for show. Later, while it was owned by Bernice Merrill, Charles Beers ran a barbershop in the basement. In 1920, a small building was constructed at the right end and was used by First National Stores. In the early 1930s, the building housed the Green Lantern Restaurant. The Esso Gas Company bought the property in 1935 and tore down the building to make way for a filling station.

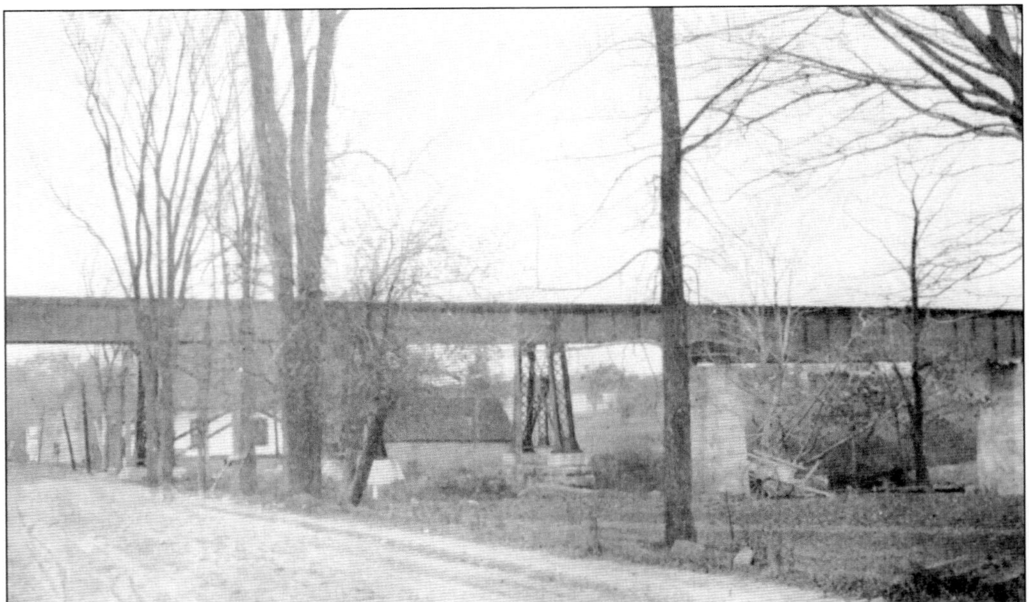

This iron bridge spanned the Lamprey River on the right and Water Street on the left. Built by the Worcester, Nashua & Portland line, the iron trestle bridge replaced an earlier wooden covered bridge. The large granite supports that lie in the Lamprey River, as well as the granite retaining wall on the opposite shore, can still be seen from Route 125 today.

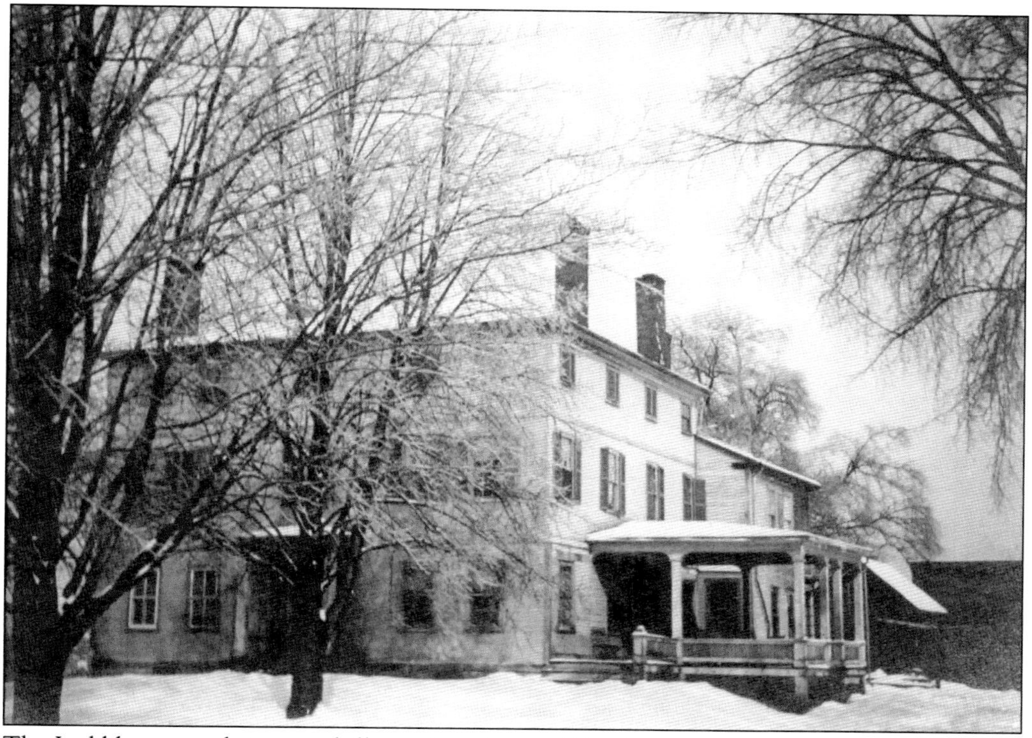

The Ladd homestead sits on a hill on Water Street. The three-story home is one of the largest in Epping. The Lamprey River runs behind the home, and Ladd's Lane, a road that branches off Water Street just after the house, has been named for the Ladd family.

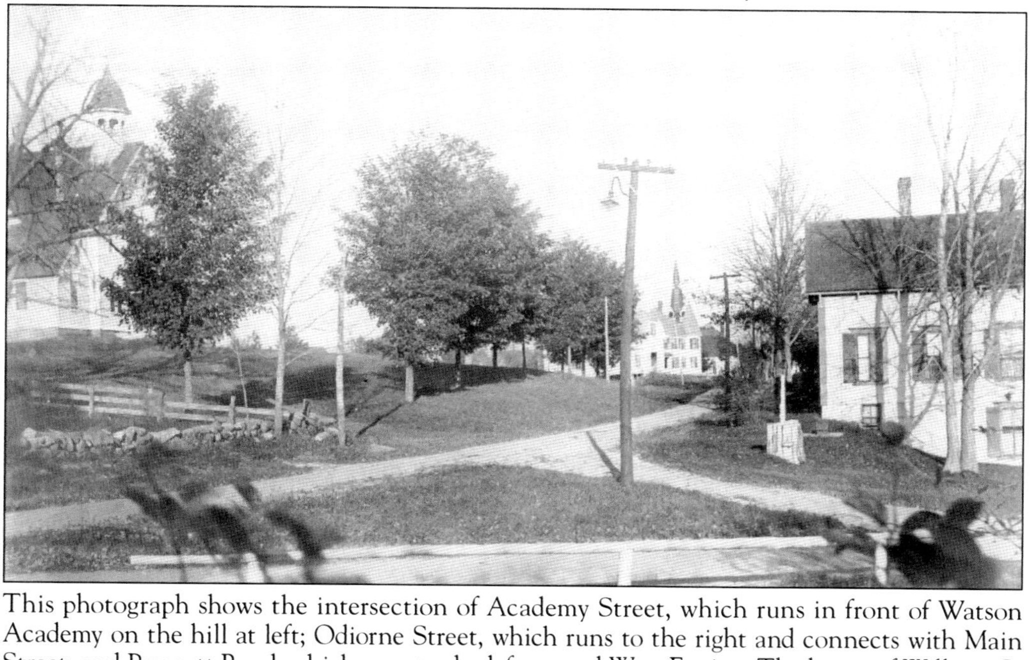

This photograph shows the intersection of Academy Street, which runs in front of Watson Academy on the hill at left; Odiorne Street, which runs to the right and connects with Main Street; and Prescott Road, which runs to the left toward West Epping. The home of William C. Brown can be seen at center at the end of Academy Street. The steeple of the Methodist church rises out from behind the house.

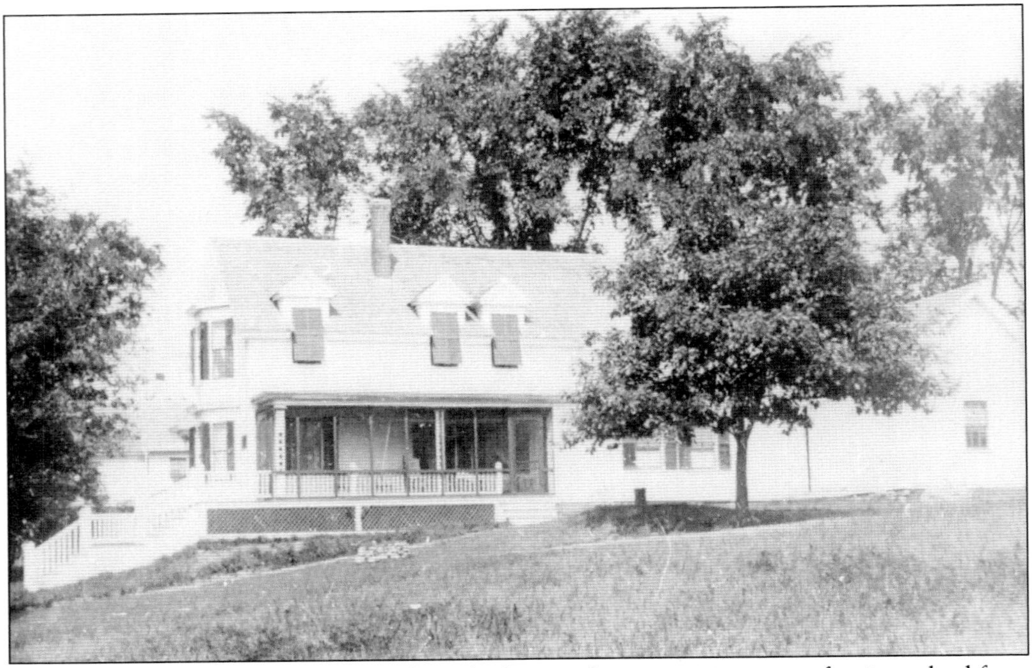

Bud Stevens's house on Prescott Road was built on a slope, requiring a set of stairs to lead from the front door down to the street. A well can be seen at center. Bud Stevens would have had a lovely view of downtown looking down from Boar's Head Hill from his screened-in porch.

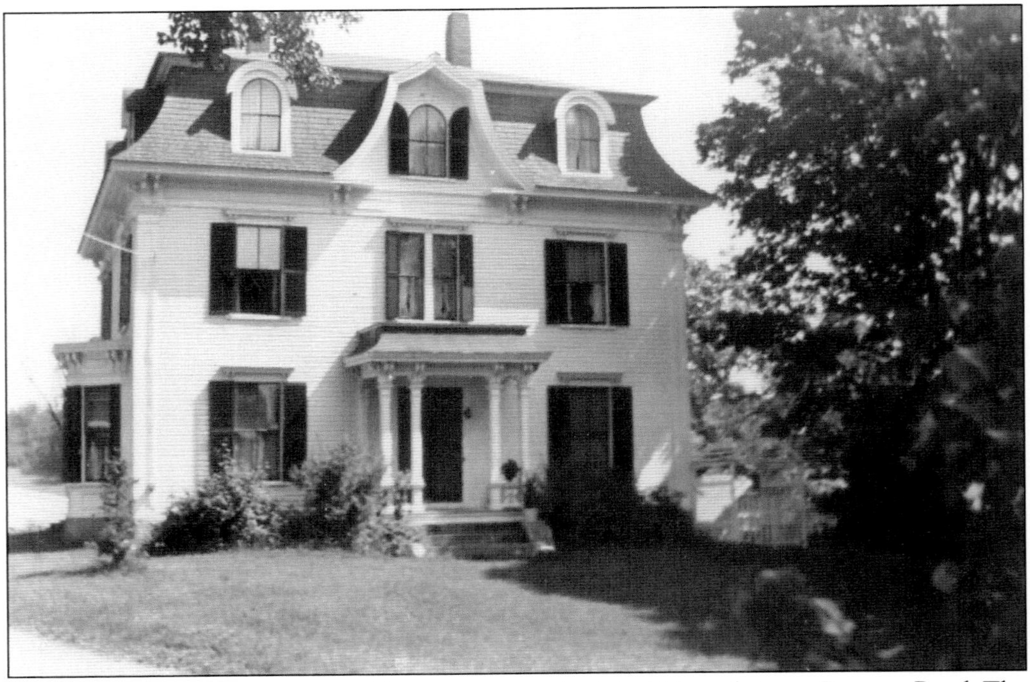

The home of Gov. Benjamin Franklin Prescott was built in 1875 and sits on Prescott Road. The house has three floors and is built in the Second Empire style with a mansard roof and detailed front portico. The Benjamin Franklin Prescott house was added to the National Register of Historic Places in 1987.

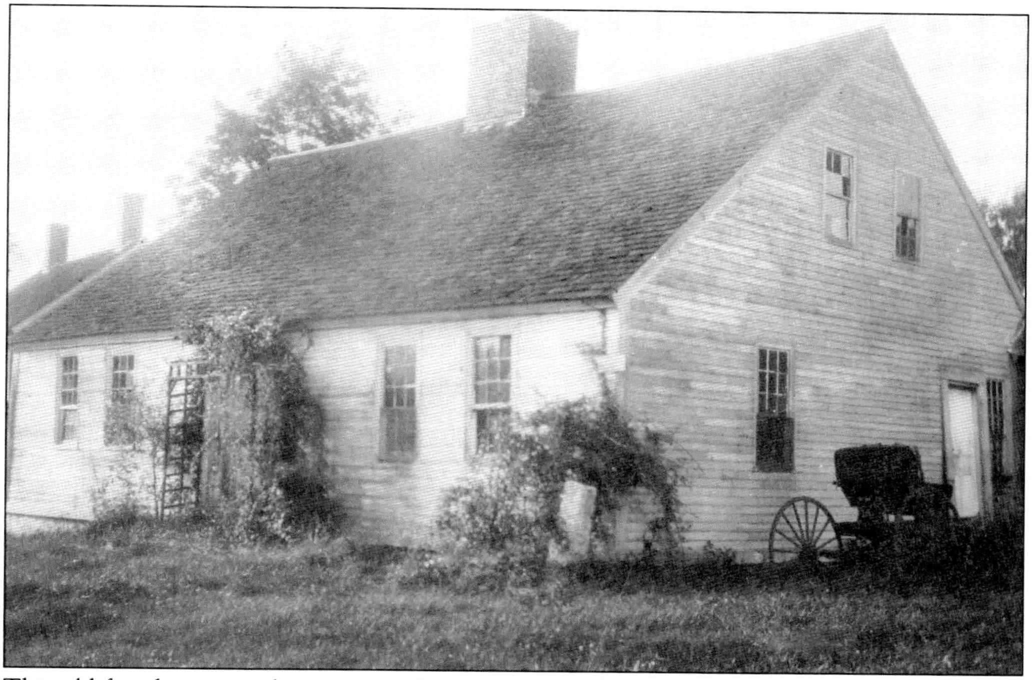

This old farmhouse on the corner of Prescott and Blake Roads has fallen into disrepair. The windows are missing panes, a carriage lies abandoned to the elements, and the grass and vines have been left to their own devices. Perhaps the owners had built a new home on their property or moved onto a new lot, or perhaps they came on hard times and took only what they could.

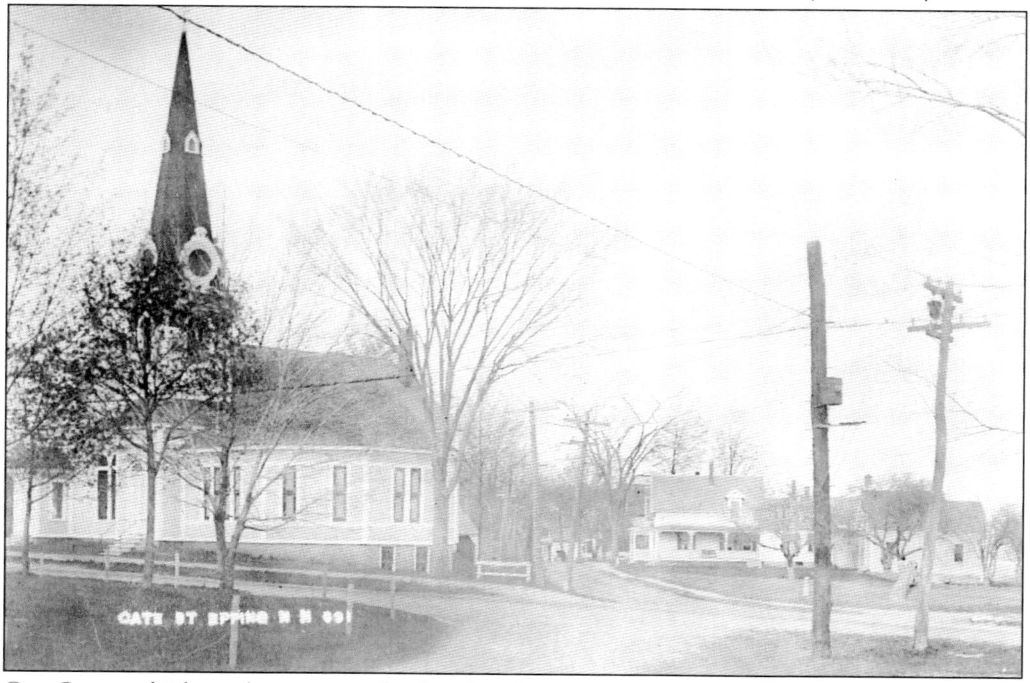


Cate Street, which can be seen straight ahead in this image, runs perpendicular to Main Street and across from Academy Street. William C. Brown's box factory was located to the right, across Cate Street from the Methodist church, for a time. The rest of Cate Street consisted of residences.

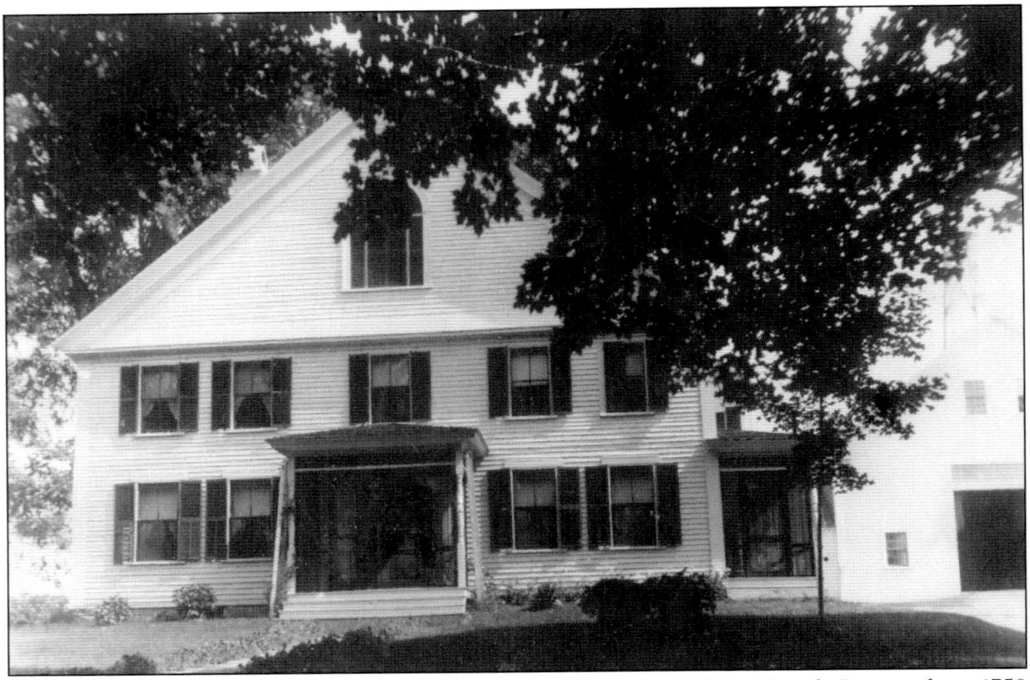

This large home on Elm Street, pictured in 1900, was the home of Rev. Josiah Stearns from 1758 to 1788. William S. Goodrich, owner and founder of the W.S. Goodrich brick company in Epping, bought the house and had brick facing from his brickyard placed over the old clapboards. The old W.S. Goodrich bricks still protect this house from the elements.

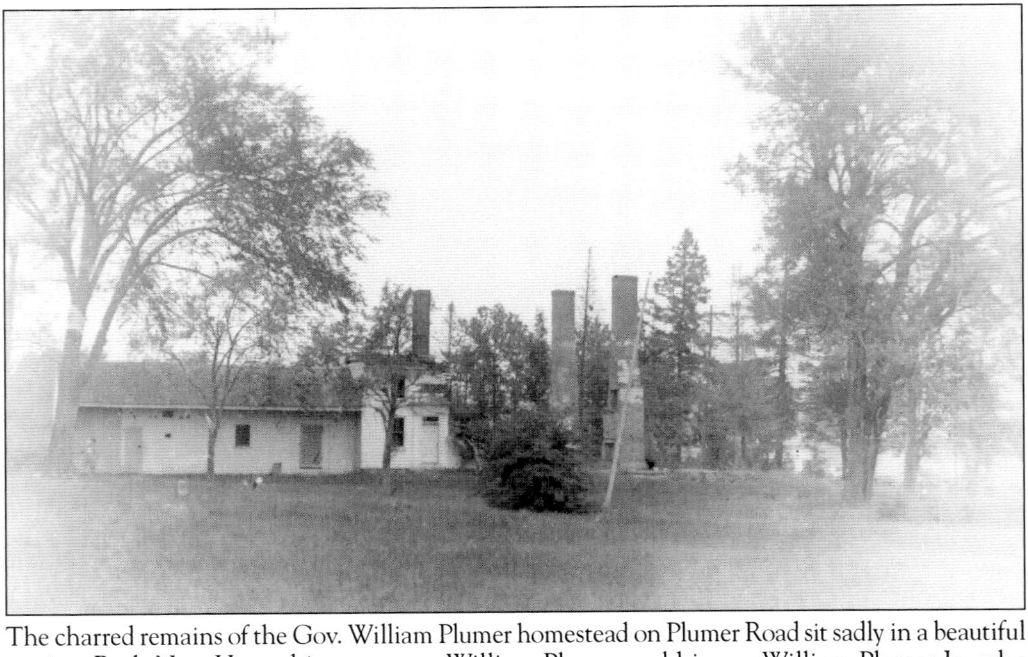

The charred remains of the Gov. William Plumer homestead on Plumer Road sit sadly in a beautiful setting. Both New Hampshire governor William Plumer and his son William Plumer Jr., who became a congressman, lived in this grand house. A man leans against a large tree at left, perhaps wondering what started the blaze and what could have been done to save the stately home.

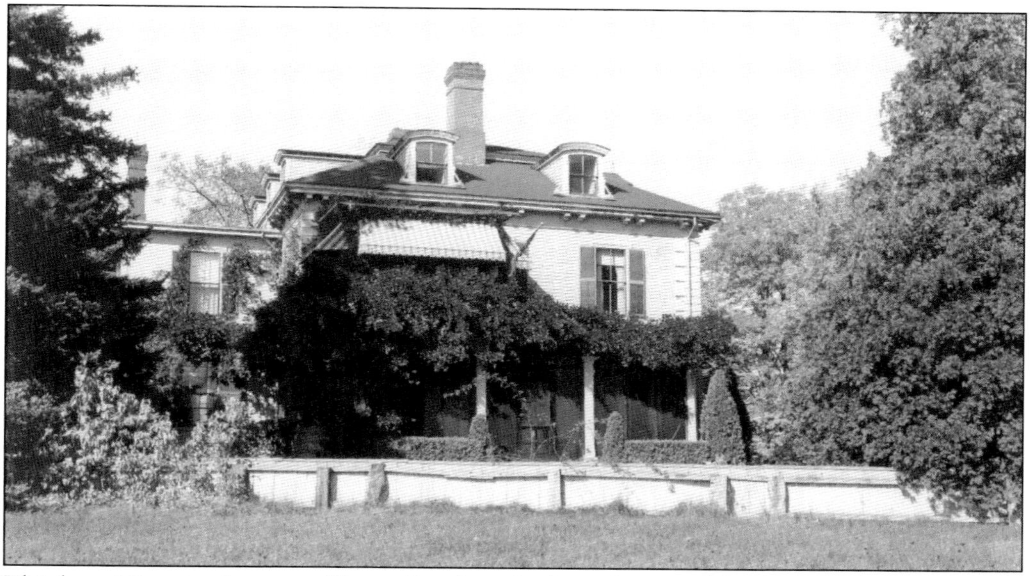

This large Victorian home on Plumer Road was built on the site of the former governor William Plumer homestead. The home was dubbed Plumercrest, and at various times, it has served as a private residence, nursing home, and bed-and-breakfast.

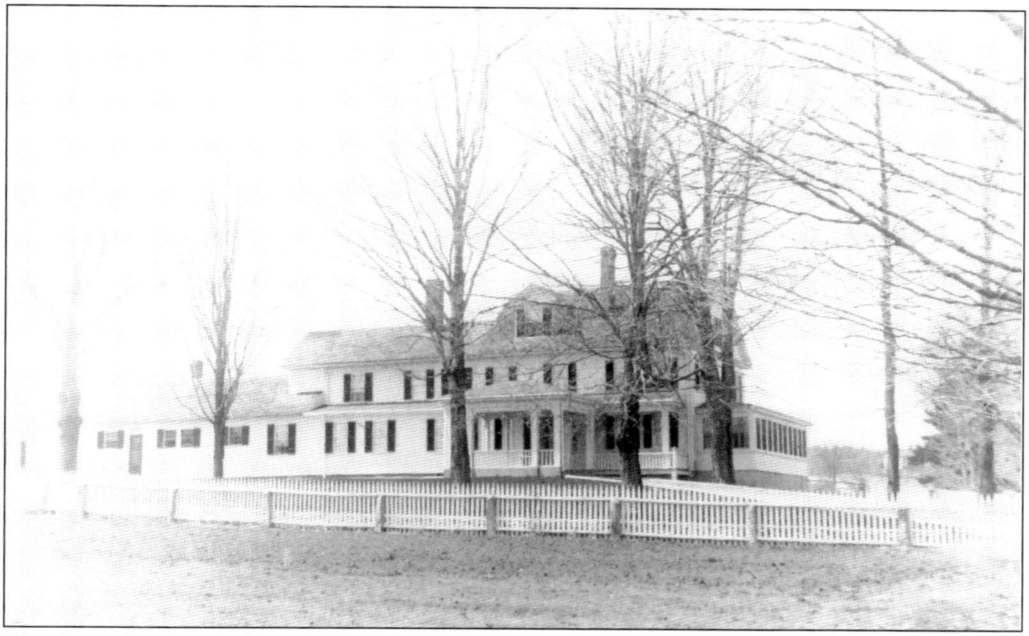

This large home on Plumer Road is separated from its farmland by a charming white picket fence. The land in the foreground has been plowed and is prepared for planting as evidenced by the furrows in the soil. The structure that comes off the side of the house at center is not a porch but a porte cochere. A porte cochere serves the purpose of allowing a carriage, or later an automobile, to pass under it so that visitors or residents can exit their transportation and enter the home while staying out of the elements.

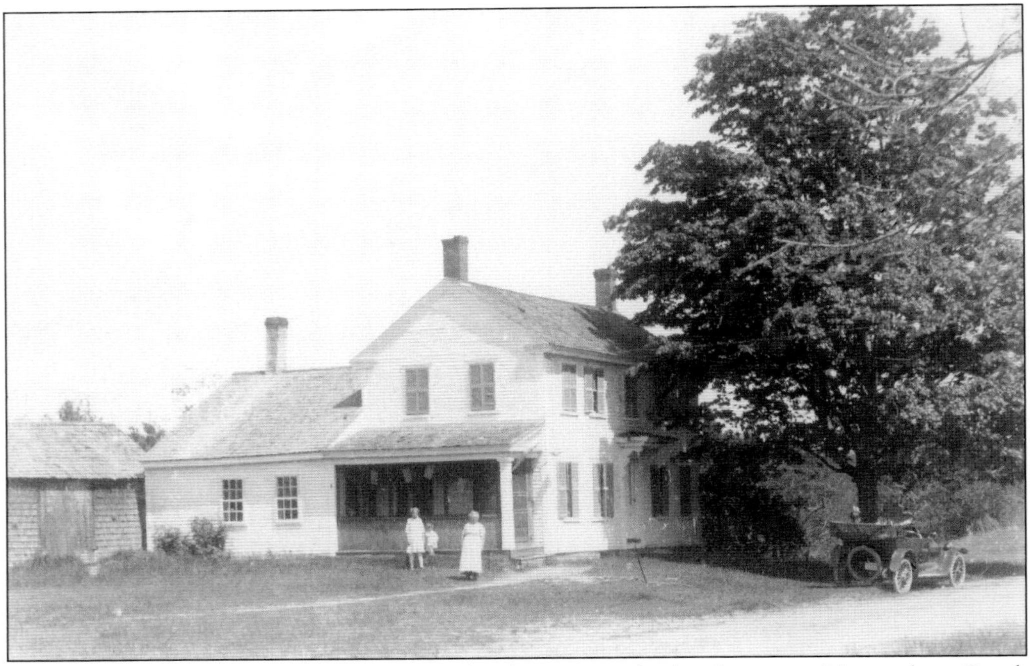

An elderly woman and two children pose for this image of a farmhouse on Nottingham Road. The back portion of this old home was probably the kitchen. As modern kitchens evolved and fireplaces became purposed more for warmth than cooking, a separate kitchen was often added off the back of the house. Two women sit in an automobile to the right, perhaps waiting for the photographer to finish and continue on their way.

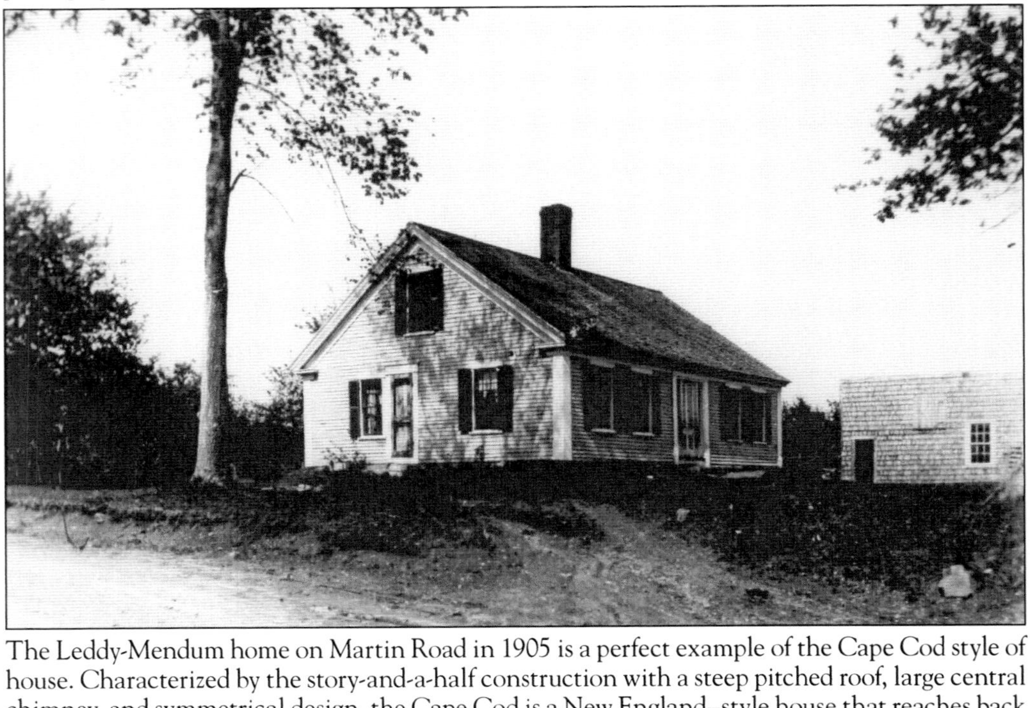

The Leddy-Mendum home on Martin Road in 1905 is a perfect example of the Cape Cod style of house. Characterized by the story-and-a-half construction with a steep pitched roof, large central chimney, and symmetrical design, the Cape Cod is a New England–style house that reaches back to the Colonial era. It was designed to withstand harsh New England winters.

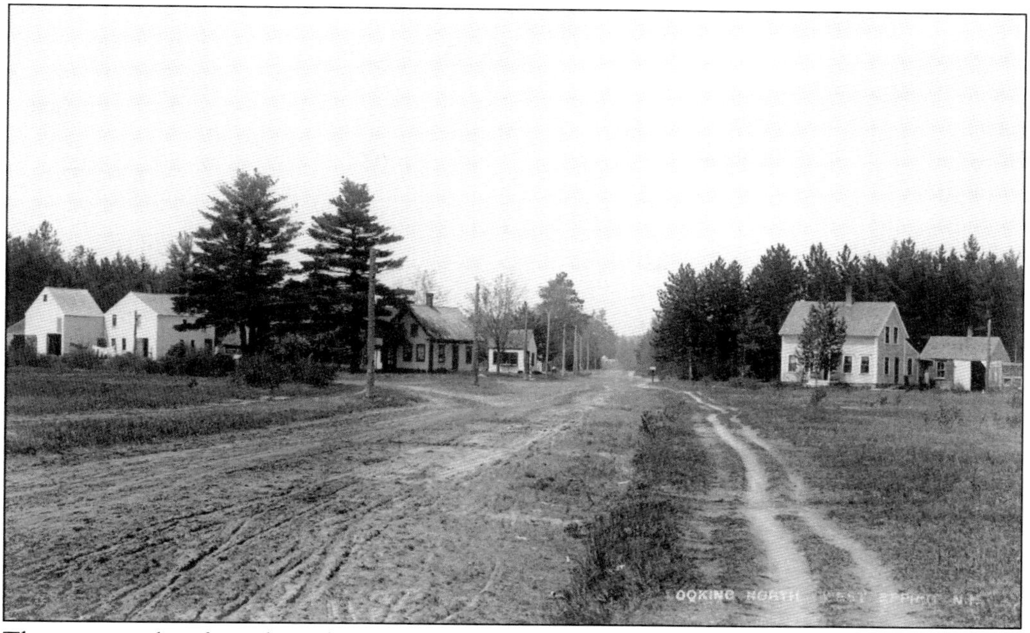

This view is taken from the railroad depot on Depot Road, looking north toward West Epping. A farmhouse to the left has laundry hanging out to dry on a laundry line. The house at center may have been the home of a mill or factory worker. The road is muddy, perhaps from a wet spring, and travelers have decided to blaze a new road to the right of Depot Road rather than get stuck in the deep mud.

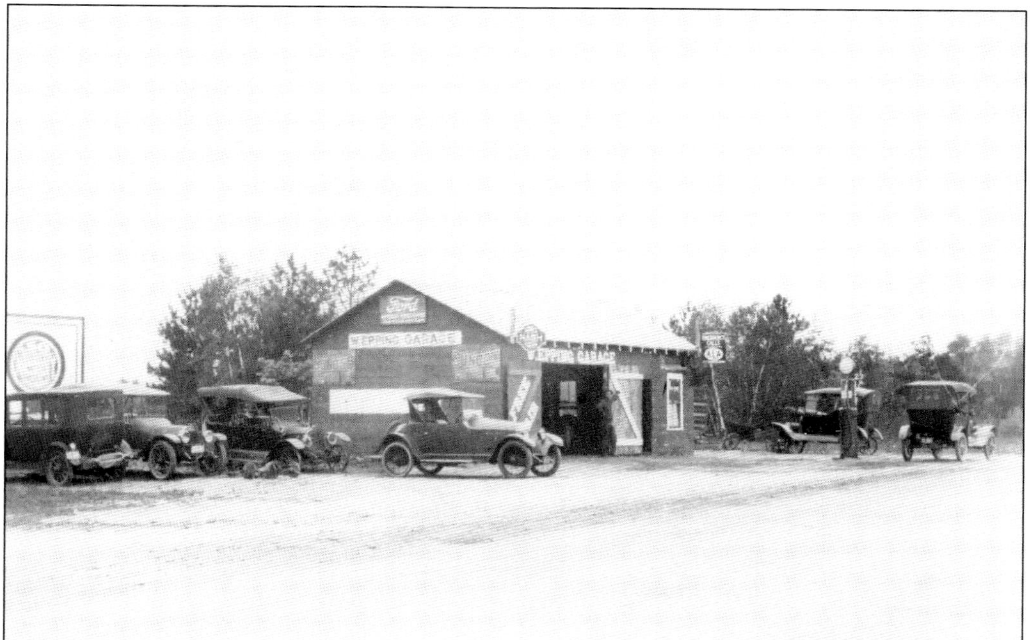

The West Epping Garage advertises free air, Sunoco Motor Oil, emergency calls, and Socony Motor Gasoline, as well as proudly displays that it is a Ford Authorized Service Station. The man leaning against the door to the garage is probably either a happy mechanic, given the six automobiles in the yard, or an unhappy owner of one of those automobiles.

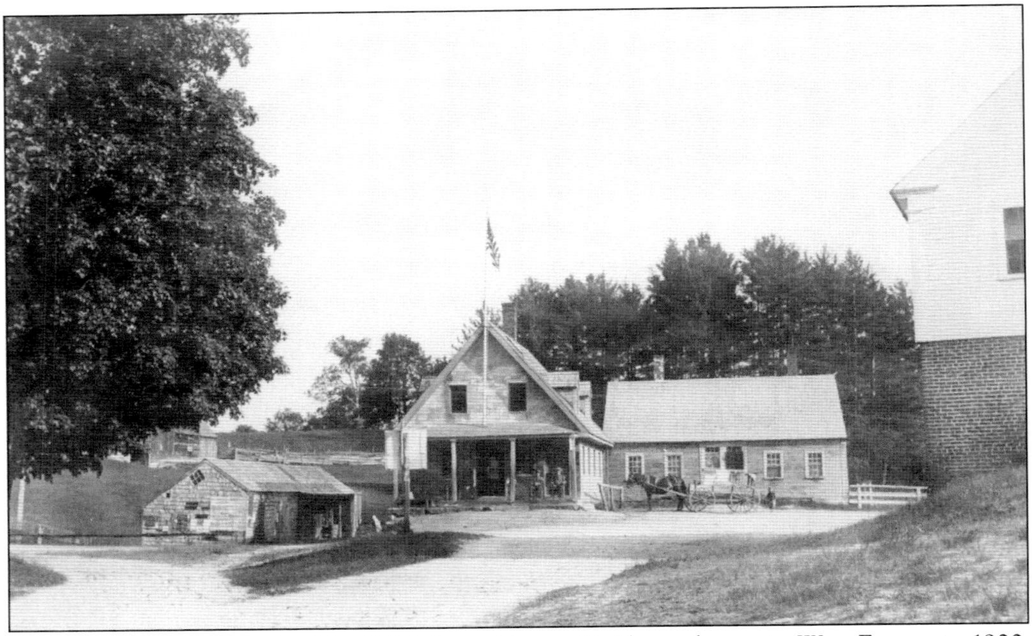

Two men sit on the porch of the W.N. Dow–George N. Shepard store in West Epping in 1900. The general store, which also served as the post office for West Epping for a time, was run by Capt. George Shepard, a veteran of the Civil War, and his partner, Winthrop Dow. Located on the corner of Route 27 and Blake Road, the store was perfectly situated for the residents of West Epping and travelers passing through.

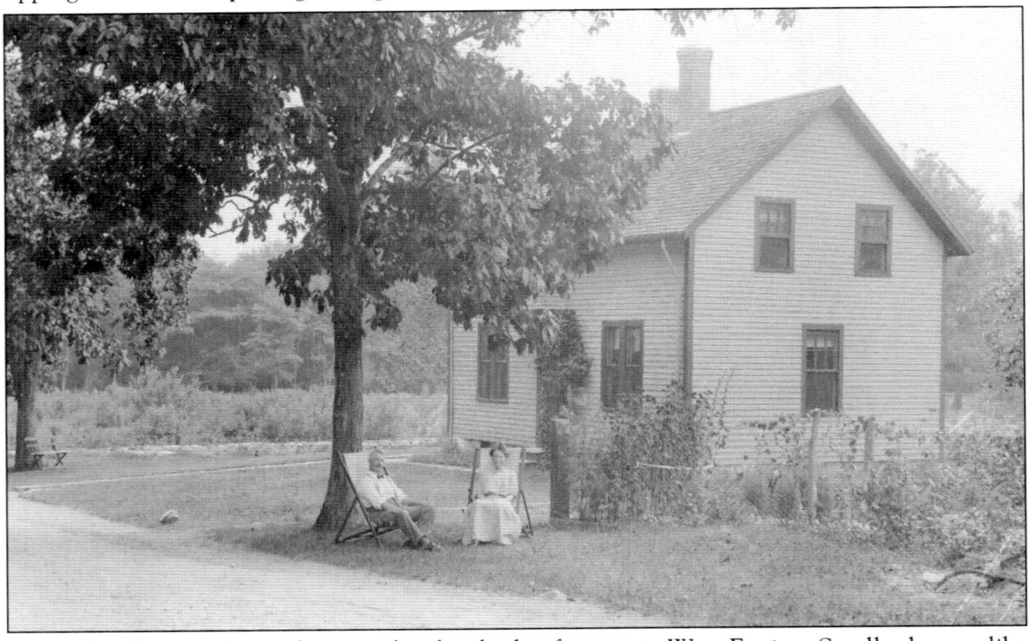

A couple relaxes in lawn chairs under the shade of a tree in West Epping. Smaller houses like these were commonly built in Epping for mill or factory workers. It looks like this couple tends a small garden to the right of the house, protected by chicken wire to keep out what may have been livestock owned by the couple or some of the many wild animals that roam Epping's forests and fields.

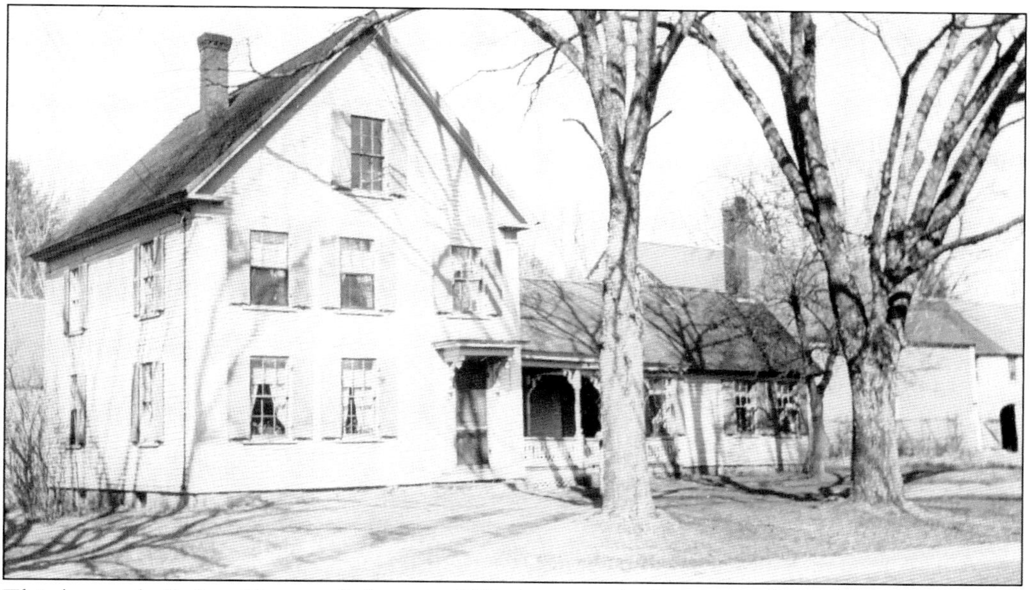

This house, built buy Thomas Folsom in 1870, became the home of Edmond G. Blair and his wife, Mary E. Blair. Mary Blair was a teacher in Epping for the better part of her life, and in 1971, she donated the land that used to be the site of the Folsom Mill to the Town of Epping for use as a public park. Today, Mary E. Folsom Blair Park is home to Epping's two Little League Baseball fields and the Folsom Dam historic site.

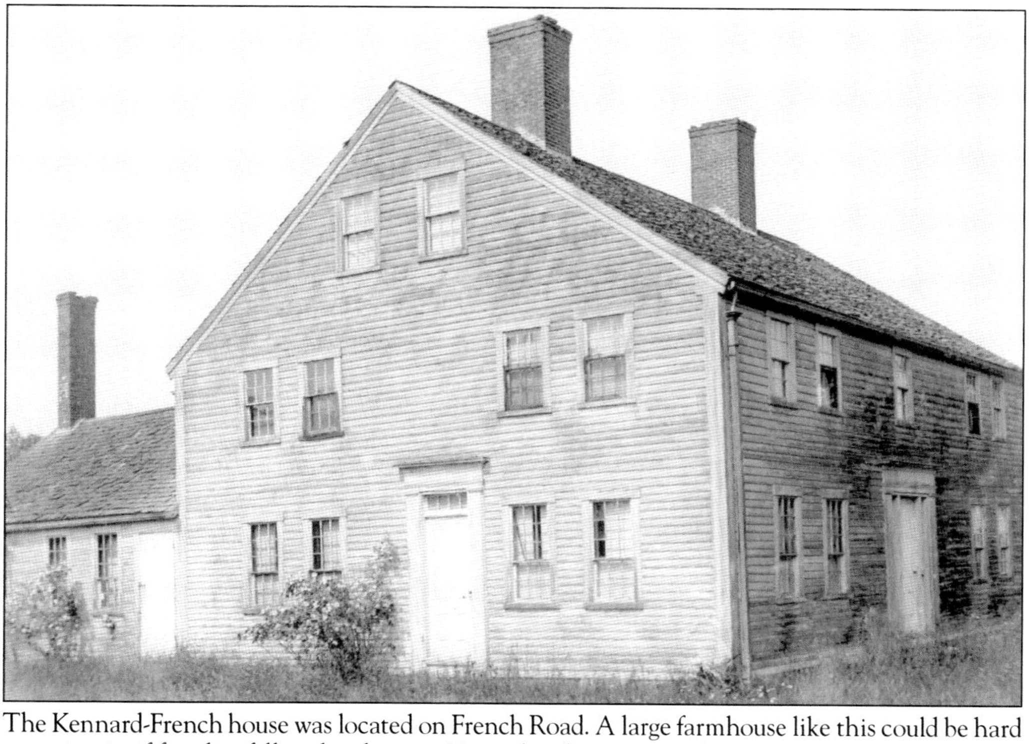

The Kennard-French house was located on French Road. A large farmhouse like this could be hard to maintain if families fell on hard times. Here, the chimneys are beginning to crack, the plants are taking over the yard, and the shingles are starting to fail. This is how the Kennard-French home appeared in 1900. It lay vacant for a time before burning down in the 1950s.

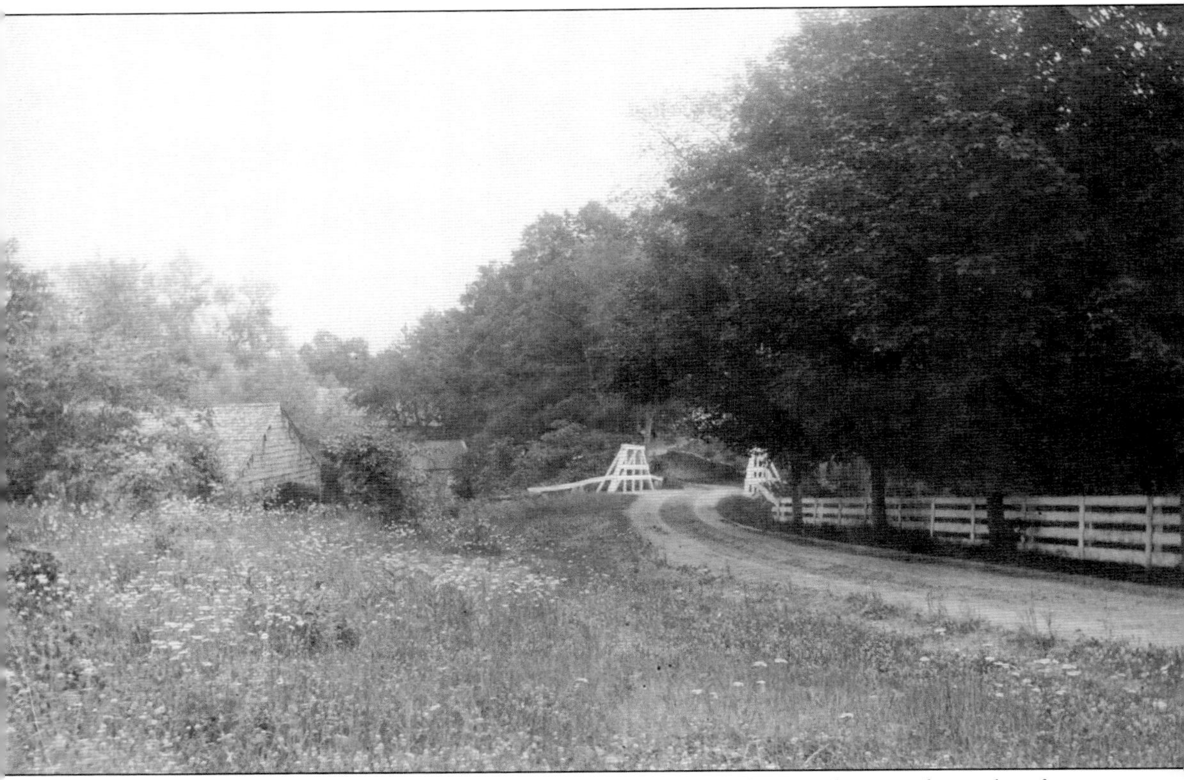

This image typifies how the back roads of Epping appeared to residents and travelers for years. Winding dirt roads glide along, lined with whitewashed fences keeping in cattle, horses, sheep, or crops. Wildflowers bloom along one side of the road while maple trees provide shade on the other. A carefully constructed bridge crosses one of the three rivers or one of the many streams that cut through the soil and clay of Epping.

# *Two*

# Places of Worship and Centers of Learning

The people of Epping worshiped far before Epping was incorporated as an independent town. Residents would make the nine-mile trek to the center of Exeter to say their prayers in the church that they supported with their taxes. One can imagine the struggle to make it through the mud, or avoid breathing in the dust, or trudge through the snow-driven road that led to the building that would save their souls from damnation. Then, when their prayers were said and the hymns were sung, they would have to turn around and make the equally difficult trip back. This round-trip journey to the center of town could end up taking the entire day.

Epping was incorporated in 1741 after the petition for independence was approved by Gov. Benning Wentworth. Epping could now establish its own places of worship, and in 1747 the Rev. Robert Cutler became the first pastor of the Congregational Church in Epping. In 1758, Epping hired on Rev. Josiah Stearns, who would go on to become one of the most successful pastors in Epping's history. A well-read, kind, and pious man with the voice of an orator and the height and bearing that put people at ease, Reverend Stearns became an influential and well-respected man within Epping and the surrounding communities.

The Congregational Church did not hold a monopoly on spiritual worship in Epping. In 1772, Joshua Folsom began preaching to the Society of Friends, or Quakers, in West Epping. In 1830, a meetinghouse for the Society of Friends was finally built for the Quakers of Epping. About 1850, the members of St. Joseph's Parish began holding their first Catholic masses in town, led by Father McDonnell. And in 1866, the Methodist Church at the corner of Cate Street and Main Street began holding meetings.

Education was just as important as worship to the citizens of Epping. In 1806, the Town of Epping established eight school districts within the town. Often meeting in small, one-room schoolhouses, students did not have a large schoolhouse until 1883.

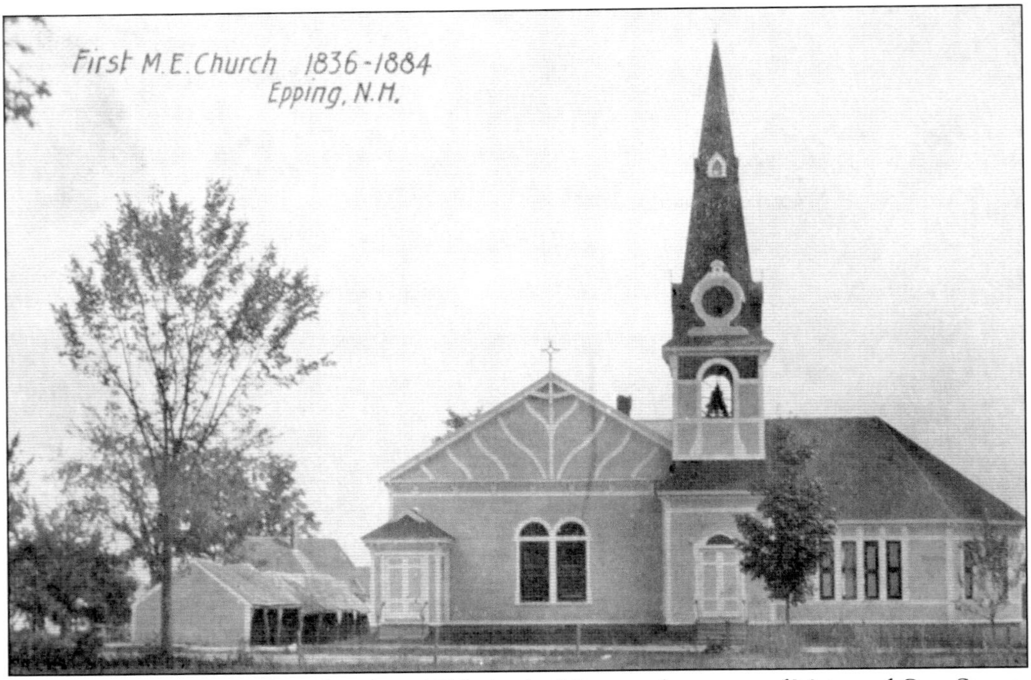


Founded as the Universalist Church in 1836, this building on the corner of Main and Cate Streets was acquired by the Methodist Church in 1866. In 1933, the Methodist congregation merged with the Congregationalists to form the Community Church, and this building was abandoned. After World War II, this building became the home of the American Legion, but it burned down in 1954 after just six years of use.

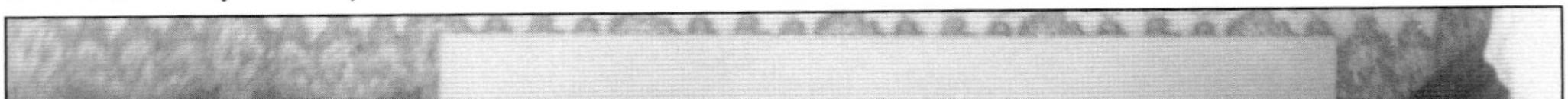

The ladies of the Methodist church choir gather for practice in 1900. This picture may have been taken inside the Methodist Church or perhaps the parsonage. From left to right above, the voices of Carrie Allen, a Mrs. Elliott, a Miss Pike, and an unidentified woman could be heard every Sunday leading the hymns of the Methodist congregation.

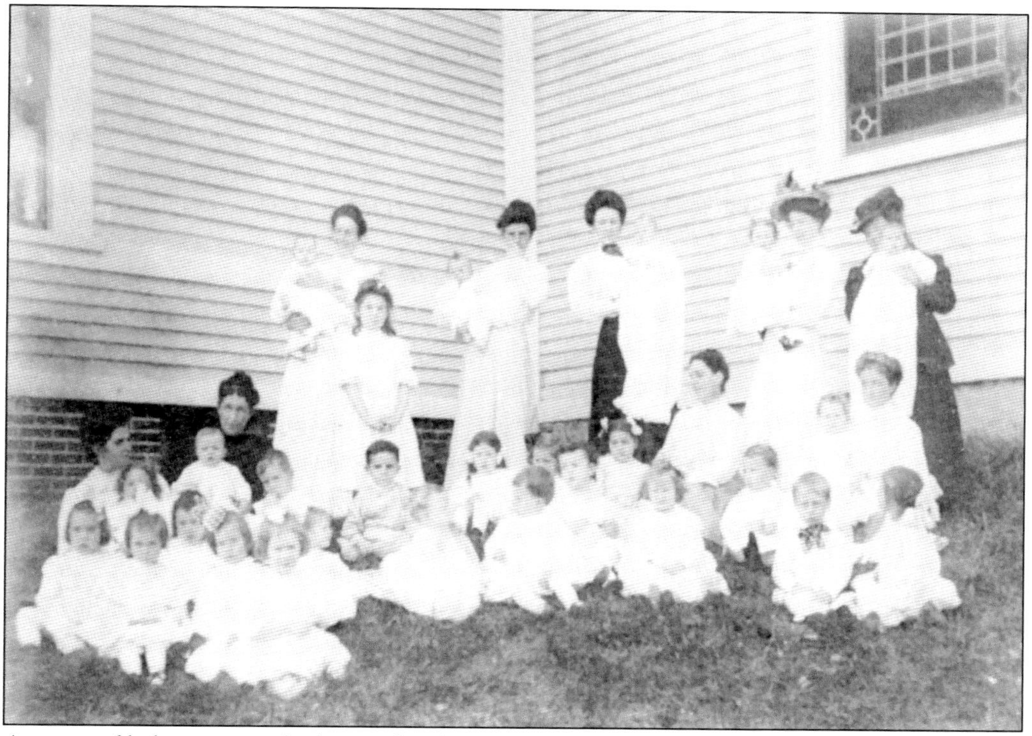

A group of ladies sit outside the south side of the Methodist church on Boar's Head Hill with a gaggle of children in their Sunday best. This may have been a Sunday school class, or perhaps the ladies are rounding the children up for a church picnic or outing. At right can be seen one of the stained-glass windows of the Methodist church.

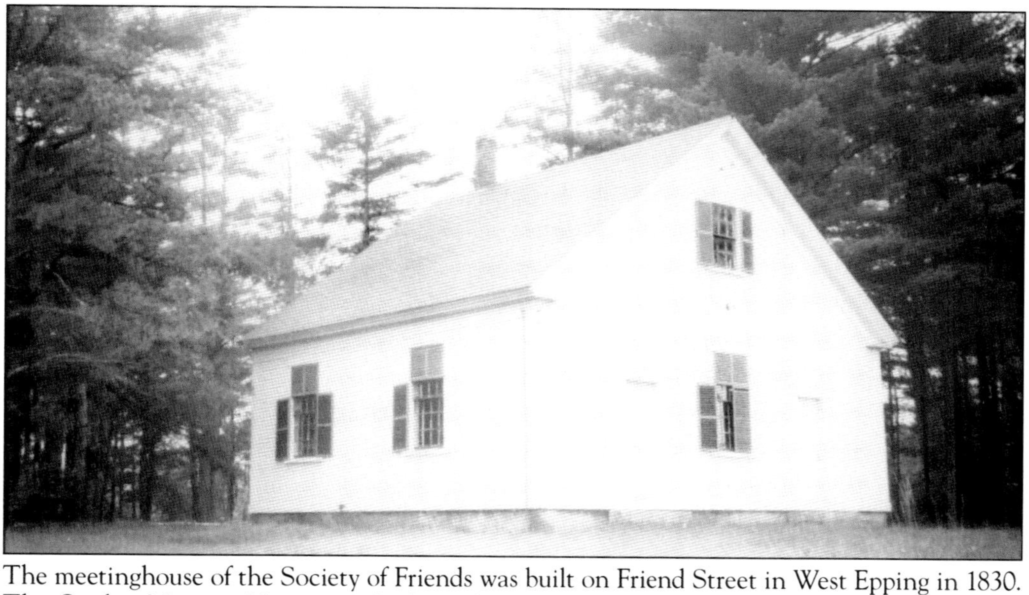

The meetinghouse of the Society of Friends was built on Friend Street in West Epping in 1830. The Quaker Meeting House was built so that a sliding shuttered wall could be slid in place and held by heavy stones to create two rooms inside. The poet John Greenleaf Whittier would frequently worship in this meetinghouse while visiting his aunt Gertrude Whittier Cortland of Lee from around 1843 to 1861.

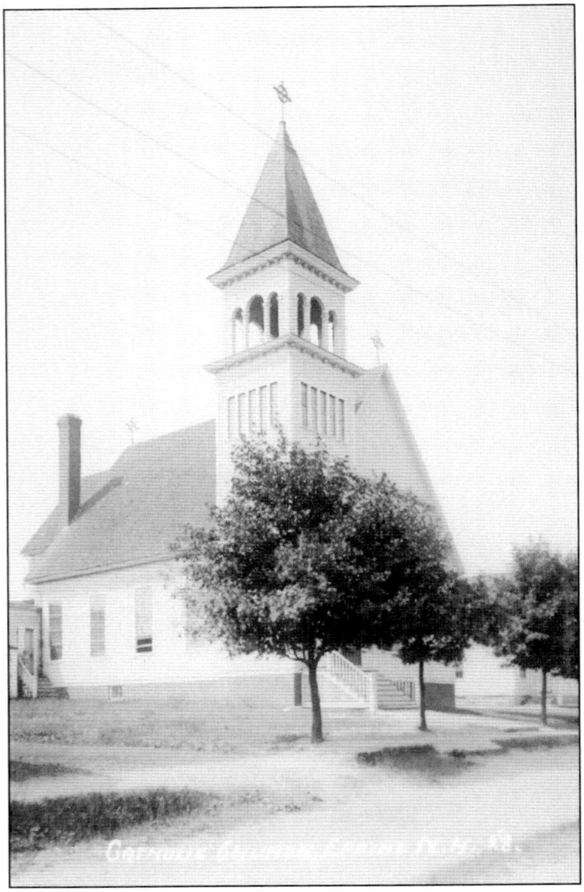

Two views of St. Joseph's Catholic Church on Main Street are seen here. This church was built in 1892 by Father O'Connor. Catholics had been worshiping in residences in Epping since 1850 and built their first independent structure in 1886. The altar of the 1886 Catholic church was preserved and placed in the new building. The parish hall seen to the right in the image below was used as a Catholic school.

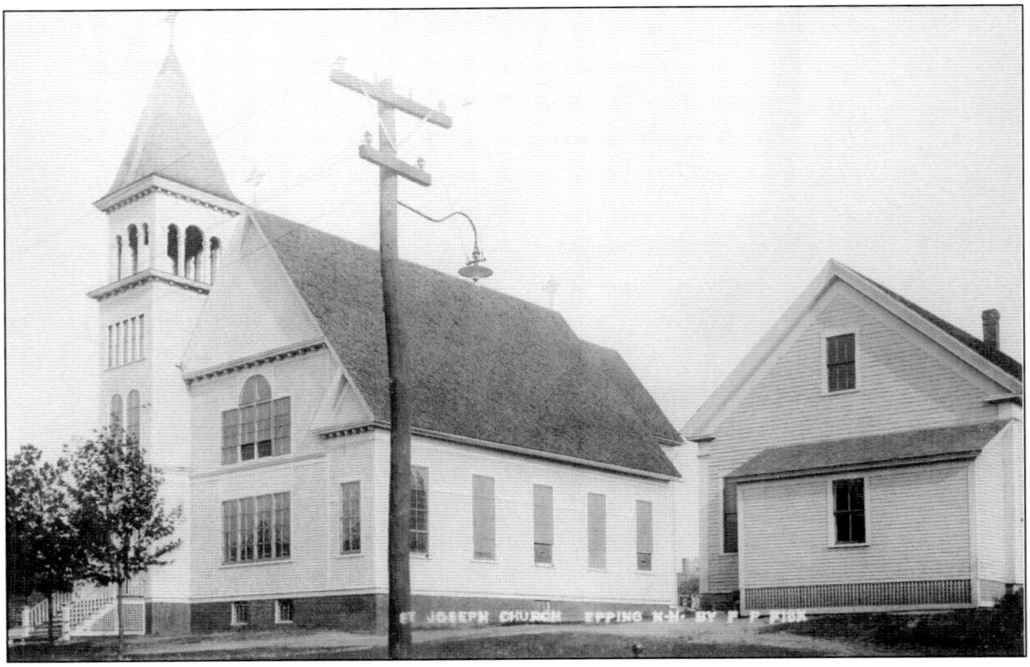

This is an early image of St. Phillip's Episcopal Church in Epping. No longer standing, the church was an impressive size and had been built in beautiful setting near an open field.

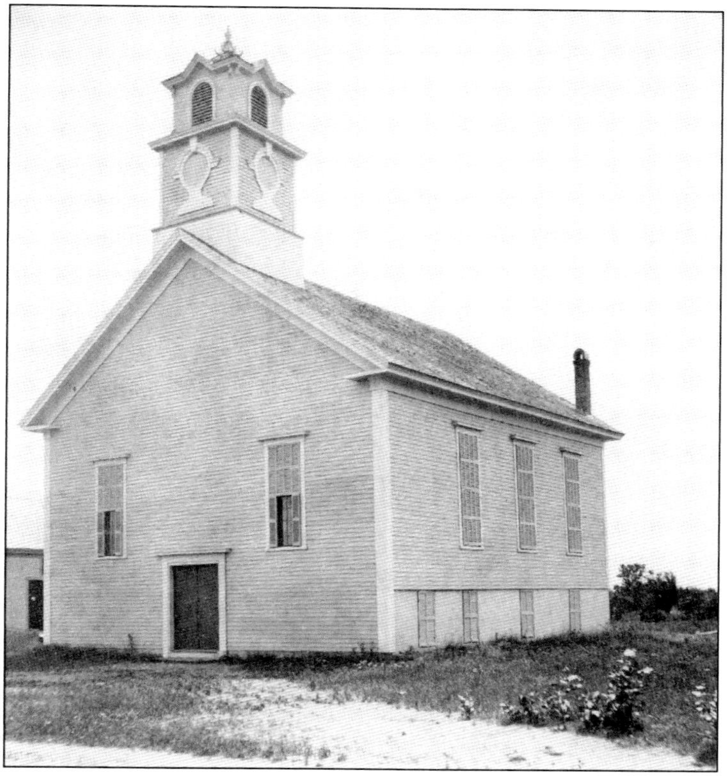

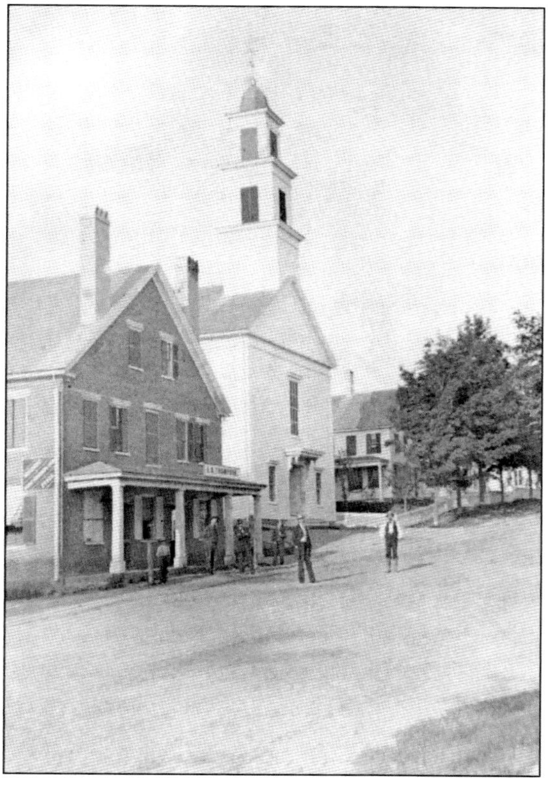

The Congregational Church sat on Pleasant Street near the downtown area. The white building beyond was a residence, and the brick building in front was the Graves Block, which was the home to White's Dry Goods Store. A group of men mill about in front of White's. Most likely they are there to pick up dry goods and perhaps visit other stores downtown. The men look pleased to be included in the photograph.

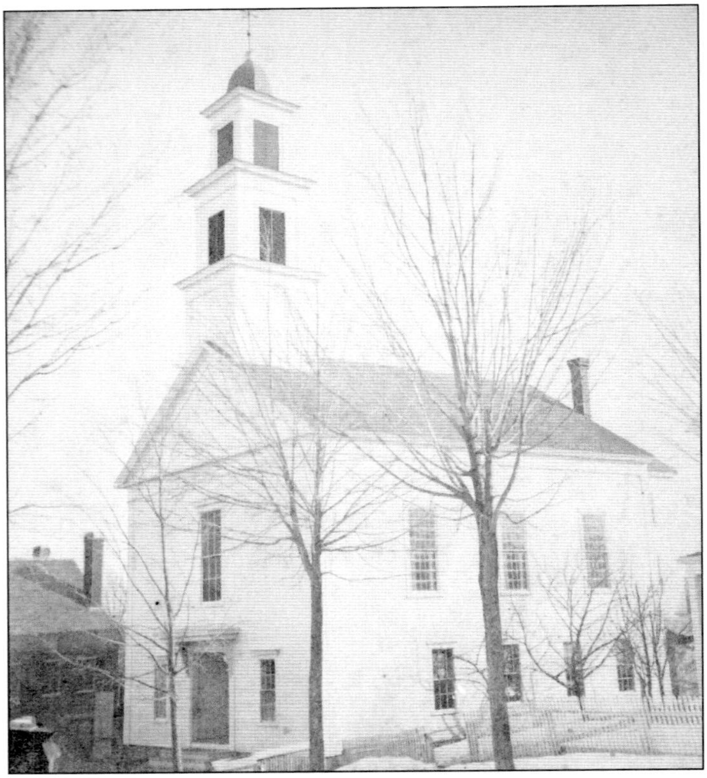

This photograph shows another view of the Congregational Church on Pleasant Street, where the church was moved to in 1875. This image was taken just before the fire of 1882, started by a kerosene lamp that broke in White's Dry Goods Store. The fire destroyed this church, the Graves Block, and a stable. Fire engines came from Rochester and Manchester aboard trains of the Nashua & Rochester Railroad and the Concord Railroad, but the church, Graves Block, and stable could not be saved.

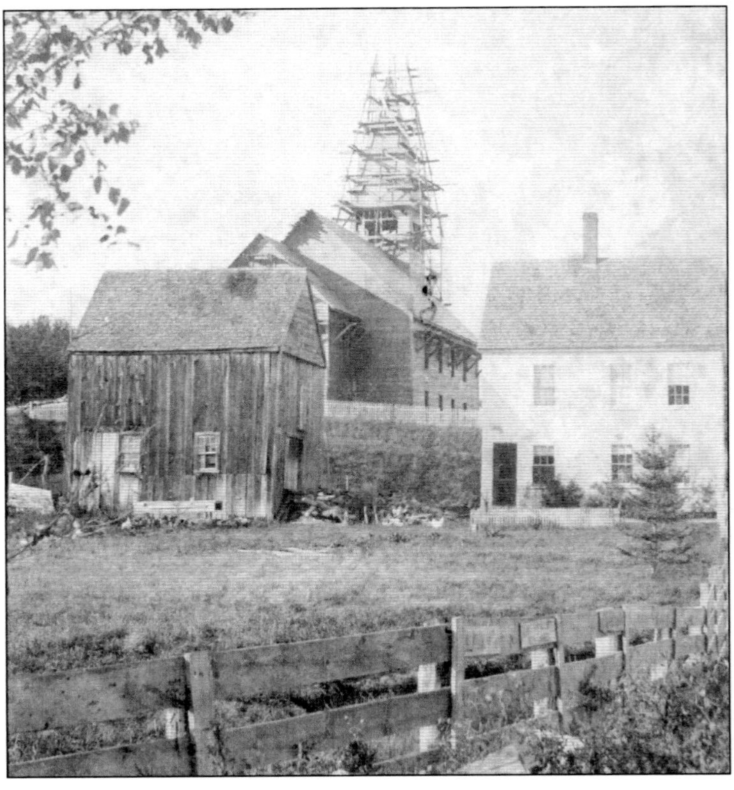

This image, taken from Main Street, shows the Congregational Church being rebuilt in 1883 after the fire of 1882. The building in the foreground at right is the home of Chavig Mallouf, with his barn to the left.

The interior of the Community Church in 1943 shows the impressive pipe organ at right, the tin panel ceiling, and the grand chandelier. The hymns have already been assigned for the next day of worship, and fresh flowers greet the eye of the worshiper. The Congregational Church became the Community Church in 1933 when the Methodists of Epping were welcomed into the congregation.

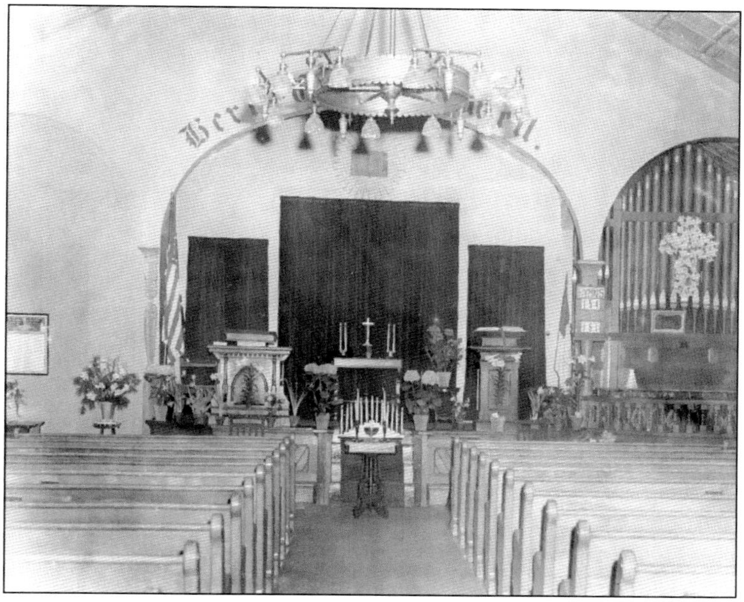

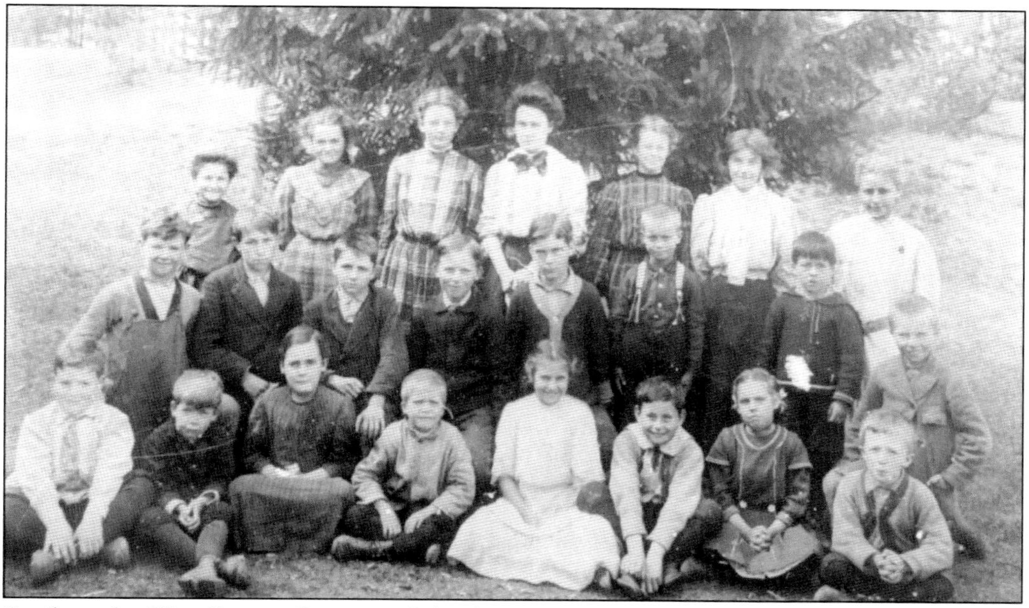

Pupils at the West Epping Grammar School convey varied emotions in this 1920 image. West Epping was School District No. Seven in Epping's original designation of eight school districts at a town meeting in 1806. These children, who varied in age, were likely all from West Epping and would study together in the small West Epping Grammar School.

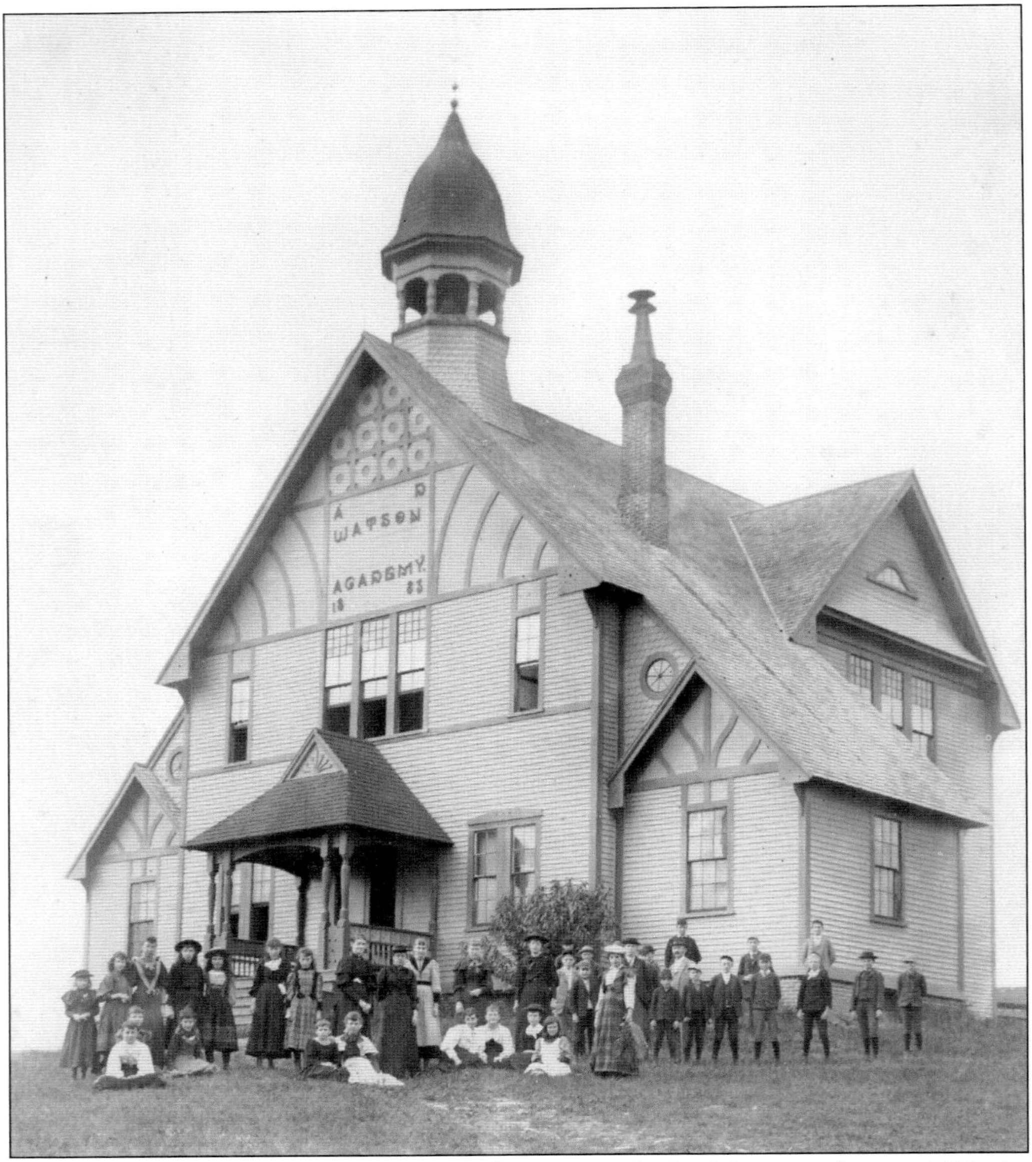


When it was decided that Epping needed a larger central school for its students in 1883, the building committee of John P. Sanborn, John Leddy, and Frank Chase awarded a contract to Beede & Shaw to build Watson Academy in three months for the price of $3,500. On September 17, 1883, a grand opening ceremony was held to dedicate the new academy, which most of the town attended. Rev. Fred White, pastor of the Methodist Church, dedicated the academy with a prayer. Rev. Josiah Stearns of the Congregational Church also addressed the crowd. Capt. George Shepherd, a Civil War veteran and president of the board of trustees, led the ceremony of the keys. Principal William H. Upton and former New Hampshire governor Benjamin Franklin Prescott gave speeches to the captive and enthusiastic audience. This image shows the boys and girls who attended Watson Academy shortly after the building's completion. The present-day Epping Middle-High School sits atop the hill behind Watson Academy.

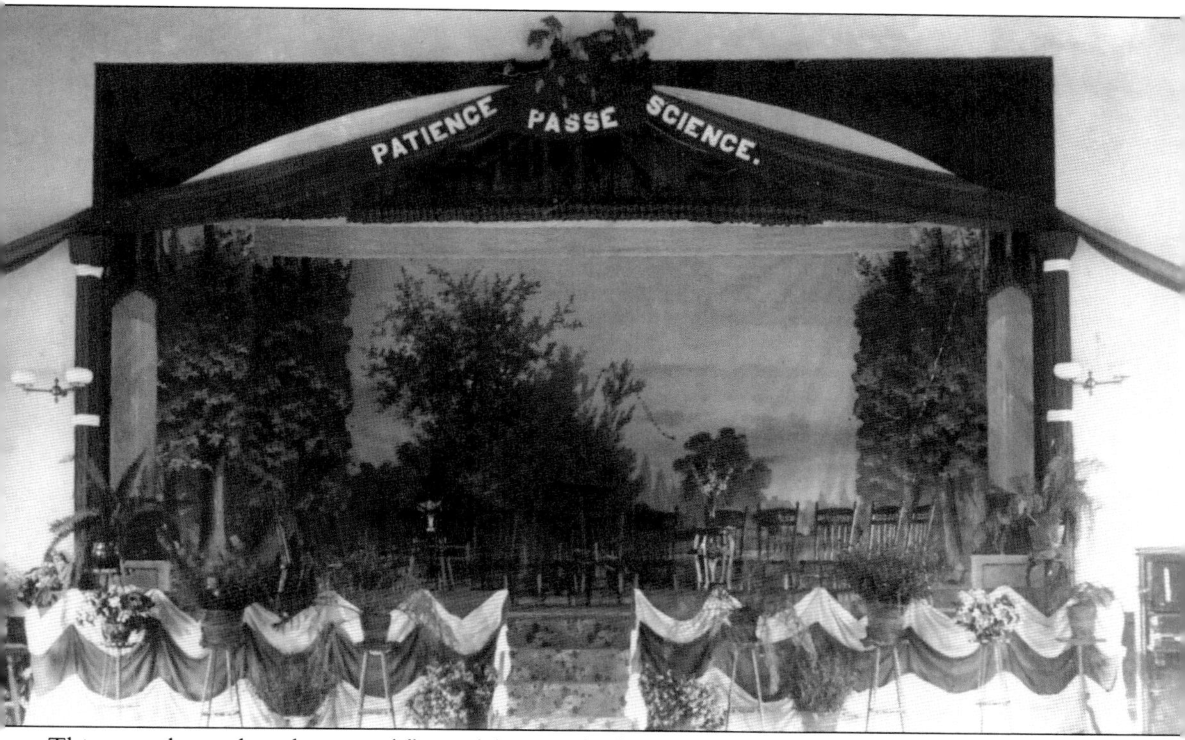


This stage, located on the second floor of the town hall, is decorated for a high school graduation. Though Watson Academy was a fine schoolhouse, it did not have a space large enough to host a graduation ceremony. The banner overhead reads, "Patience Passe Science," which is the French form of the proverb "Patience Surpasses Knowledge." The backdrop behind the graduating students depicts a romantic landscape while the stage front is covered in bunting. Flowers crowd the stage, and a piano can be seen at right to be played while the graduates marched on and off the well-appointed stage.

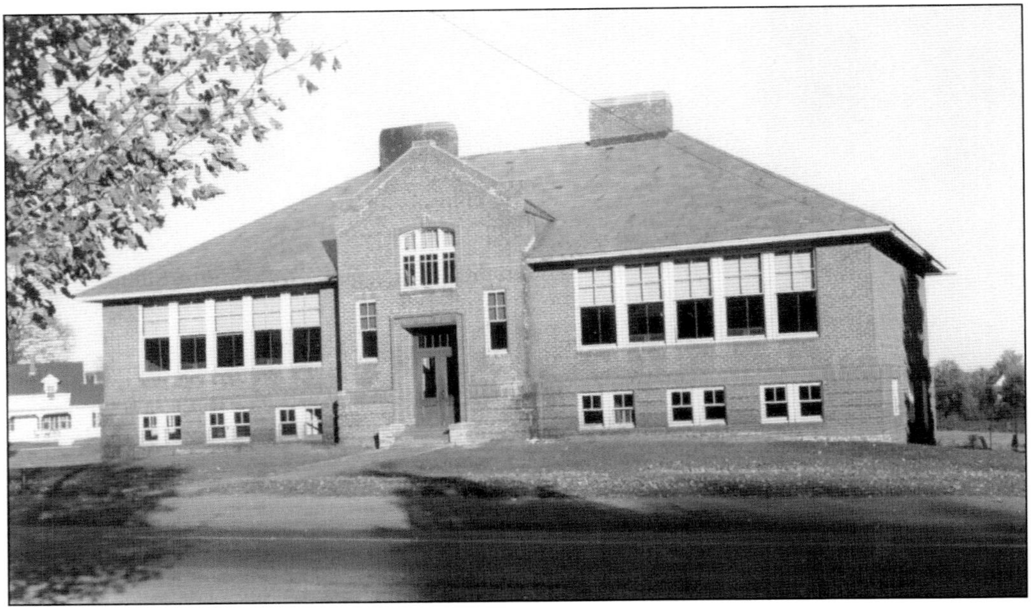

The Epping Central School is located on the corner of Main and Cate Streets. Once the location of William C. Brown's box factory, the Central School is just across the street from Watson Academy. When it was first built in 1915, the Central School consisted of four rooms. In 1940, two additional rooms were added, and the school contained seven grades of students. The Methodist church was located on the other corner of Main and Cate Streets. When the former Methodist church, by then the American Legion Post, burned down in 1954, the Central School escaped damage. The Central School still stands and has been used by the Epping Recreation Department. It now houses the offices for the Epping School District.

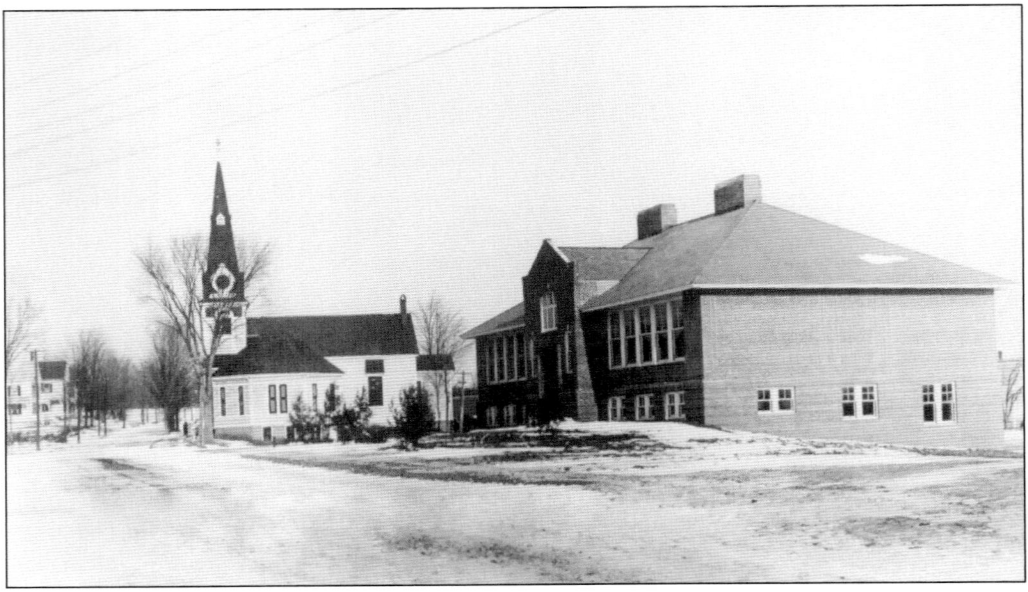

# *Three*

# HEDDING

The grounds of the Hedding Camp Meeting Association were first surveyed by Rev. James Thurston in 1862 in order to find a new venue for Methodist camp meetings that had been meeting in South Newmarket. The South Newmarket grounds, used since 1857, had become too small for the growing number of camp attendees. The lease for the grounds was also due to expire. And so, in 1862, land was purchased from Ezra Barber in Epping in order to secure a larger, more permanent location for future camp meetings.

The meeting ground in Epping, named Hedding after Bishop Elijah Hedding, was successful throughout its early years. Attendees came from all over New England with tents and stoves to set up on auctioned off plots. Rail lines offered a special discount to those traveling to the camp meetings, as well as collected an extra 5¢ as a donation to the camp. A special spur was constructed off the rail line that ran through Epping to bring in camp followers. About 6,000 people attended the camp meeting of 1863, rising to about 12,000 by 1868. Hedding was a resounding success.

Hedding grew in area as well as attendance. Over the years, more acreage was purchased, and permanent buildings began to pop up among the tents. In 1870, stables were built to house the horses of travelers who decided to forgo the trains. Cottages began to replace the tents on avenues that got their names from Methodist reverends. Even the founder of the Methodist Church, Rev. John Wesley, was honored in Wesley Park on the west end of the campground.

Hedding Campground survives today as a sort of town within the town. Tucked away in a wooded lot in the east of Epping, the Methodist tradition of camp meetings lives on in the charming little cottages and large central meeting hall of Hedding.

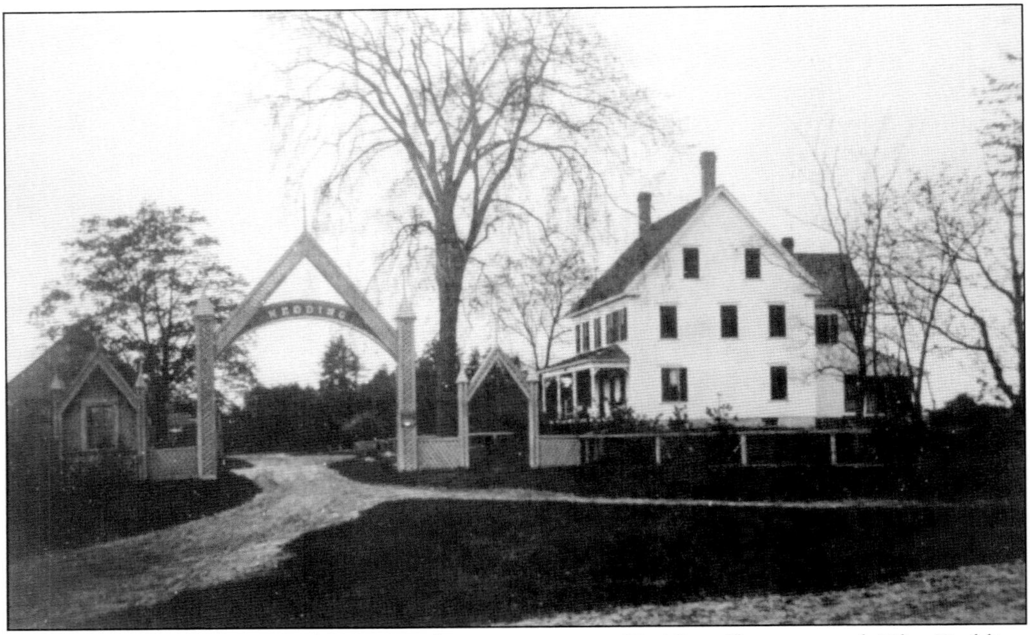

The Barber farmhouse stands next to the entrance into Hedding Campground. The Hedding Camp Meeting Association purchased the land for its camp meetings from Ezra Barber, whose family had long been residents of Epping, in 1862. Thousands of attendees to the camp meetings flowed under the ornate latticed archway and into the grove to set up tents for the multiple days of worship and fellowship.

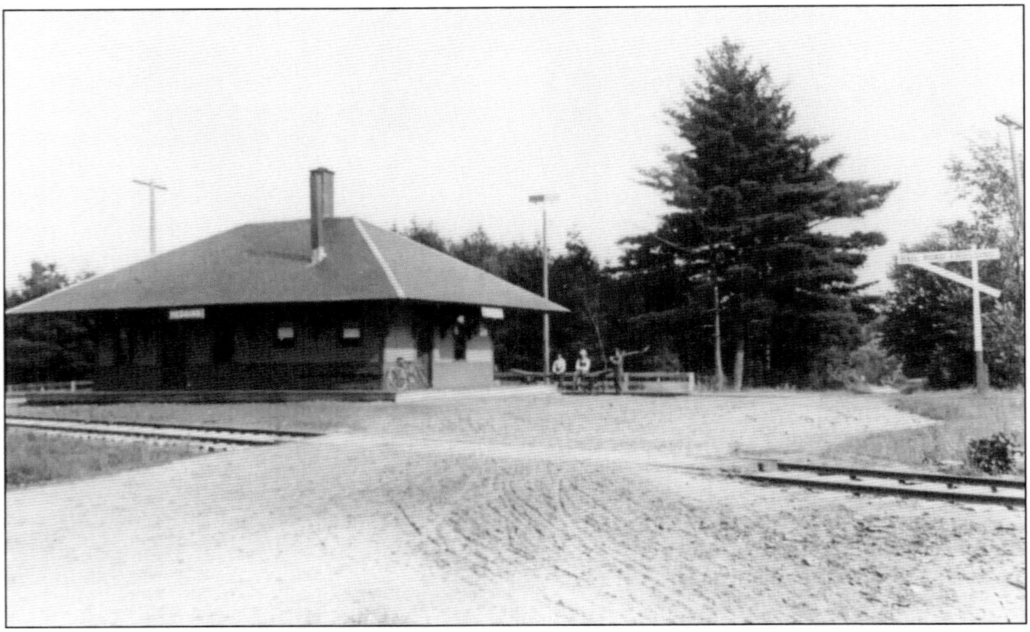

A special spur was built off the railroad line that ran east-west through Epping to bring camp attendees directly into Hedding. Two men relax on a fence while talking to a man with a shovel and wheelbarrow at the Hedding railroad depot. A bicycle, perhaps the mode of transportation for one of the men, leans against the depot. The spur was discontinued, and the track was taken up in 1901.

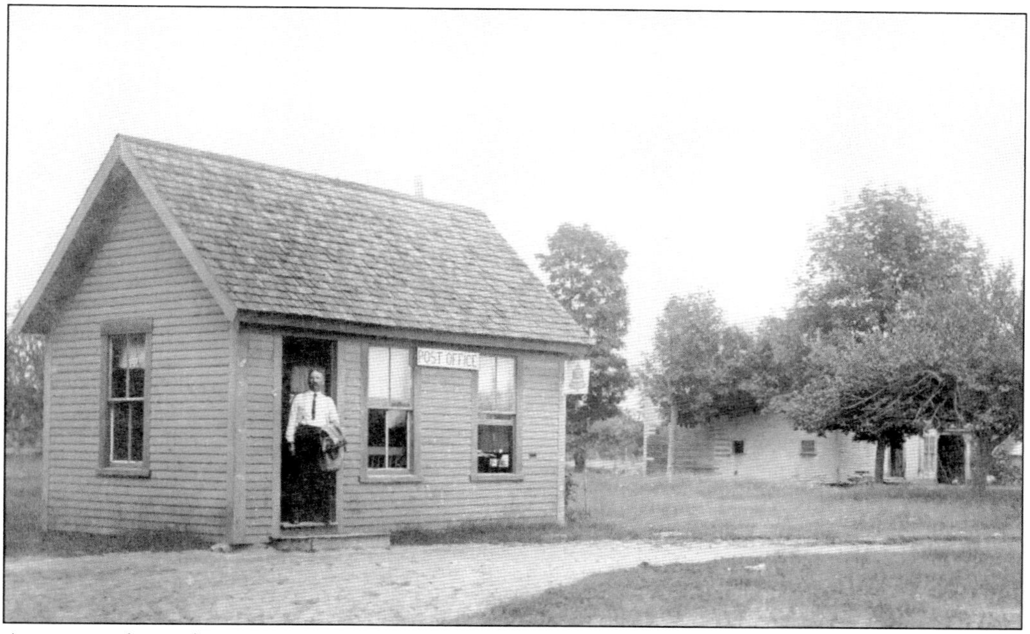


A man, perhaps the postmaster or just a patron, stands in the doorway of the East Epping Post Office. The first East Epping Post Office building was opened in 1876 to service the rapidly growing Hedding Campground. This later building has a sign hanging that advertises a "Local & Long Distance Telephone."

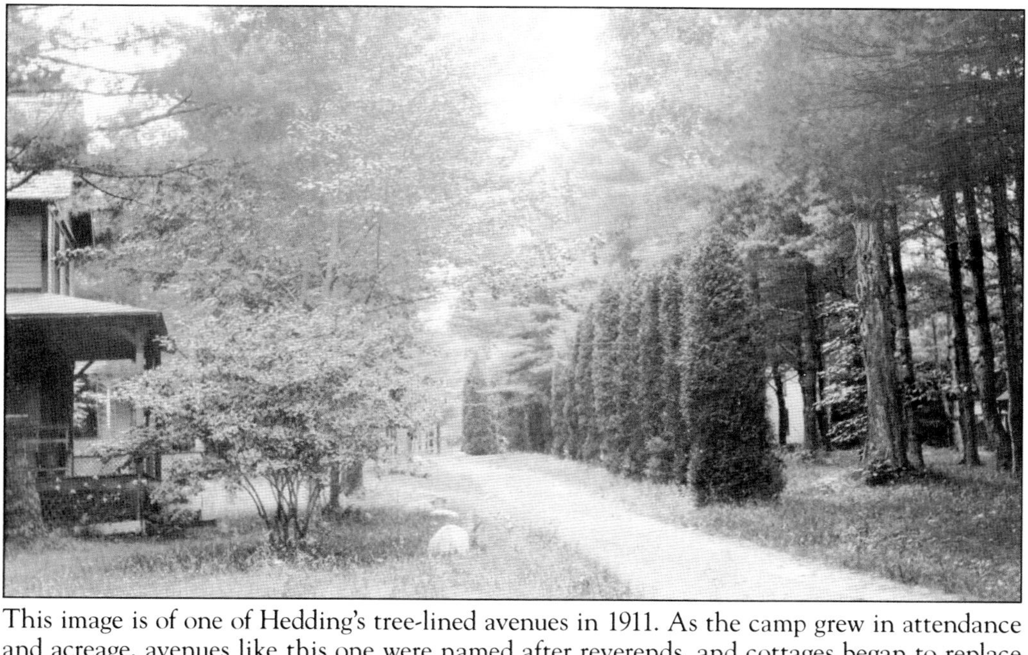

This image is of one of Hedding's tree-lined avenues in 1911. As the camp grew in attendance and acreage, avenues like this one were named after reverends, and cottages began to replace tents. The cottages are built in the middle of the groves of trees, providing shade as well as a rustic campground feel.

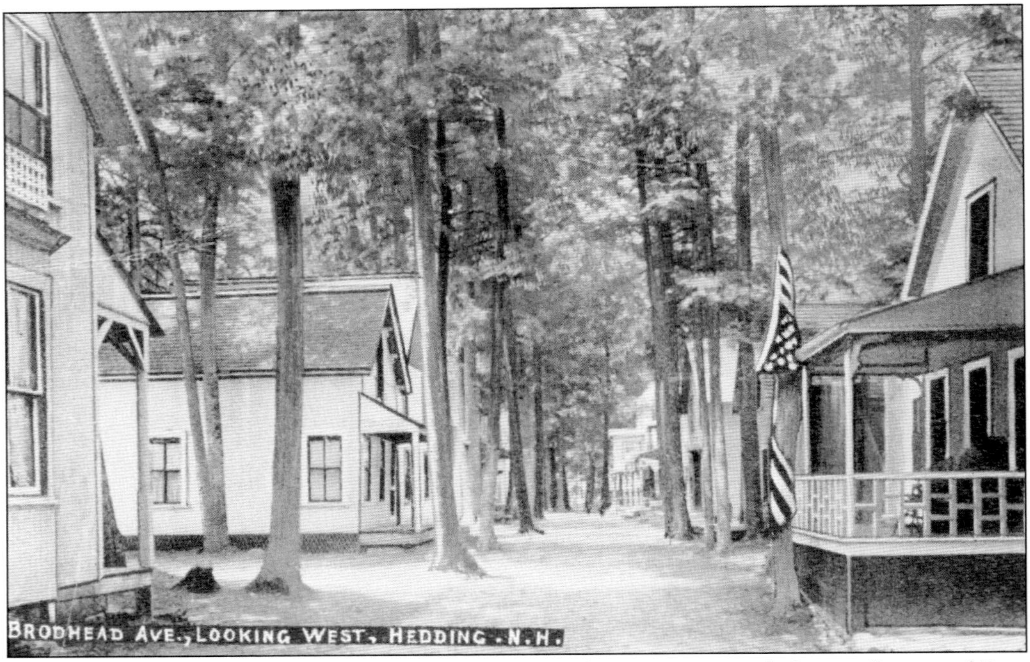


This view of Brodhead Avenue is looking west in Hedding Campground. Originally named First Avenue, Brodhead Avenue was renamed for Rev. John Brodhead. Cottages line the avenue in close proximity, some very plain, some with porches, and some elaborate and ornate. All of them are nestled within the trees of the grove.

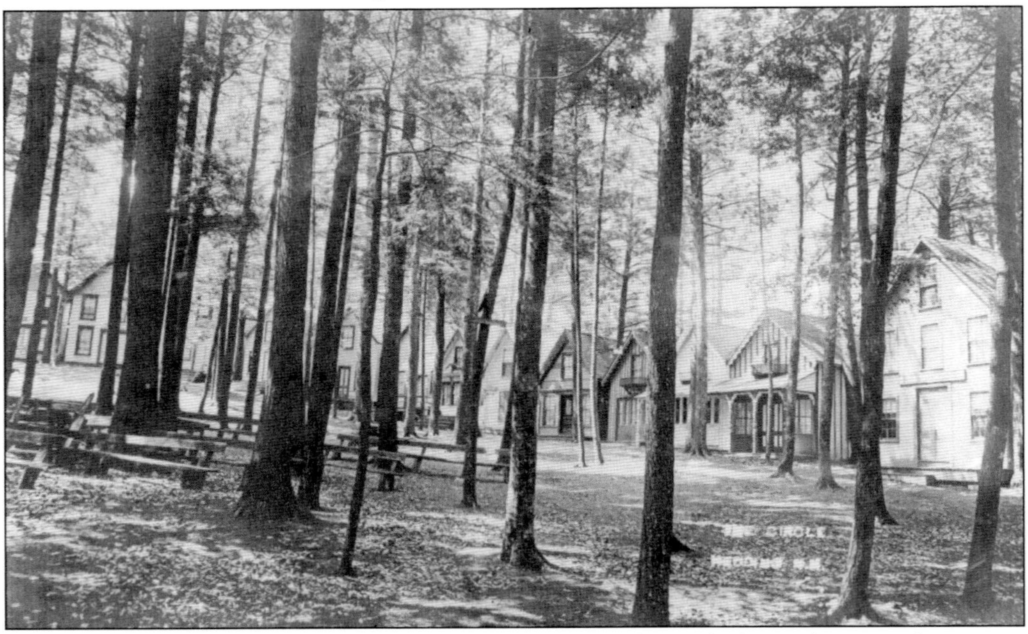

The Public Circle in the center of Hedding stretched even beyond what is shown in this image. The buildings are, running from left to right, the West Hampstead house, First Church Manchester house, Salisbury house, Smithstown house, North Salem house, and Epping Society House. The Newfields house is on the far right, with some cottages in between. The benches of the outdoor auditorium are seen in the foreground at left.

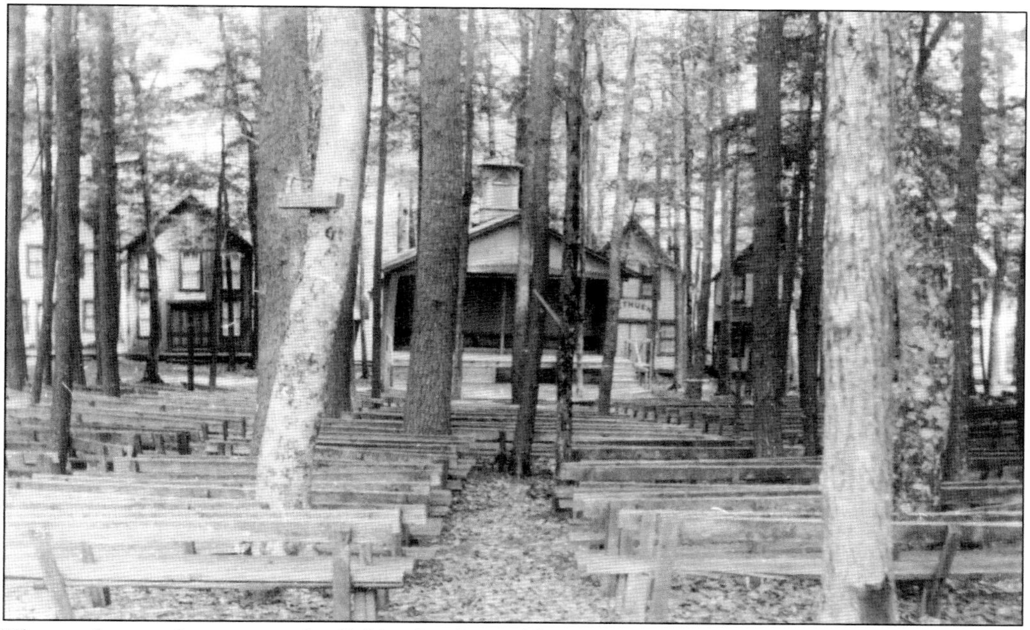

The outdoor auditorium in the Public Circle could seat as many attendees as could squeeze onto the benches. Even more attendees would be standing behind the benches. As with the cottages, the seats are built in among the trees of the grove. The preacher's stand helped to throw the speakers voice outward, toward the crowd.

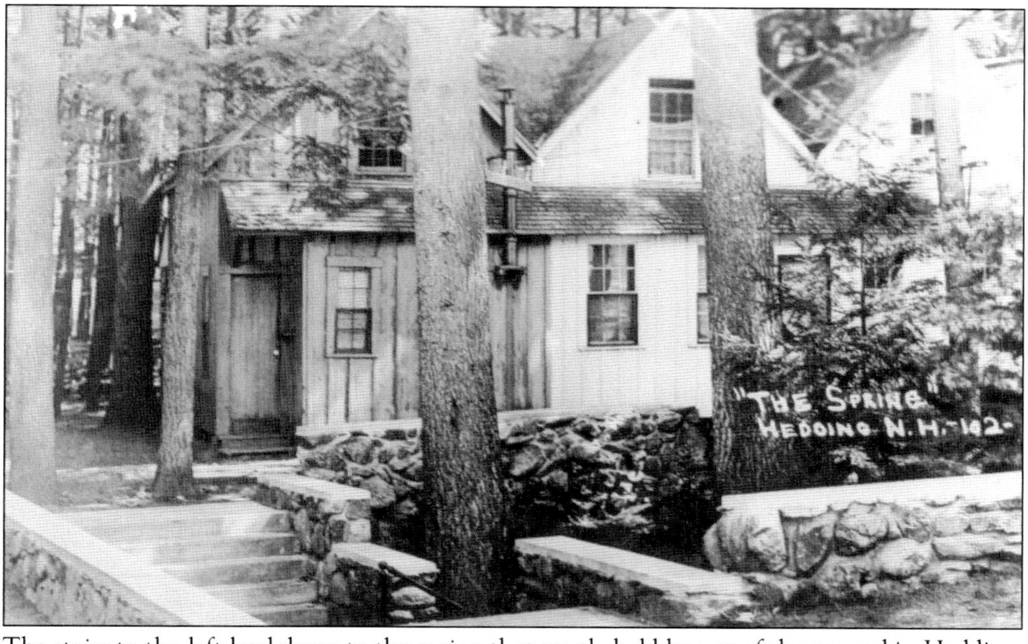


The stairs to the left lead down to the spring that gently bubbles out of the ground in Hedding. The spring, then simply a stream of water darting among the trees, absent of the stone wall built around it with rocks taken from the Barber farm, was one of the attractive features that drew the Hedding Camp Meeting Association to the grove. The spring water was valued for its purity and was believed to have medicinal value.

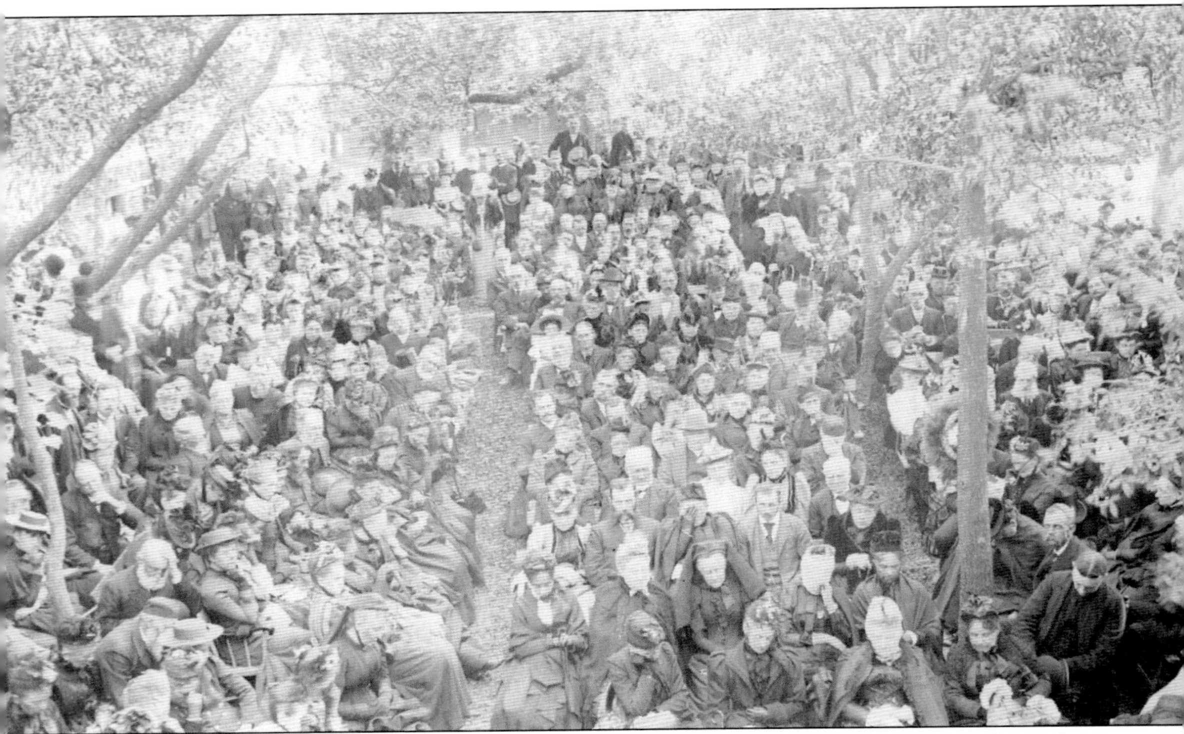

Camp attendees crowd into the outdoor auditorium seating to listen to sermons. Some bow in prayer, others seem to be in deep contemplation, and others simply look into the camera. Hedding attracted thousands of attendees, rising steadily from around 6,000 in 1863 to about 12,000 by 1868. It was no small wonder that the population of Hedding came to demand a spur on the rail line as well as its own post office. The spring supplied water to the camp and stores were also founded to provide food and other provisions.

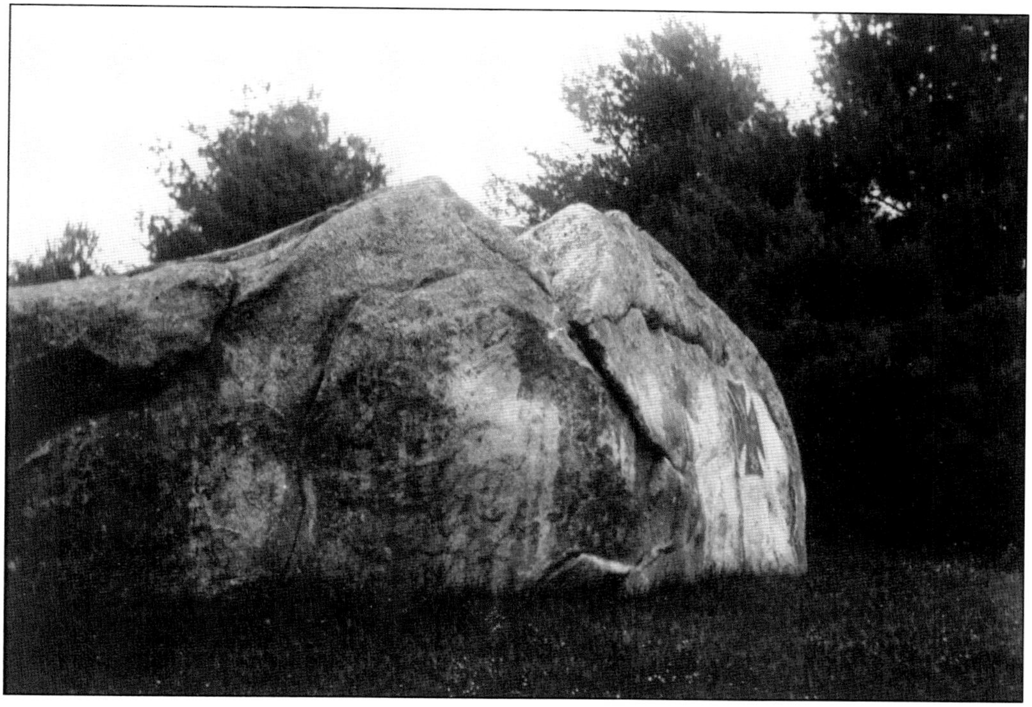

Vincent Rock in Hedding Campground was named for the founder of Chautauqua University in New York, Bishop John H. Vincent. Vincent Rock became a popular spot for children to climb around and families to picnic. These two men show just how large the rock is. A remnant of New Hampshire's glacial past, this large rock was left behind when the thick rivers of ice receded at the end of the Ice Age. The symbol of the Epworth League has been painted on the broad, flat side of the rock.

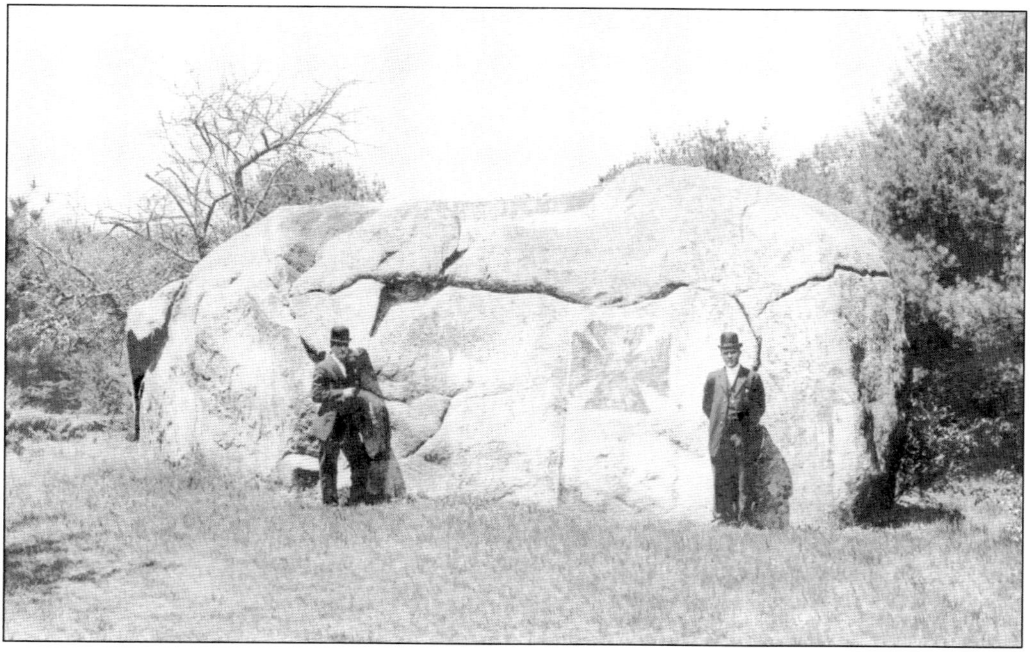

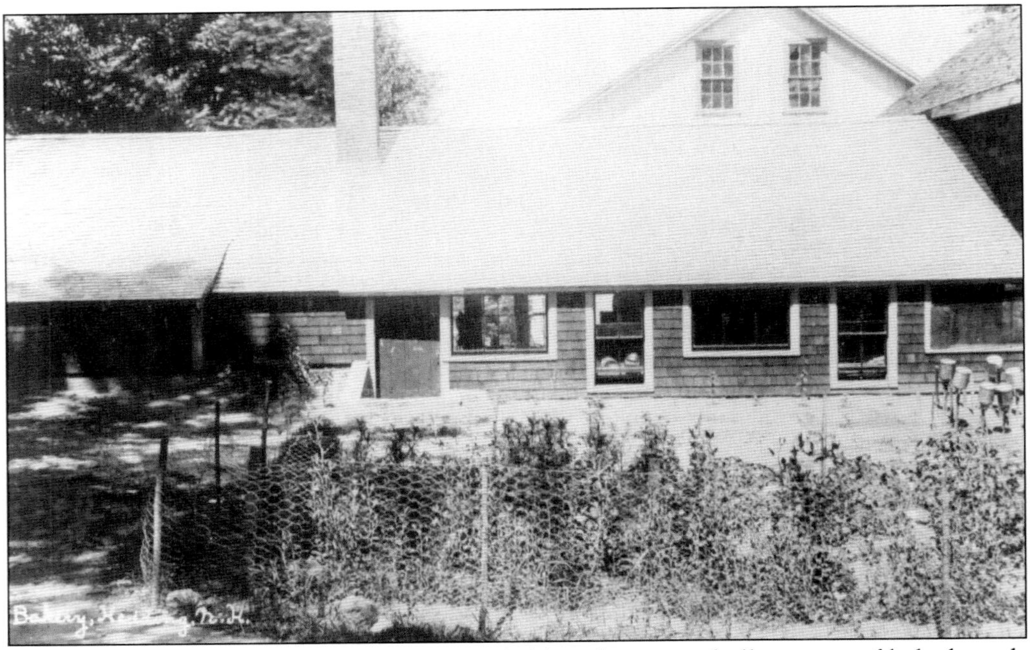


This building housed the bakery that provided bread, pies, and all manner of baked goods to the attendees of Hedding. A small garden, protected by chicken wire, can be seen in the foreground.

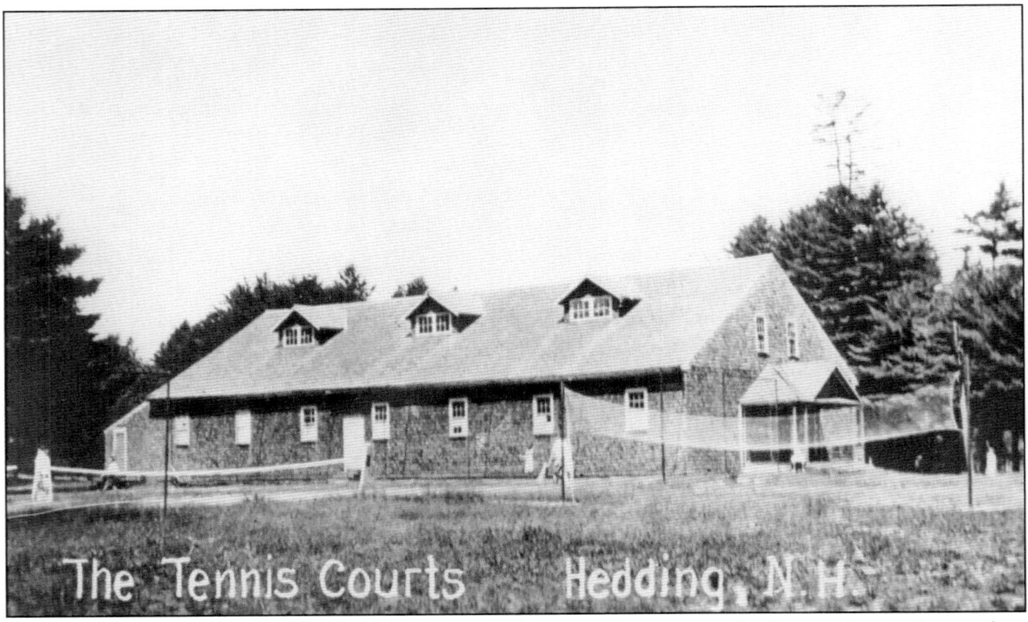


The tennis courts in front of the large meetinghouse, Chautauqua Hall, could also be used to play volleyball. As the cottages of Hedding began being opened throughout the summer, the Hedding Camp Meeting Association bought Chautauqua Hall, originally built as a roller-skating rink in Exeter, in 1887 and placed it in Hedding to provide a meetinghouse where attendees could worship in poor weather.

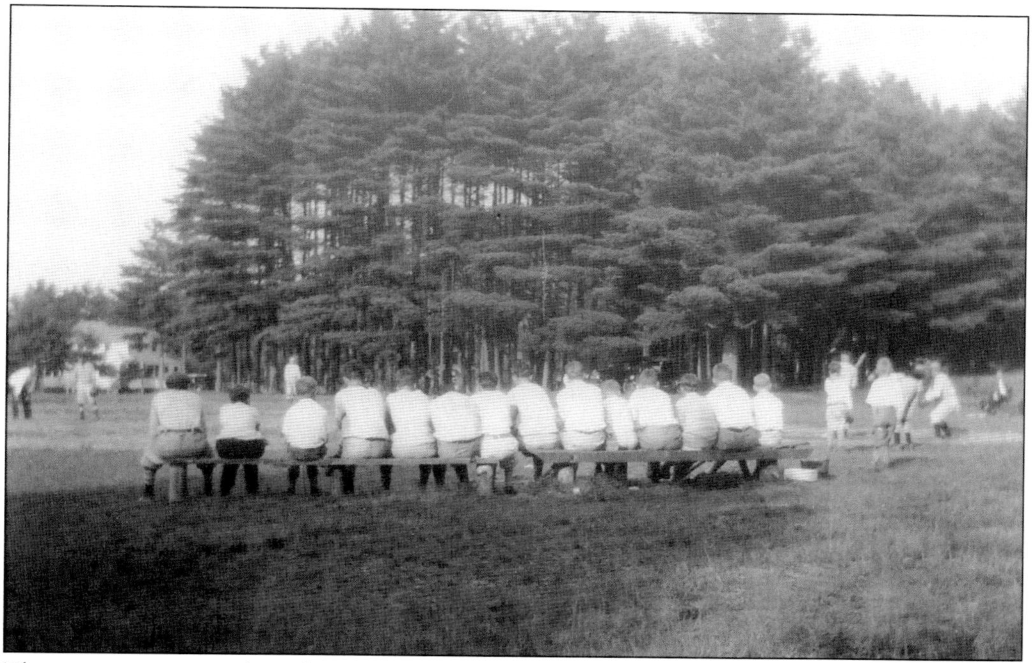

There was room enough in the center of Hedding Campground for a baseball field to be created. Hedding teams played the national pastime against one another, against teams from other Methodist organizations, against teams from Epping, or against other neighboring towns. While competitive, the games were always held in a sporting spirit.

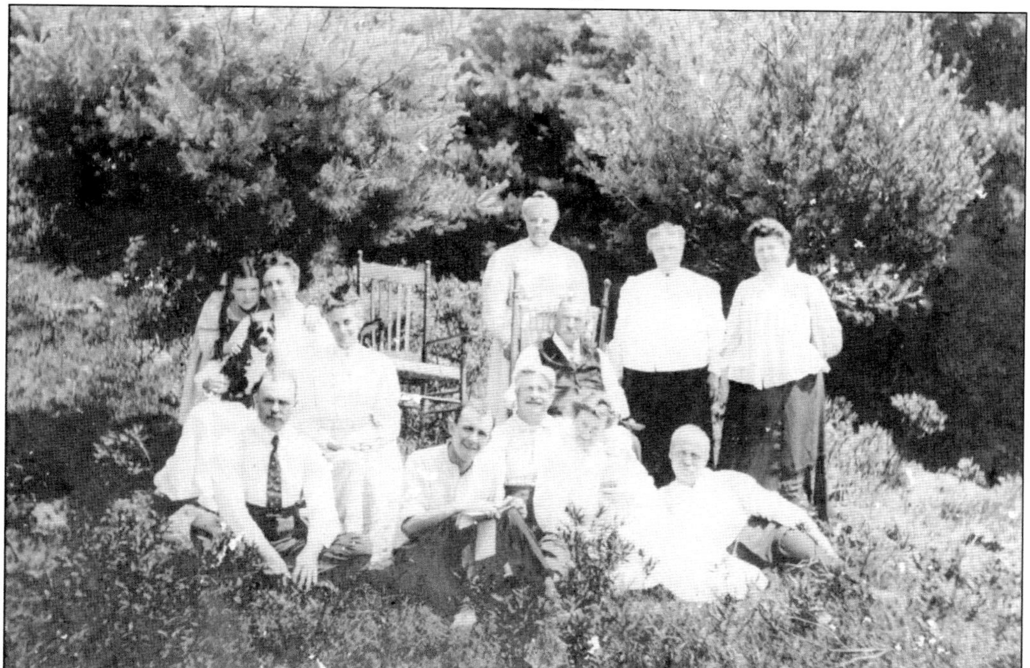

Hedding contained enough acreage that attendees could easily slip away into the woods to find a clearing for a picnic. This group brought along a couple chairs for the older members of the group. A happy dog was also welcomed by the outing party.

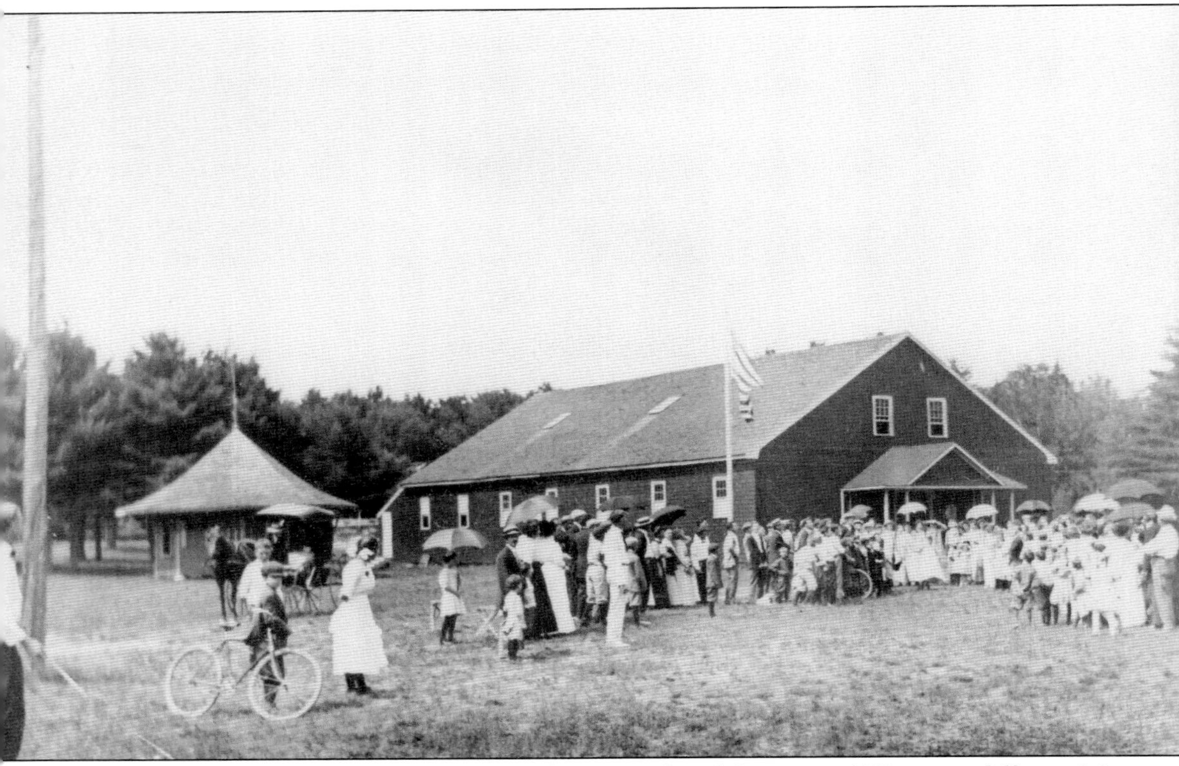

Old Home Day at Hedding always drew a large crowd, and this one in 1912 was no different. Men with straw boating hats, women with parasols, and patient children—one with a bicycle—listen to an address to open the festivities. The pagoda to the left of Chautauqua Hall was built as a stand to provide refreshments to camp goers.

# *Four*

# FARMING

Epping has a long history of farming. Native Americans farmed the fields while fishing along the banks of the Lamprey and hunting in the forests of Epping. When European settlers began settling the western part of what was then the town of Exeter, they cleared fields, plowed the earth, and built the many stone walls that run along roads, through the forest, and across the fields of Epping. The same stones that were turned up and fashioned into walls were used to construct the foundations for the farmhouses and barns that would come to house residents and their livestock.

Epping has been home to working farms for the entirety of its history. The longest-running farm, founded as Applehurst Farm, has grown produce and raised livestock atop Red Oak Hill uninterrupted since 1755. Epping's farms have grown corn, beans, gourds, apples, and all manner of produce, as well as raised sheep, pigs, chickens, and cows. If one take a ride down Prescott Road today, one might see the highland cattle of Whitegate Farm, with their long wavy coats of hair and broad horns, grazing on the green grass of the rolling hills.

Epping, like many New England towns, was founded on farming. While industry and urbanization took over parts of Epping and helped the town grow, farming has always remained a lynchpin of the community.

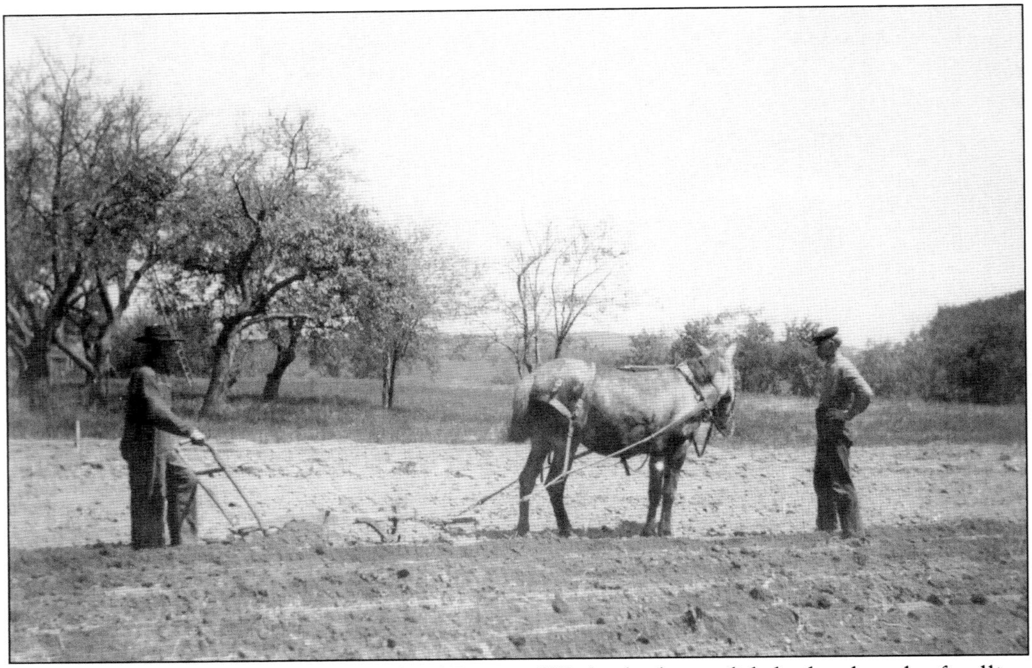

Two men plow furrows into the earth of Epping. While the horse did the hard work of pulling the plow, guiding the plow and horse to create straight and even furrows was an art form. Fruit trees can be seen in the back with a ladder propped against one to aid in reaching the high-hanging fruit.

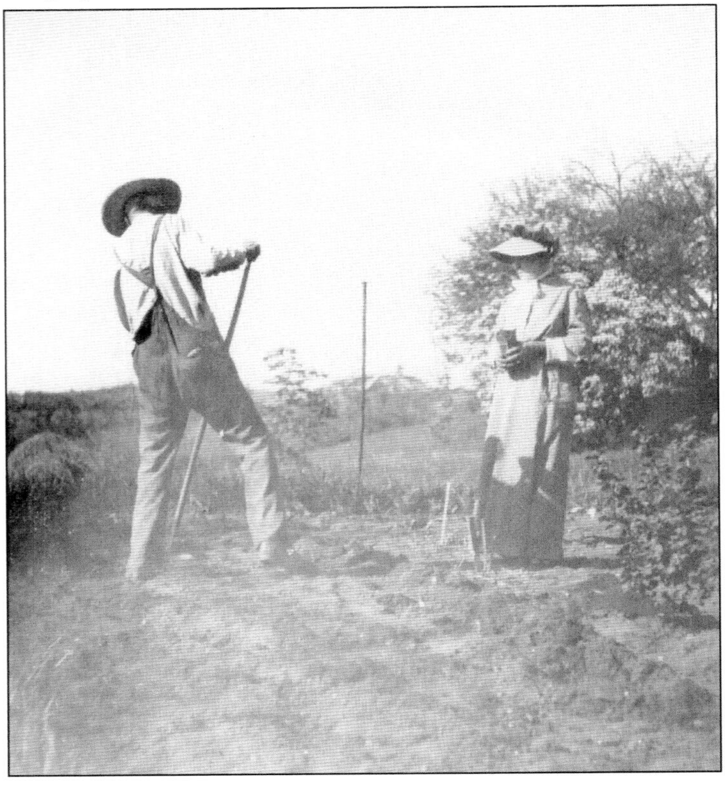

Some produce requires more attention than others. Here a farmer carefully hoes between rows while his wife stands at the ready with seed. It was important to start early in the short New England growing season to ensure a successful harvest.

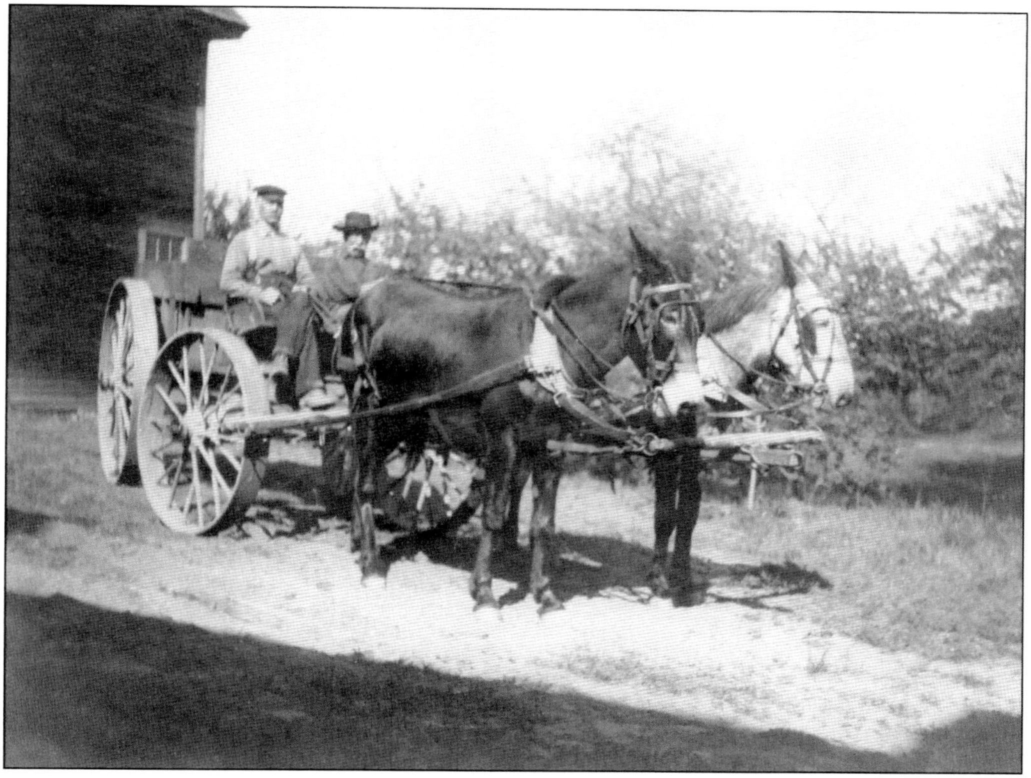

Horses and oxen were worth their weight in gold for farmers. A team like this was needed to plow hard-packed earth; remove heavy stones, stumps, and logs; and bring the fruits of a farmers' labor to market. This wagon might be on its way to collect supplies, inspect a field, begin the harvest, or bring produce to market.

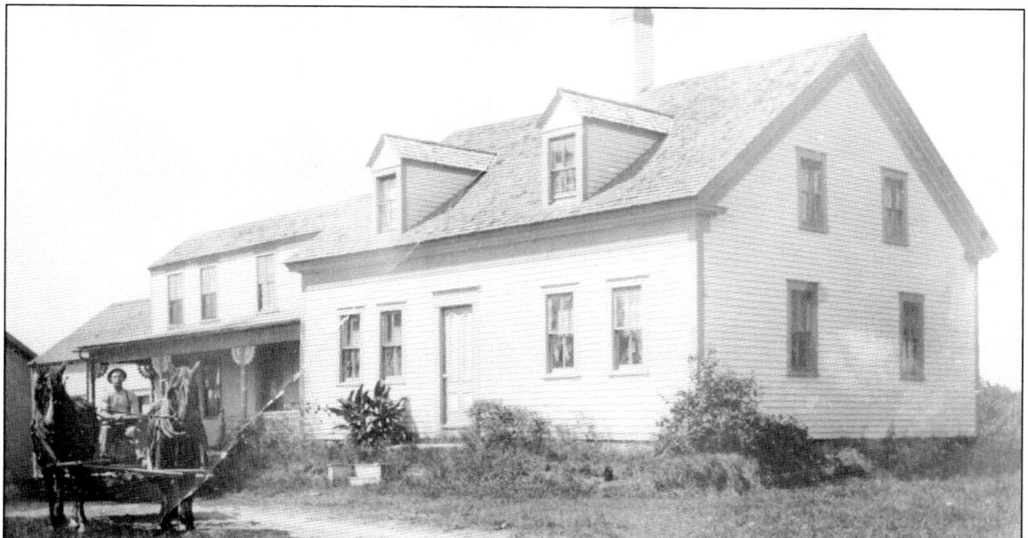

A farmer with his team of horses poses outside Brookside Farm around 1914. Farmhouses with large central chimneys for cooking and warmth were common in New England. As the family grew, or more space was needed, additions like the ones to the left could be put on.

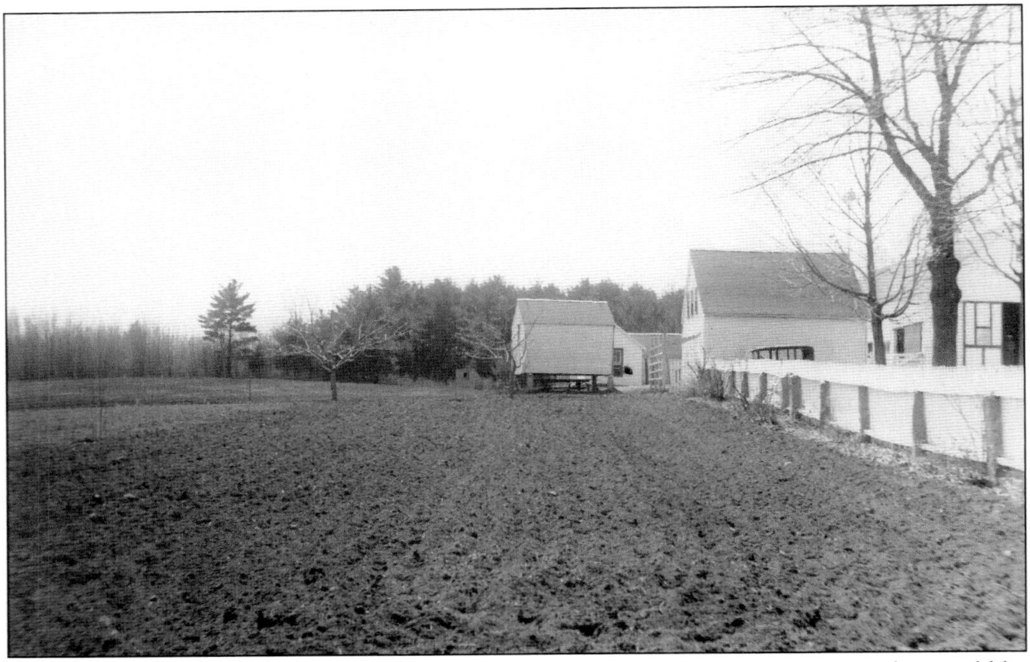

A freshly furrowed field on Plumer Road is ready for planting. The more acreage that could be readied for planting, the higher the chance for a farm to produce a successful crop yield. Planting a variety of produce was another way to ensure success. For example, if an early frost killed off a crop of tomatoes, a field of gourds, more resistant to cold, could save the farm from ruin.

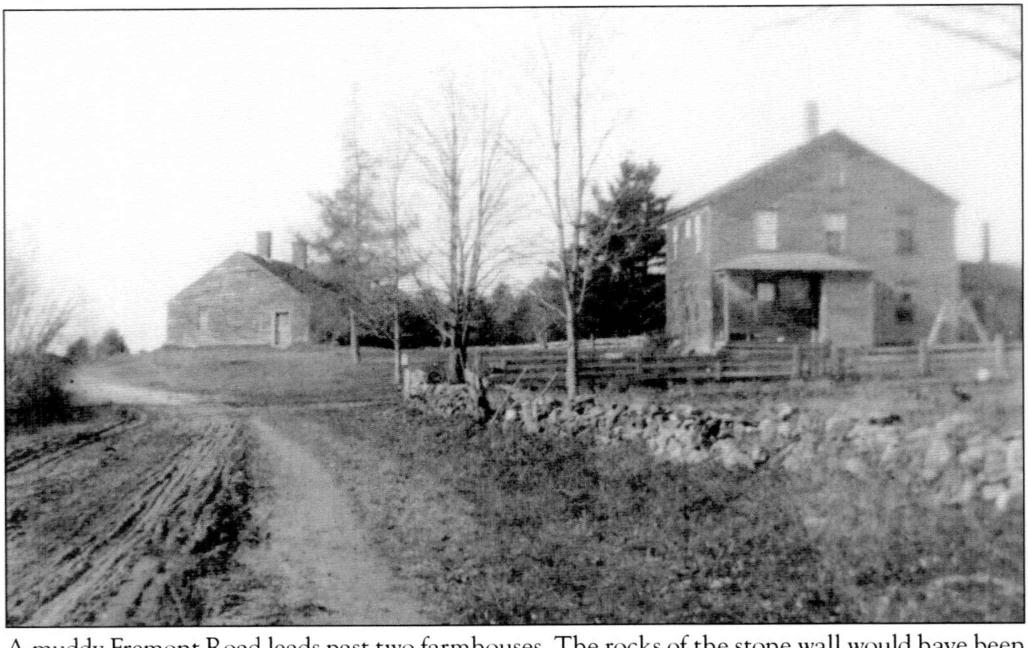

A muddy Fremont Road leads past two farmhouses. The rocks of the stone wall would have been dragged out of the rocky New Hampshire soil and placed along the property line to separate fields. Having close neighbors could be a godsend when an extra hand or a piece of equipment needed to be borrowed. Neighbors often supported one another by helping out when needed and calling in favors that were owed.

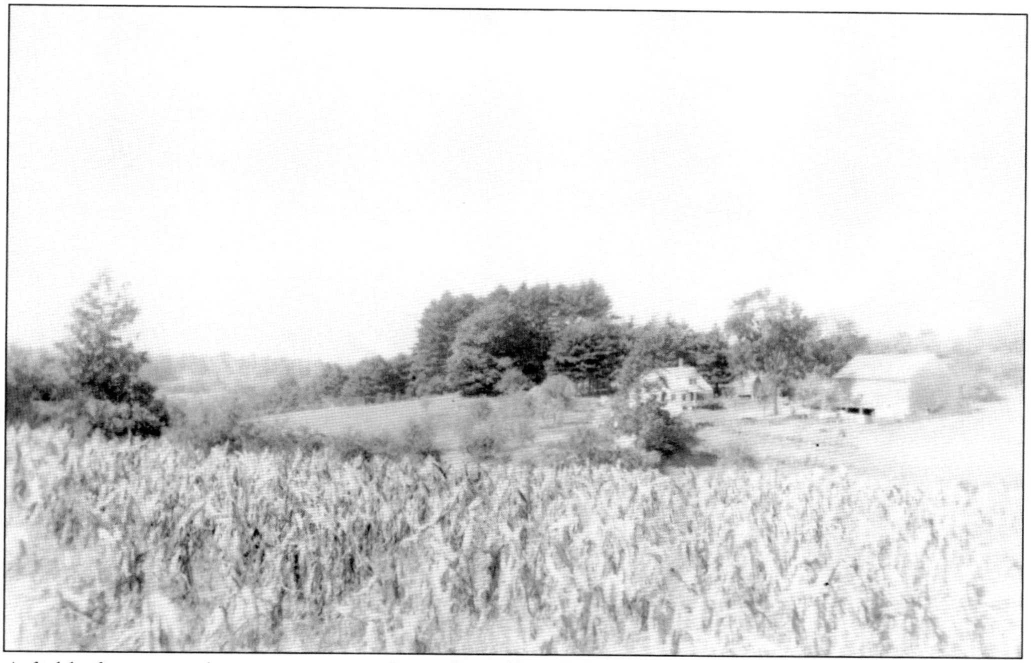

A field of corn can be seen growing along the rolling hills of Epping in the back cornfield of C.W. Woods around 1900. Corn could be ground into flour in gristmills, the first of which in Epping was built in 1746 by Joshua Folsom, or sold for food for both humans and livestock alike. The farm in the distance is that of Arabella Harvey.

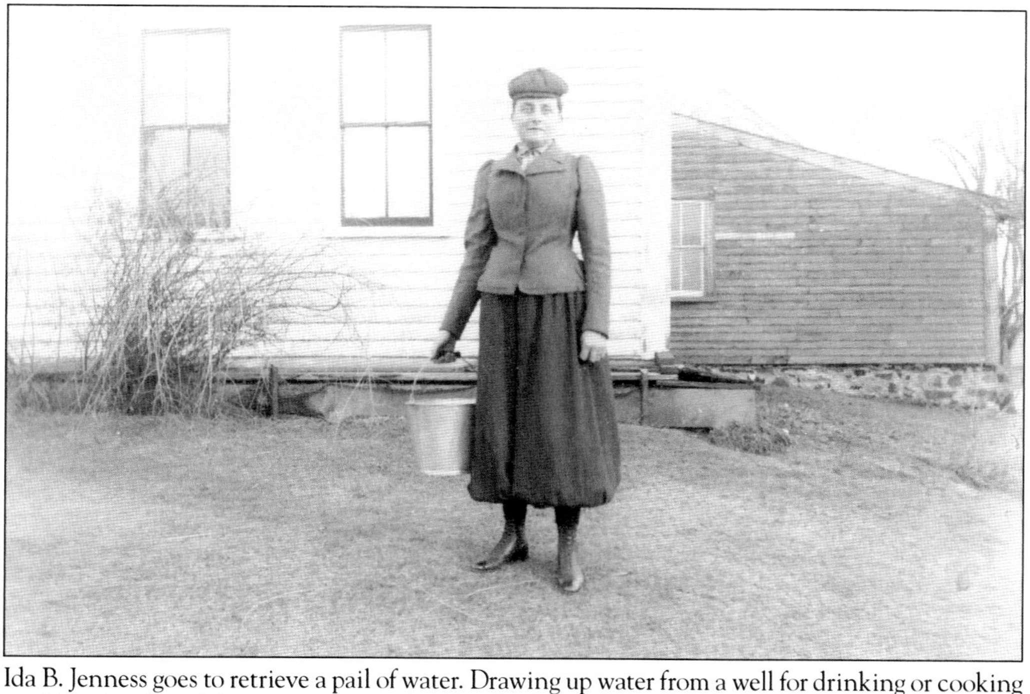

Ida B. Jenness goes to retrieve a pail of water. Drawing up water from a well for drinking or cooking could be hard work but was necessary. Animals were usually watered from streams or ponds on the farm. Ida Jenness's wool hat, jacket, and bloomers would have been heavy enough to keep her warm through spring and fall.

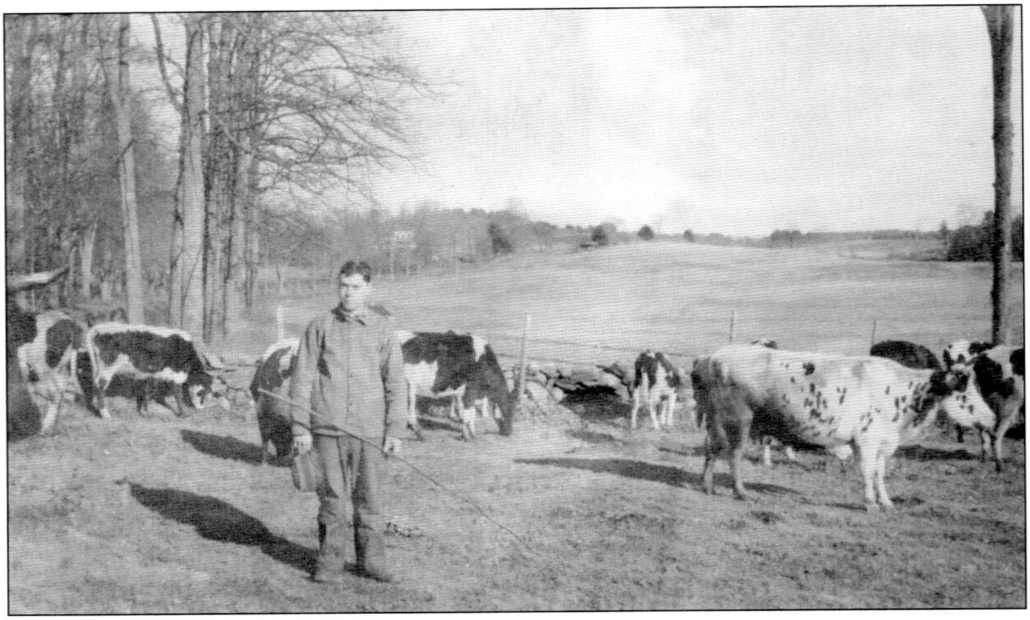

A young man with a switch tends to a herd of cows. The rolling fields in the background were perfect for planting long rows of crops or for use as grazing land for cows and sheep. The young man would be in charge of keeping the cows moving from field to field for grazing and making sure none wandered away. The stone wall could be a property line or used to separate two fields utilized for two different purposes. Below, Madge Pike poses with one of her favorite cows from the family herd. Orchards like the one Madge Pike stands in could also be used as grazing land before the growing season and after the harvest.

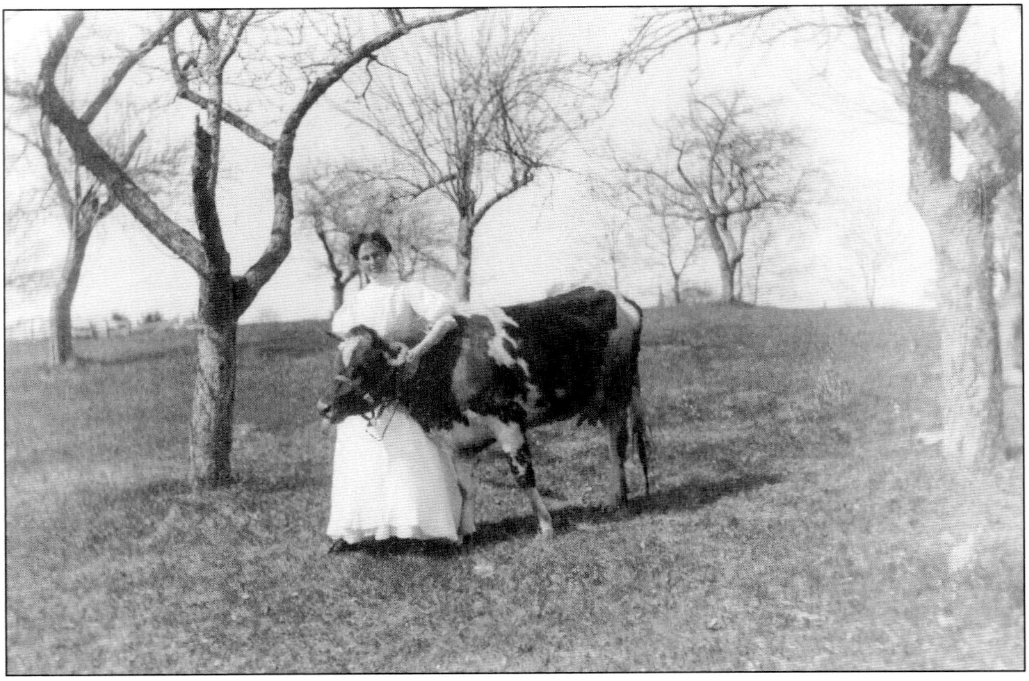

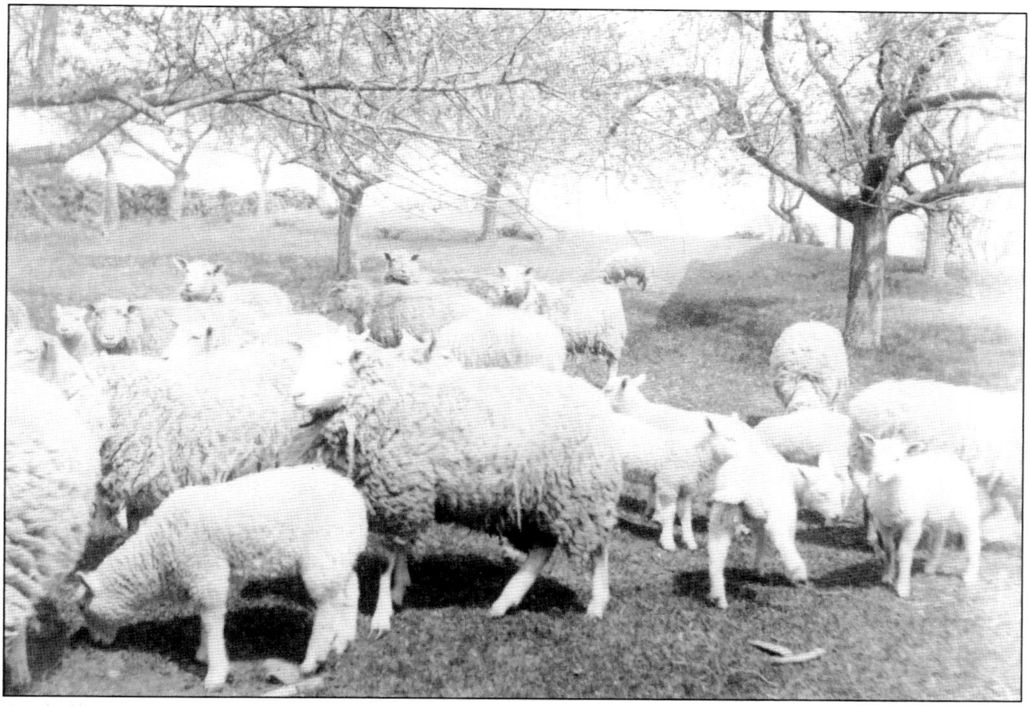

Arabella Harvey's sheep graze among the orchard trees on Red Oak Hill around 1900. Harvey and many other farmers raised sheep for both their wool and their mutton. Epping was home to a woolen mill founded in 1840 by Enoch Pearson that ran until about 1920. Wool could be sold to this mill or to residents who could spin their own yarn.

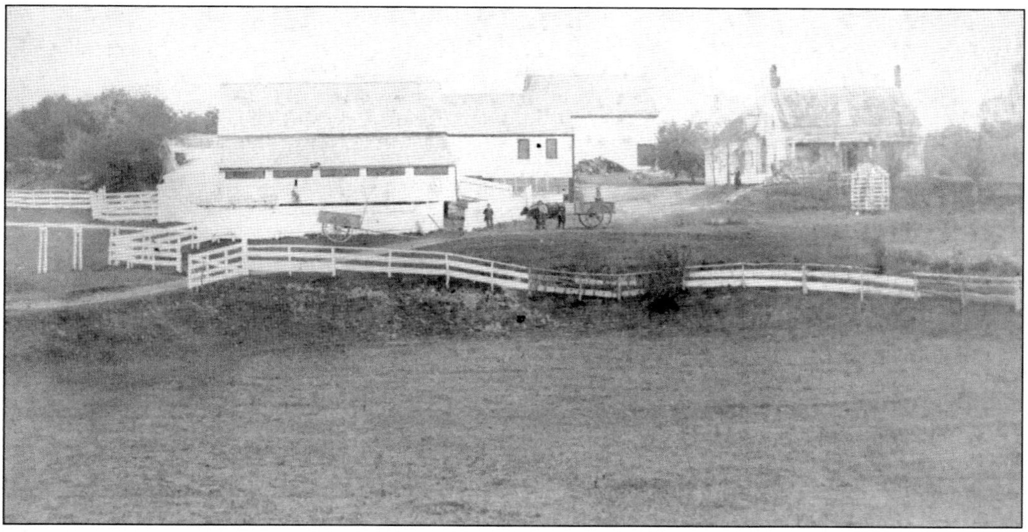

This image from 1890 shows just how large Epping's farms could be. Multiple barns housed livestock, feed, and equipment. Three men pose with a team of oxen hitched to a wagon while a woman stands by a tree up by the house. This farm would have taken a lot of work to maintain, and it is probable that it was run by either a large family or that farmhands were hired to do some of the work.

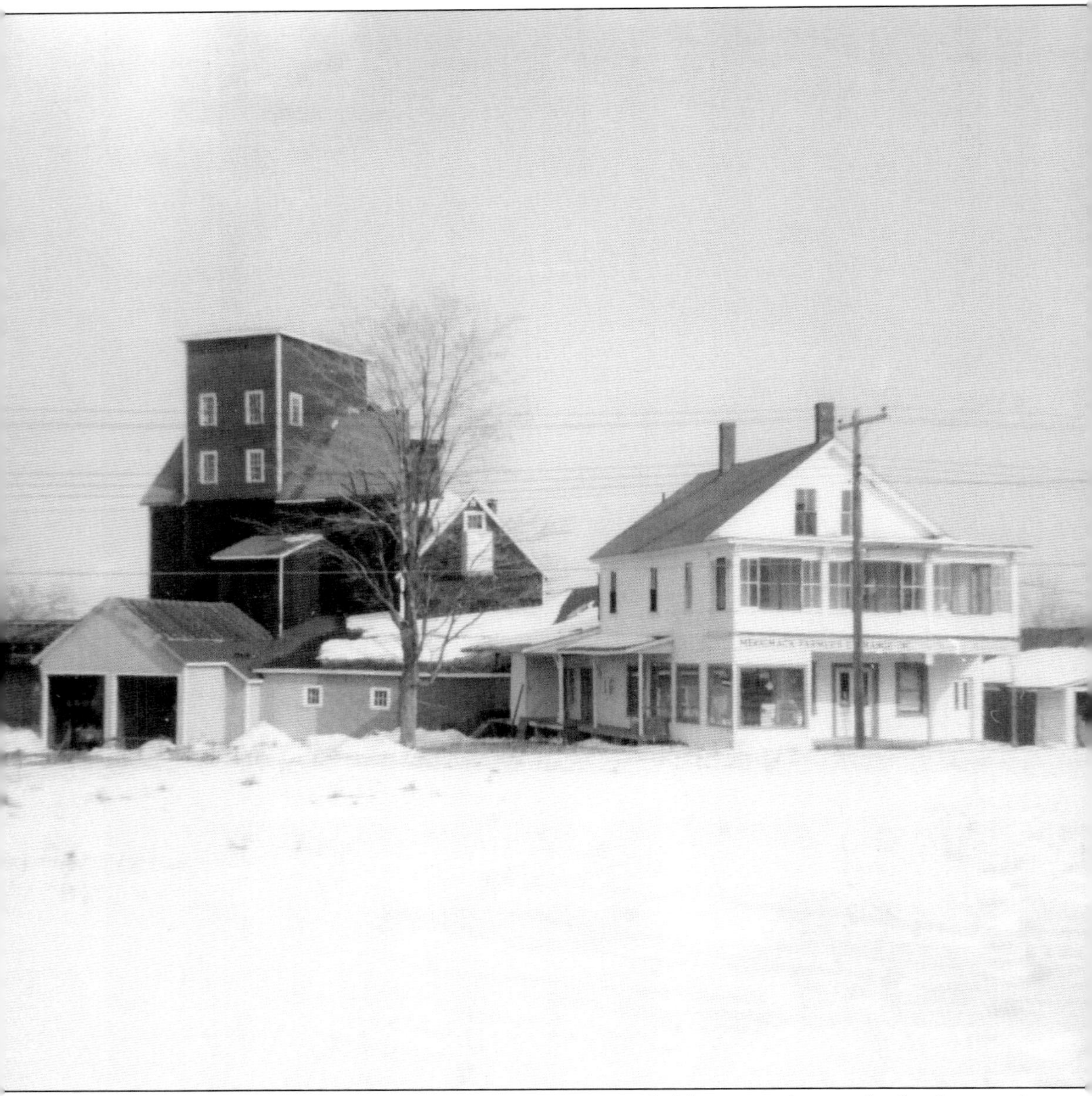

The Merrimack Farmers' Exchange on Main Street provided farmers with an outlet for their goods. Placed along the rail line, farmers could load their produce or livestock onto train cars from the farmers' exchange. They could also buy goods that were brought into the farmers' exchange from the same trains. The farmers' exchange also did a brisk business in milling for the farmers. The tall part of the building in the rear is a grain elevator that has since been removed. The building now serves as office space.

# *Five*

# The Lamprey

The Lamprey River winds through the center of Epping before curling north toward Lee. For centuries, the banks of the Lamprey have provided water, food, power, and recreation to the inhabitants of Epping. Before European colonization, Native Americans lived and camped along the banks of the river as far back as 8,600 years ago. They probably dug for freshwater mussels and built weirs to trap fish, turtles, and the American brook lamprey, which is native to the river and gives it its name. The American brook lamprey, a type of freshwater jawless fish, was prized among the Native Americans and later the European settlers as a food source. The American brook lamprey is now considered an endangered species by the New Hampshire Fish and Game Department, but they were once plentiful in the Lamprey River.

In 1746, Joshua Folsom began the first mill on the Epping section of the Lamprey River. By 1806, maps showed mills on both sides of the river at the Folsom Mill site. The Lamprey came to support gristmills, woolen mills, shoe factories, lumber mills, a plaster mill, and an ax-handle factory all along the Epping section.

Aside from food, water, and power, the Lamprey has long provided recreation to Epping residents. Swimming, boating, fishing, and ice-skating have made the river a popular spot in all seasons. The annual Lamprey River Canoe Race is held in Epping every spring. The steady, cool water is often shaded by an overhanging canopy of trees that line the sandy and rocky banks. It is no small wonder that the Epping section of the Lamprey River has been added to the National Wild and Scenic River System.

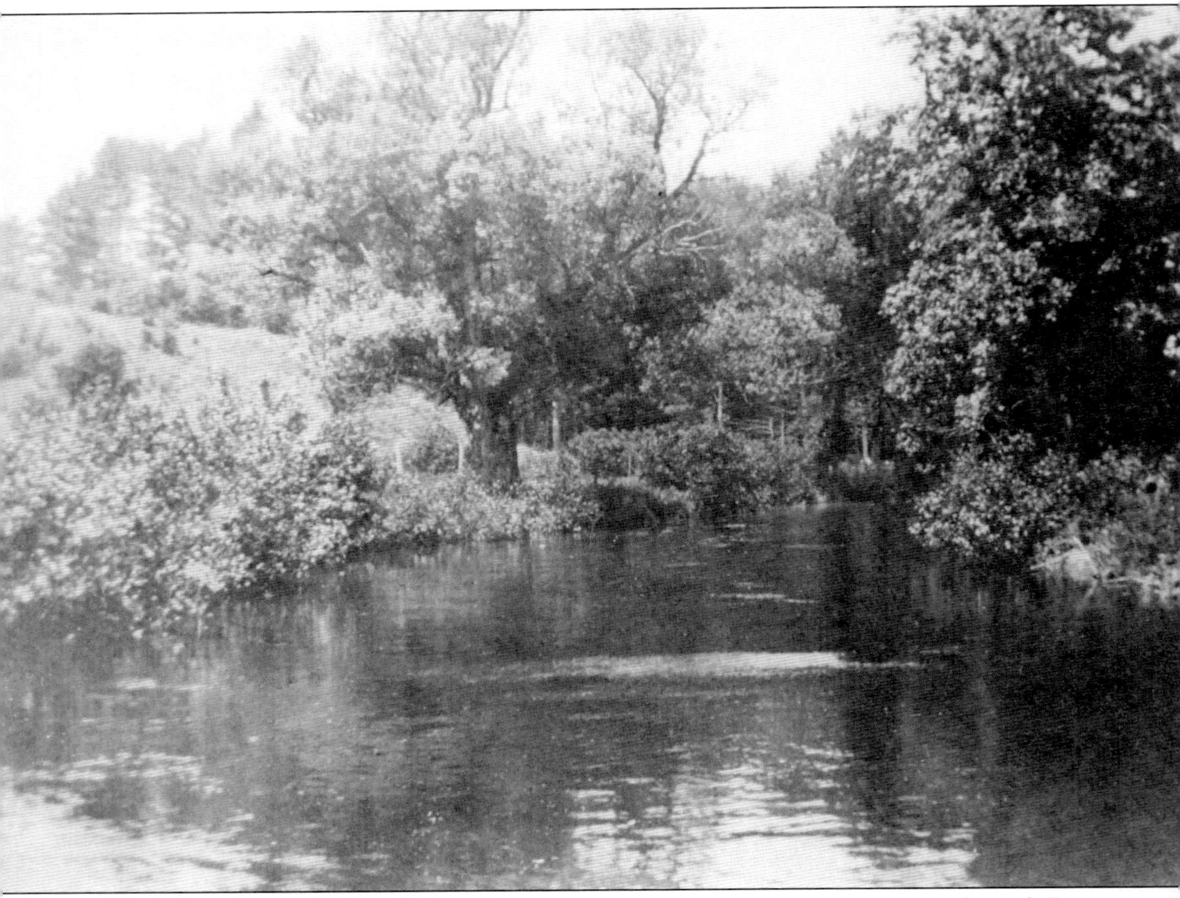

The Lamprey River gently flows into one of the many curves of its windy course through Epping. Scenes like this are still common, with sandy beaches and rocky banks shaded by large trees and low bushes. The river flows past both forest and field alike, some of which is farmland.

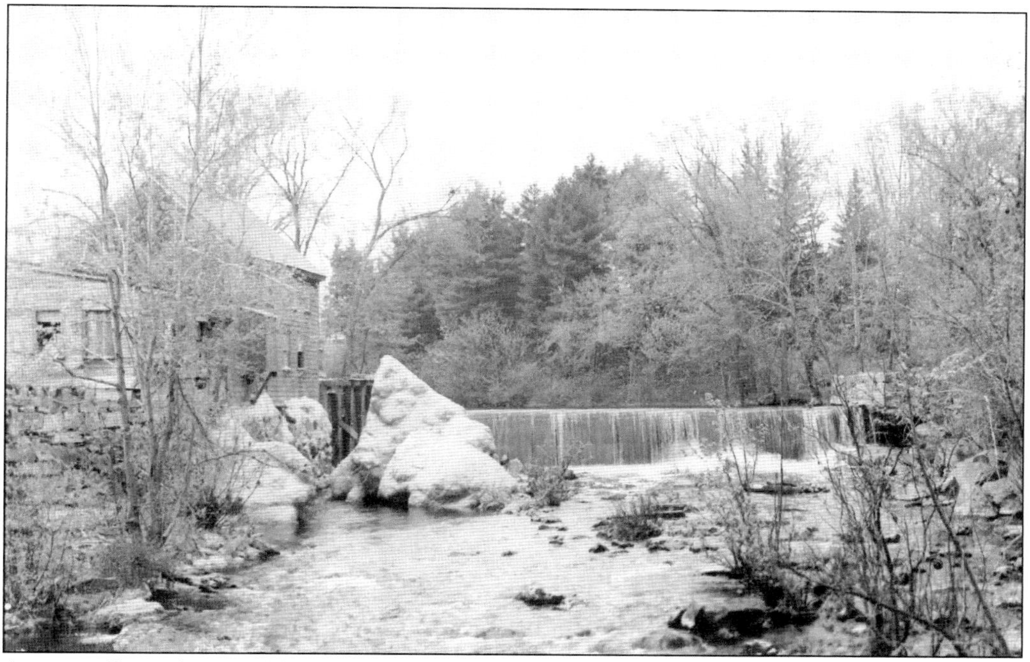

A gristmill was first established on the Folsom Mill site in 1746 by Joshua Folsom. Located at a sweeping bend in the river, the mill site proved to be a good one as the water power was found to be more than sufficient to power gristmills, woolen mills, a plaster mill, and lumber mills. The mill in these images is a lumber mill and shows the power of the Lamprey at both low and full power. The image above shows the river probably in midsummer, when the river is at its lowest but still powerful enough to mill logs into planks. The conical formation to the right of the mill in the image above is a large pile of sawdust leftover from milling. The image below shows how powerful the Lamprey could be with spring runoff or in summer and fall with heavy rains.

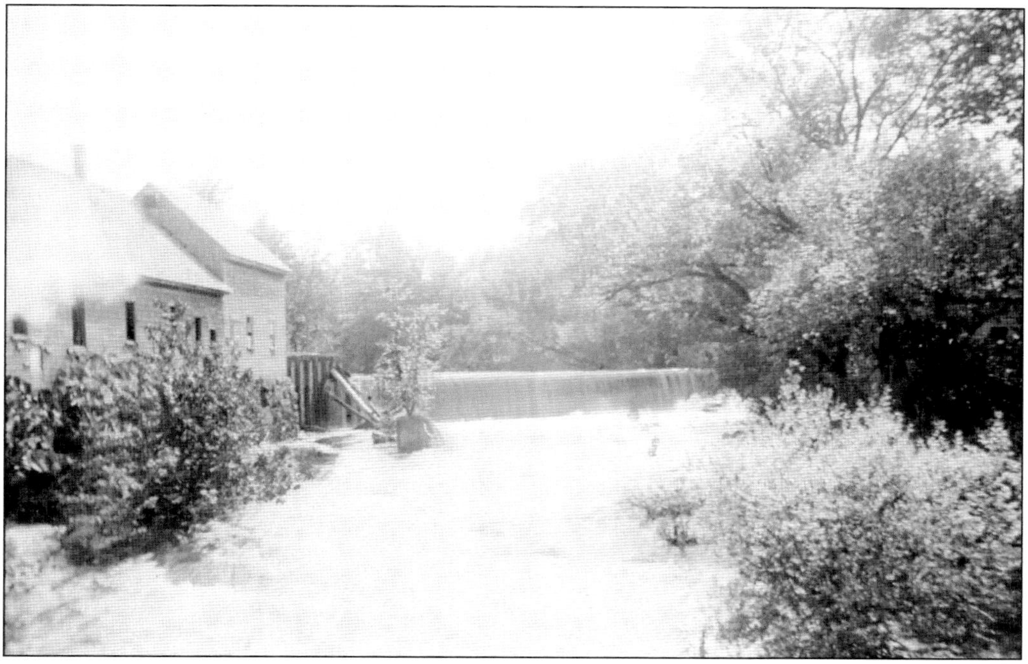

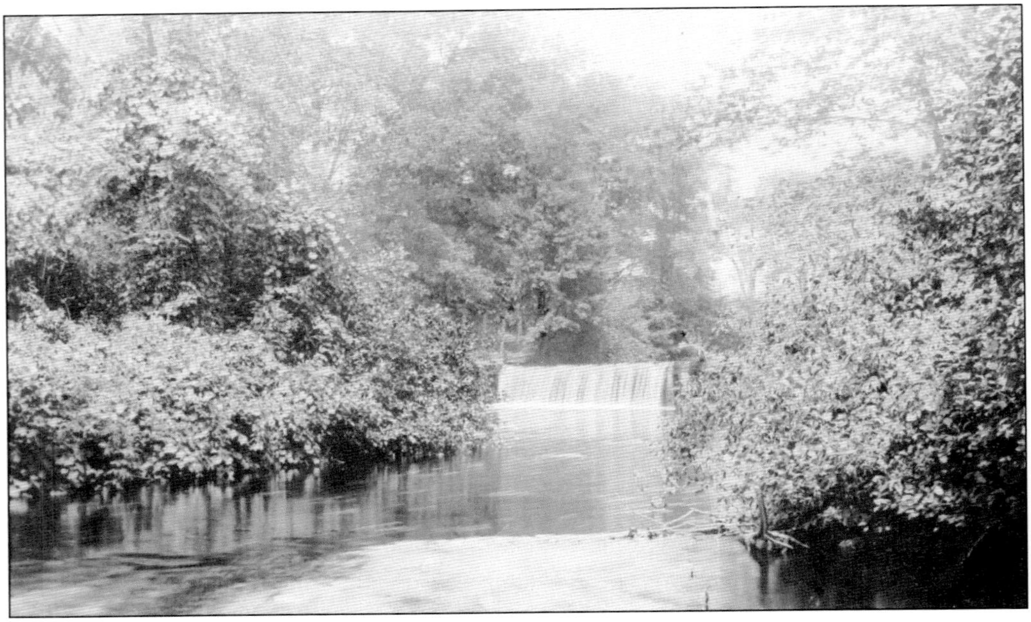

The Mill Street Dam supported shoe factories, lumber mills, and an ax-handle factory. The image above shows the Mill Street Dam at its largest. It was later downsized, and in the image below, it is hard to see that there is a dam at all. Regardless of appearances, the dam could still generate enough power to support the mills.

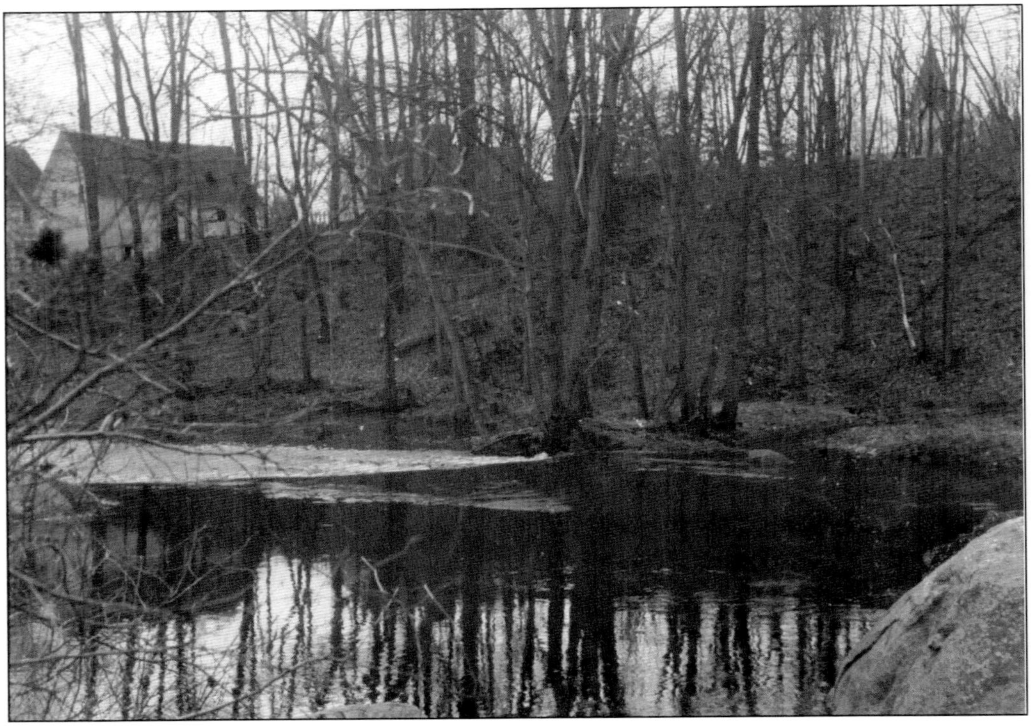

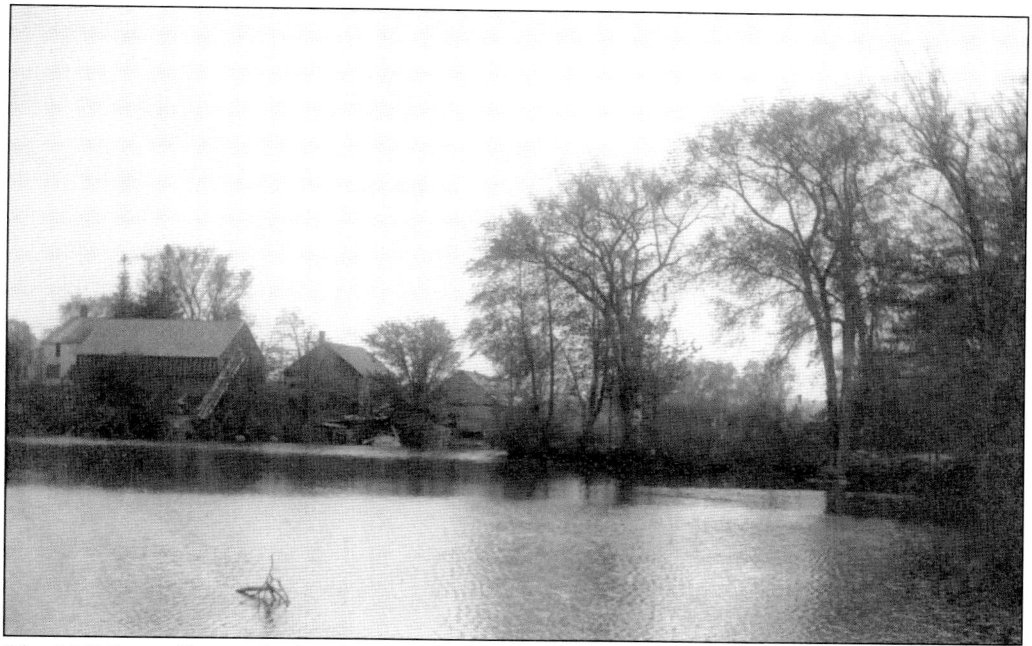

The Mill Street Dam, which is located just beyond the trees at center, created this millpond in the Lamprey River. Millponds provided habitat for wildlife and fish but could disrupt spawning runs, leading to the development of fish ladders. The buildings, from left to right, are the icehouse, an ax-handle factory, and a sawmill.

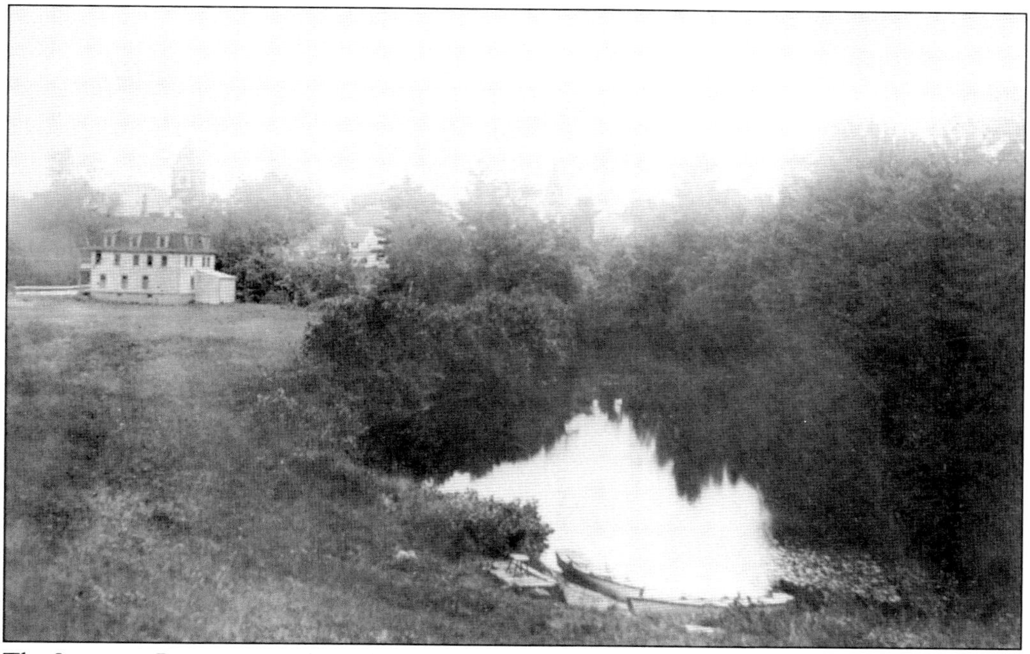

The Lamprey River curves through downtown Epping and under the Main Street bridge. The bridge is in between the old Grange Hall, seen at left, and the town hall just beyond. The two buildings sit diagonally on opposite sides of Main Street and opposite banks of the Lamprey River. The steeple of the Congregational Church can be seen in the distance at center.

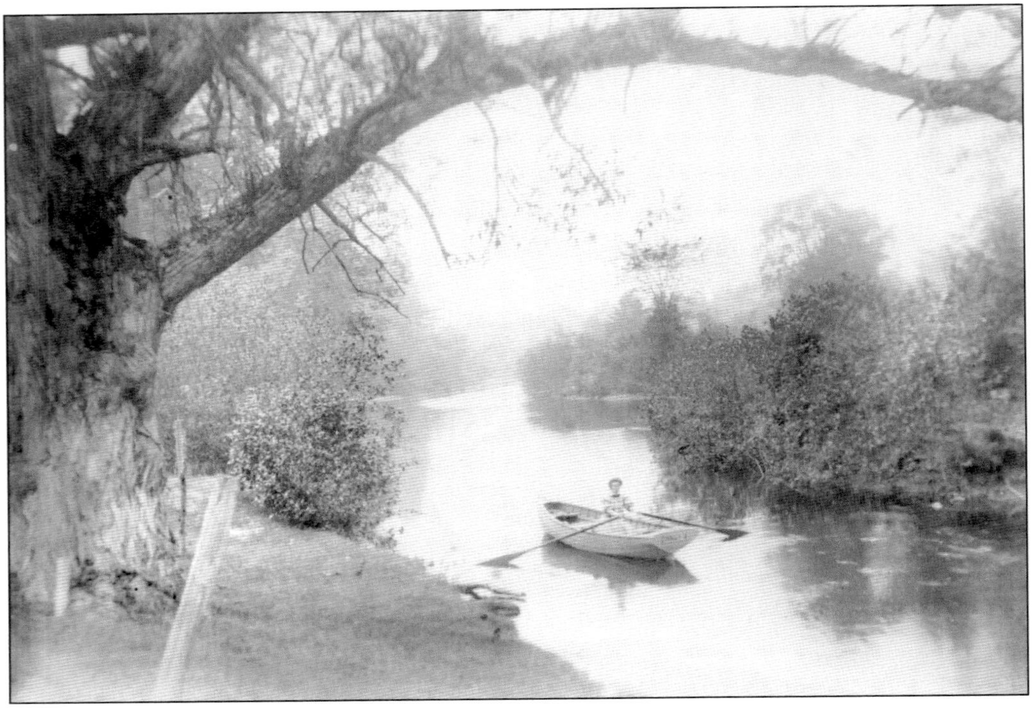

Rowboats have always been a popular way to enjoy the scenic Lamprey River. Mabel Willard enjoys rowing her boat, the *Dolly B.*, down this gently flowing section of the Lamprey in the above image. Not to be outdone, below, Hannah Ahern and a friend row a boat built by Walter P. Sanborn, avoiding the occasional rock and enjoying the overhanging trees.

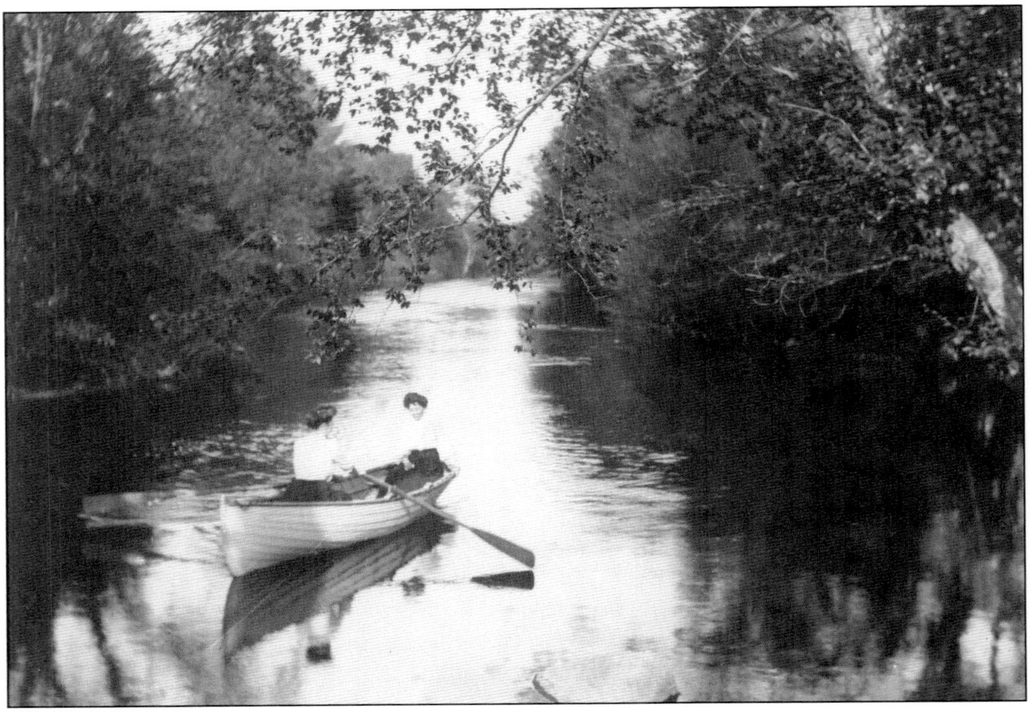

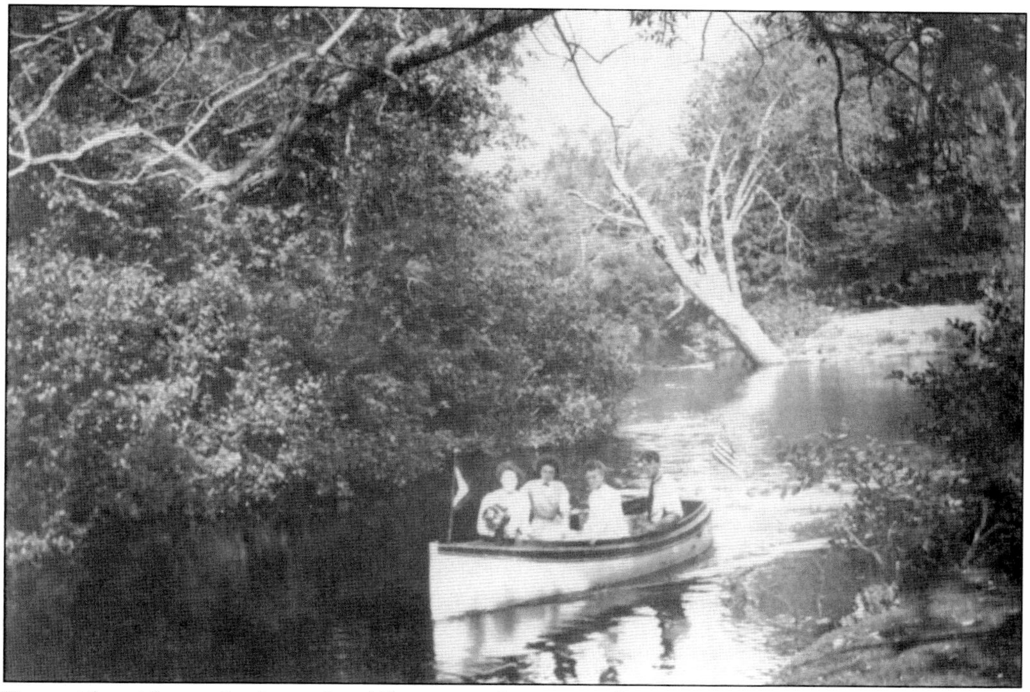

For a ride without the fuss of paddles, motorboats are the way to go. These ladies are being chauffeured around by a young gentleman working the motor. This boat, also built by Walter P. Sanborn, comes complete with a lamp and a nautical flag on the bow and an American flag on the stern. A sandy beach can be seen upstream in the image above.

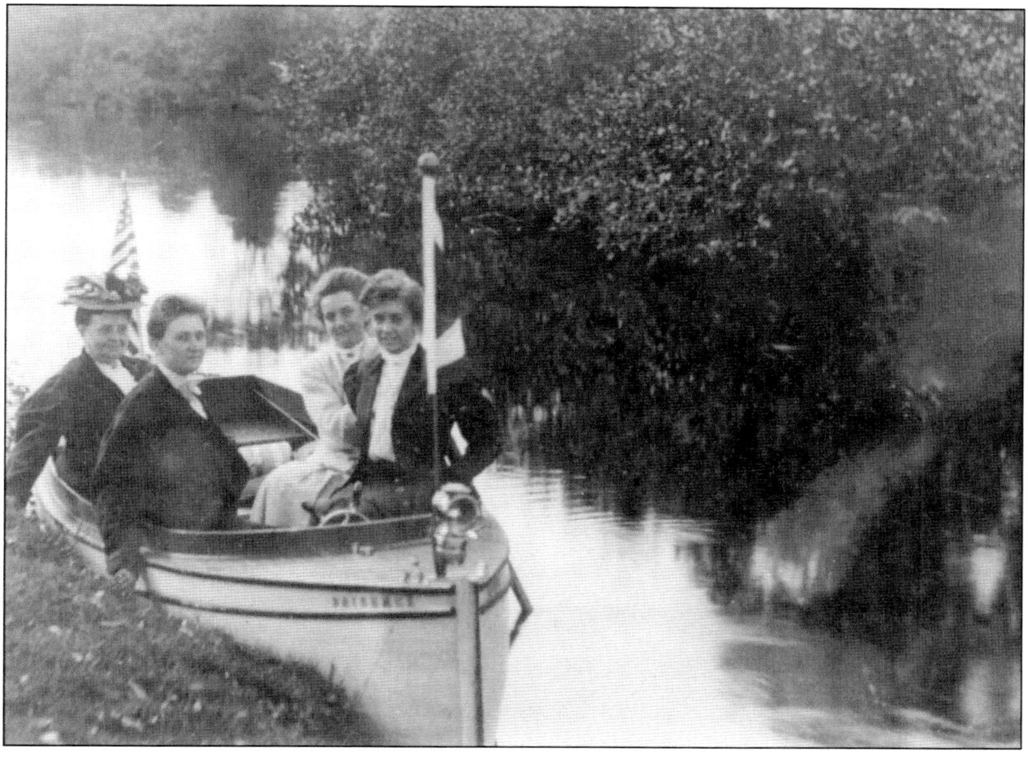

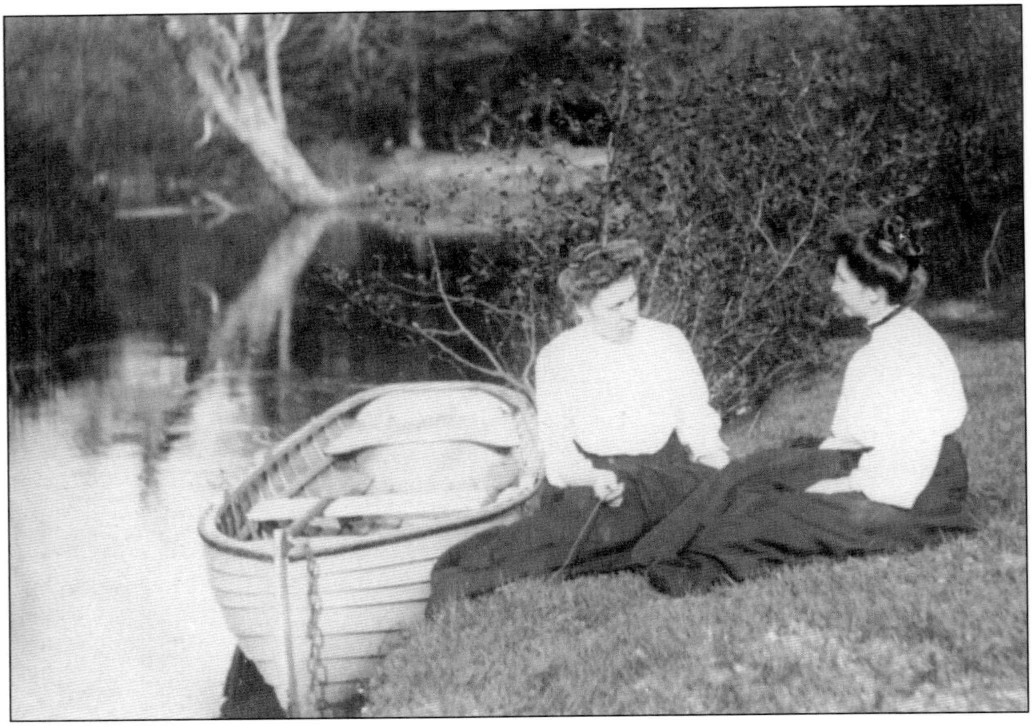

While boating on the Lamprey River is nice, stopping to enjoy the water rushing past while lounging underneath a large tree can be just as rewarding. What better spot is there to sit and talk to an old friend or a new boating partner? The image below is titled "Two School Teachers Beside the Lamprey River."

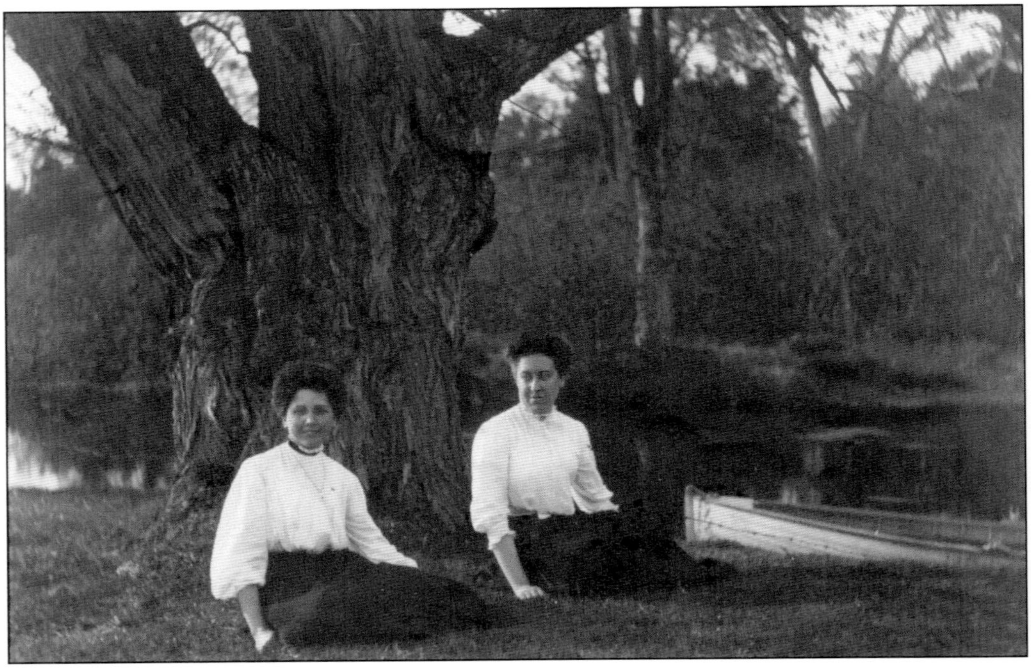

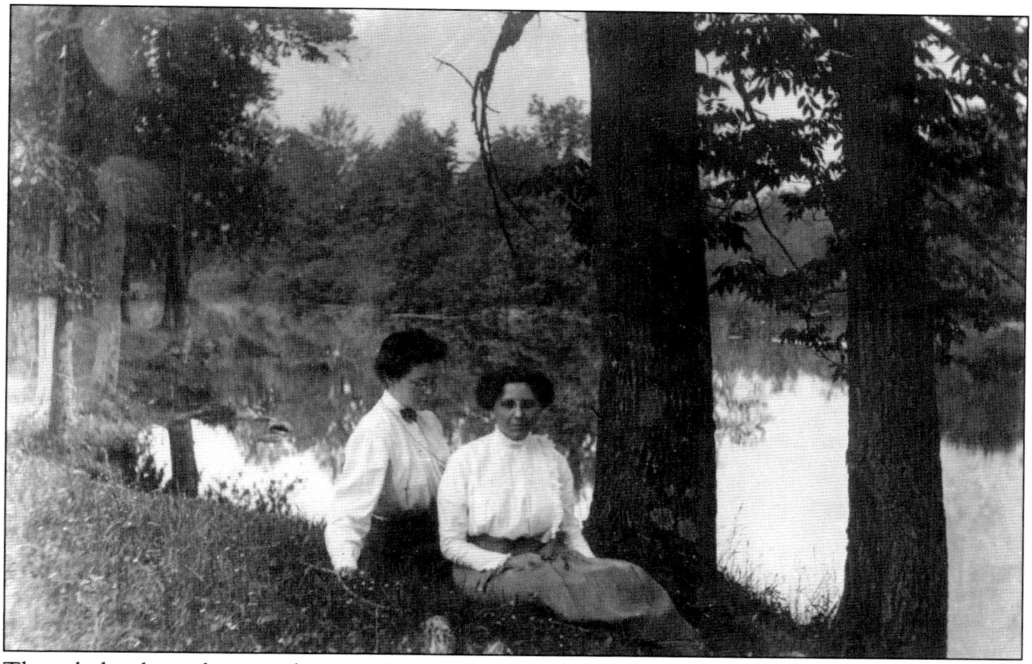

These ladies have forgone the use of a boat and simply chose to sit on the banks of the Lamprey. The river may look calm in this image, but the current can pick up a lot of speed at sections. While erosion is an ever-present battle between water and land, the trees that line much of the Lamprey help to keep the power of the water at bay.

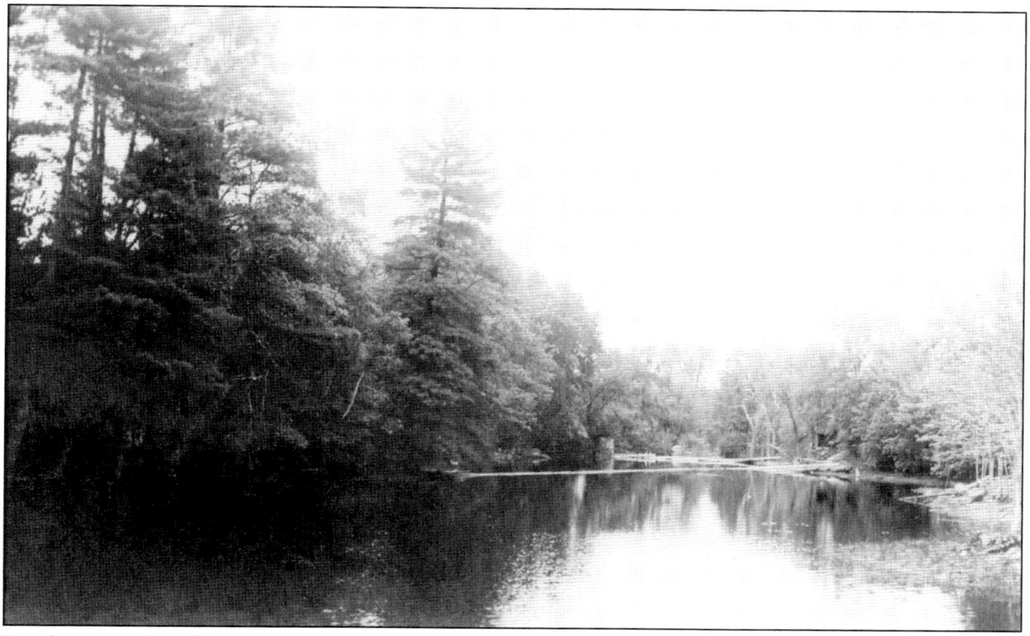

Bunker's Pond in West Epping was created by the mill dam built at the Folsom Mill site. Although it is not known exactly what the first dams at this site were made of, evidence suggests that they were a combination of granite stonework, wooden cribbing, and earth. Those who built the early mills would have to be confident of their engineering, as a burst dam was as dangerous then as it is now.

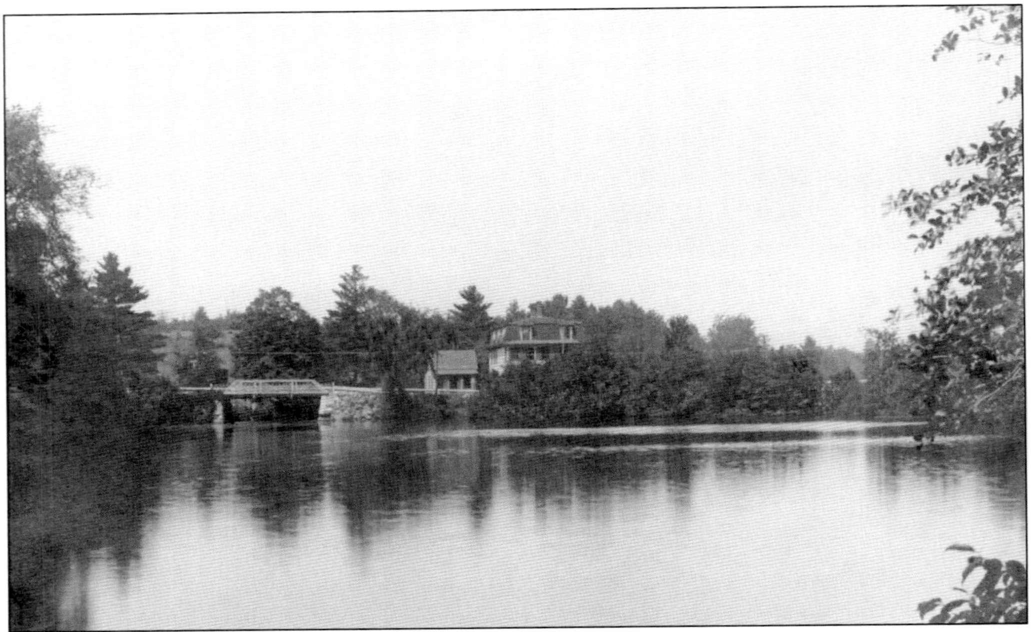

The millpond created by the Mill Street dam stretched upriver to the Main Street bridge. The bridge, with its granite support walls and latticed iron truss, was thought to be very beautiful in construction and appearance when it was built in 1893. The small print shop and large old Grange Hall can be seen on Main Street in this 1917 image.

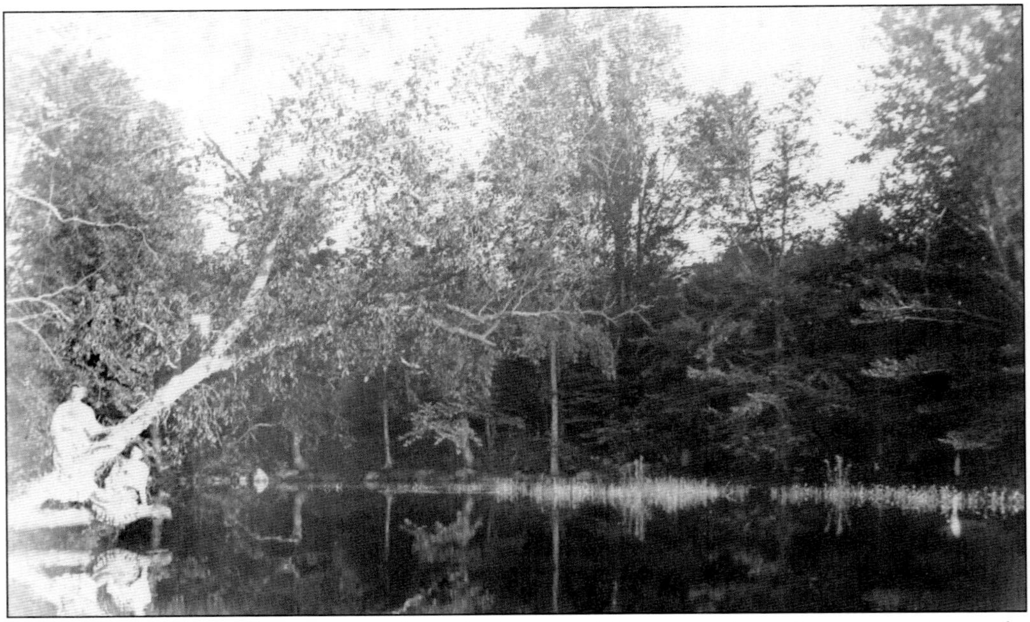

The millponds created by the dams along the Lamprey River created excellent swimming pools. Elizabeth Sanborn (left) and Mable Willard (right) have climbed out over one of the millponds on an overhanging tree. Perhaps they are contemplating coming back and diving in for a swim to cool down.

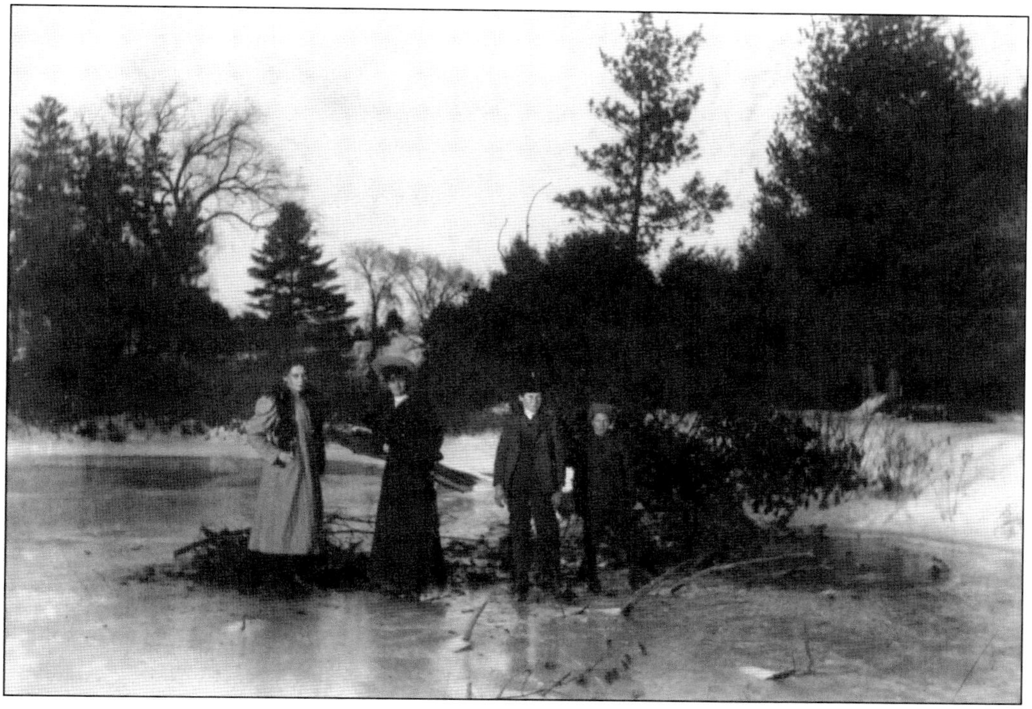

In the winter months, the Lamprey afforded another mode of recreation. Ice-skating was popular with both men and women, and the Lamprey provided the perfect location once the cold New Hampshire winters froze the river solid enough. The skating party above might have been a family outing, or perhaps the two young boys are attempting to court the young ladies. Below, Ada Allen (left) and Bernice Swain (right) show their skills as they skate with Boar's Head Hill in the background.

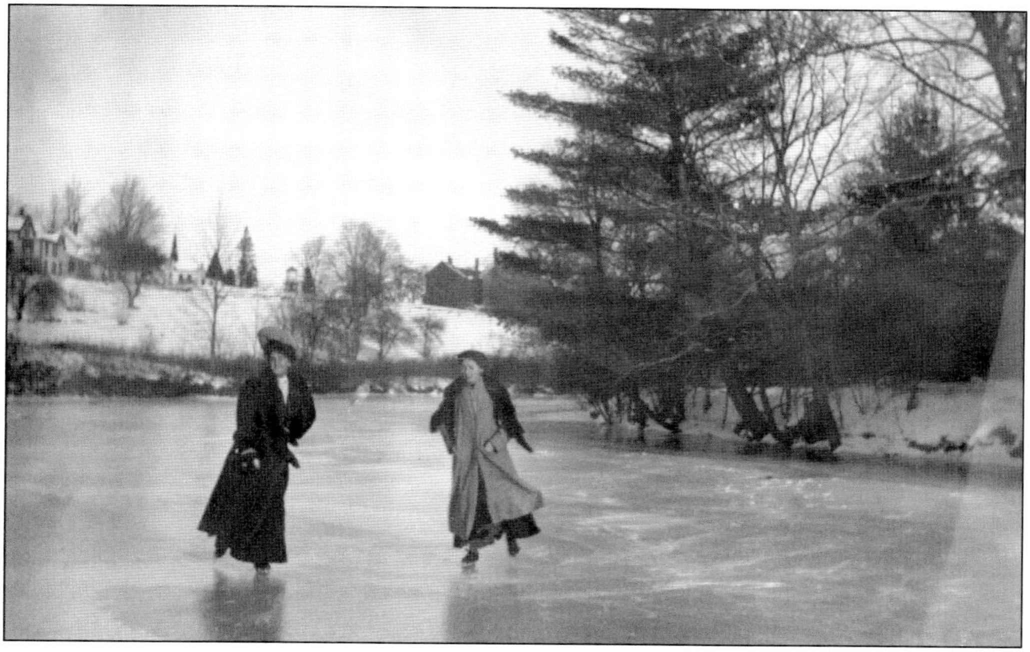

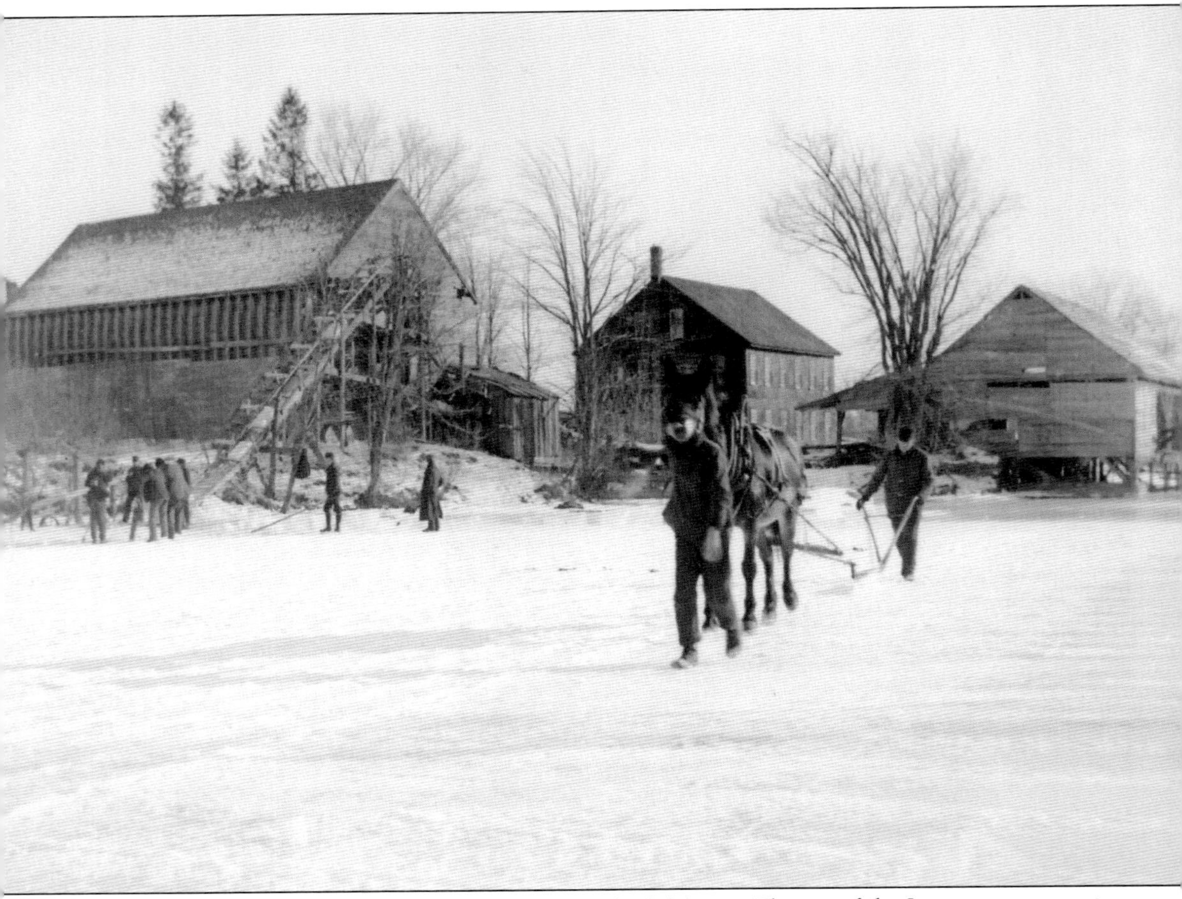

The Lamprey provided water in both liquid and solid forms. The ice of the Lamprey was not just for skating. Here, Charles Tarbox leads a horse pulling a plow used to mark the ice for cutting. The marks in the ice can be seen making square blocks. In the background, men use long polls to slide the ice into position to be fed up the conveyer belt, run by Walter Sanborn, and into the icehouse. Once in the icehouse, the blocks would be covered in sawdust, easily attained from one of the lumber mills in Epping, which would help insulate the blocks and keep them from melting too quickly. Farmers used a large amount of ice throughout the year to keep milk from spoiling, and stores and residents would use the ice in their iceboxes to keep their food and drinks cool. The buildings are, from left to right, the icehouse, an ax-handle factory, and Howard Mile's sawmill.

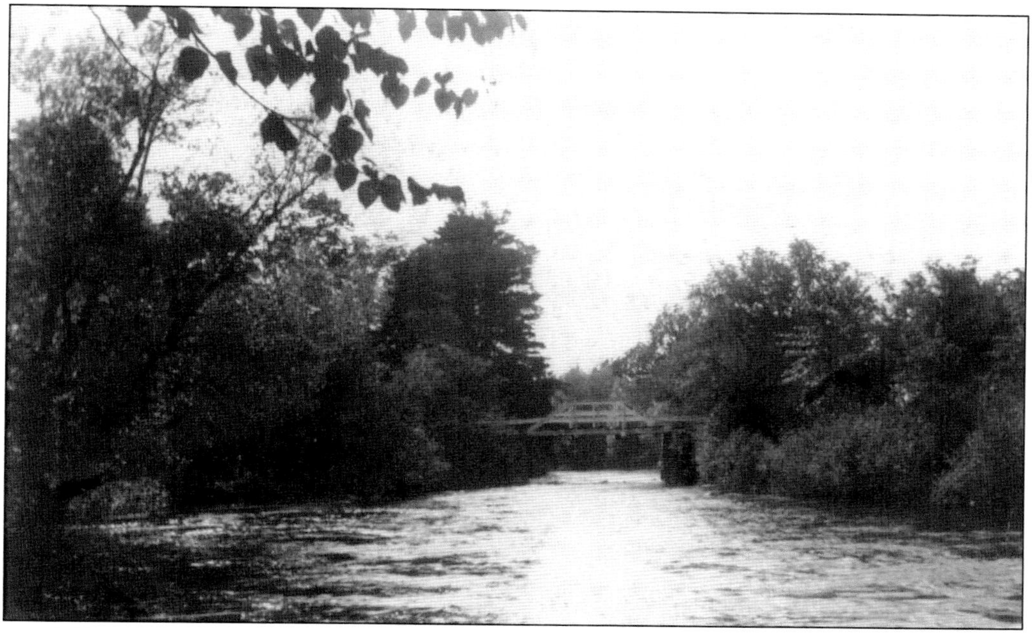

Bridging the Lamprey River was always necessary for the residents of Epping. The river almost splits the town in two, so multiple bridges were needed throughout the history of Epping. Bridges could range from the simple to the complex. The bridge above is an unsophisticated timber plank bridge on Blake Road. While simple, the bridge did its job remarkably well. The bridge below is of the more complicated sort. This railroad bridge required a granite retaining wall along one side of the Lamprey River, which can be seen at right; two large granite support columns; and an iron construction. The granite retaining walls and columns can still be seen today.

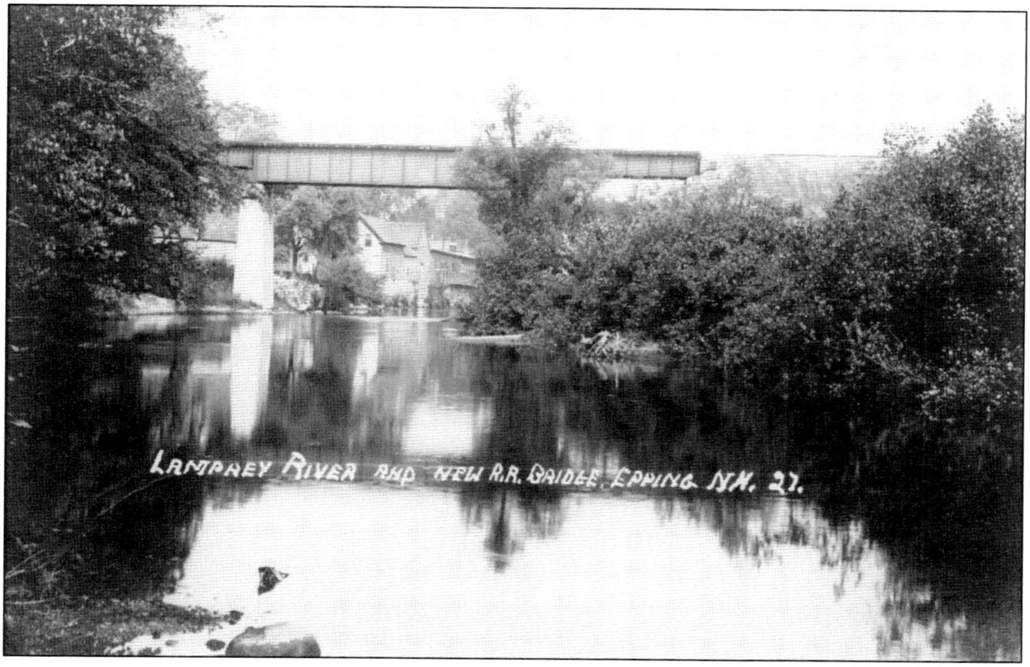

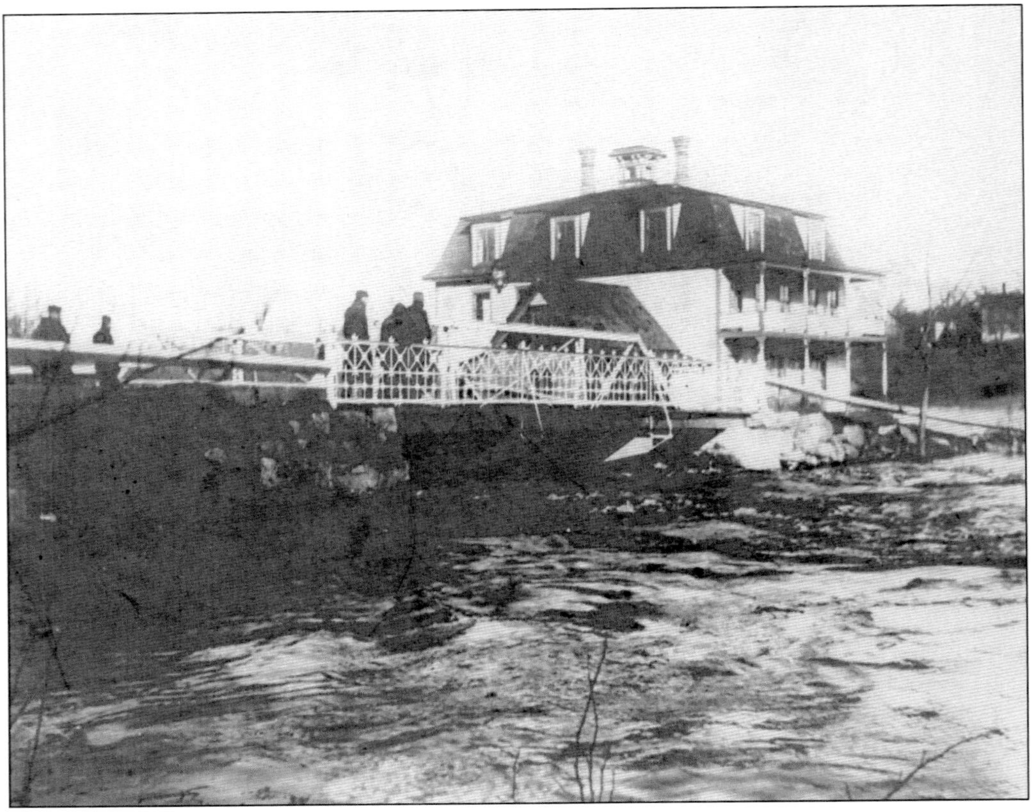

For all the good that the Lamprey River provides to Epping, it can also be a dangerous and costly hazard. A crowd nervously gathers on the Main Street bridge to inspect the high waters of the Lamprey. The image below shows the damage of the flood of March 1936. This section of Main Street, next to the old Grange Hall, has been completely washed out as the waters of the Lamprey find a way to flow forward no matter the obstacle.

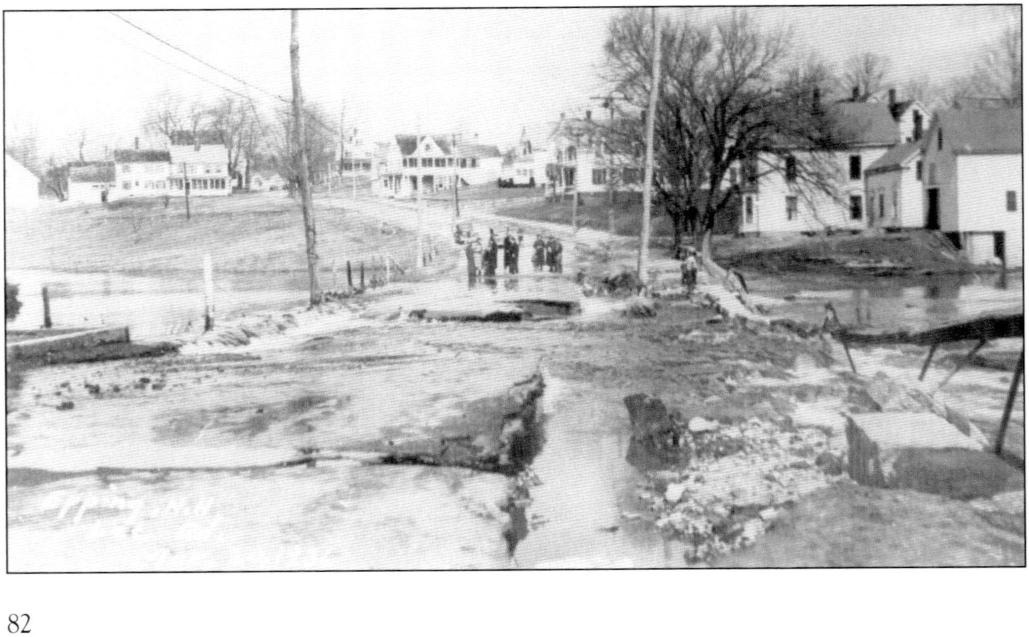

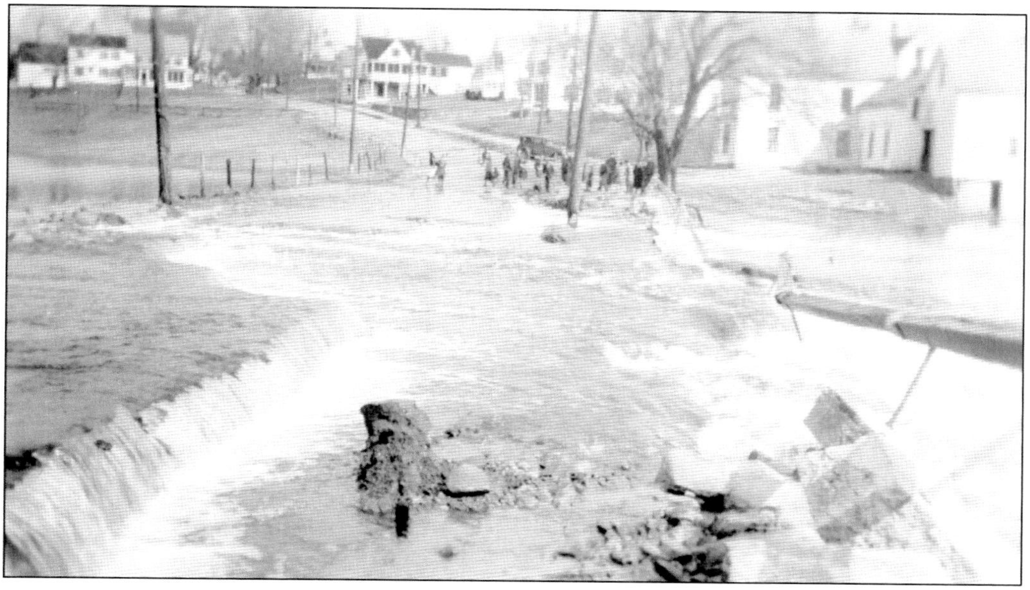

The flood of March 1936 caused considerable damage. Even more of Main Street was eaten away by the raging waters of the Lamprey River. The old Grange Hall that sits to the left was damaged by water but survived the flood. Below, the aptly named Water Street is completely submerged by the flood. It appears that no one would be getting any gas or lunch at this Water Street station for some time.

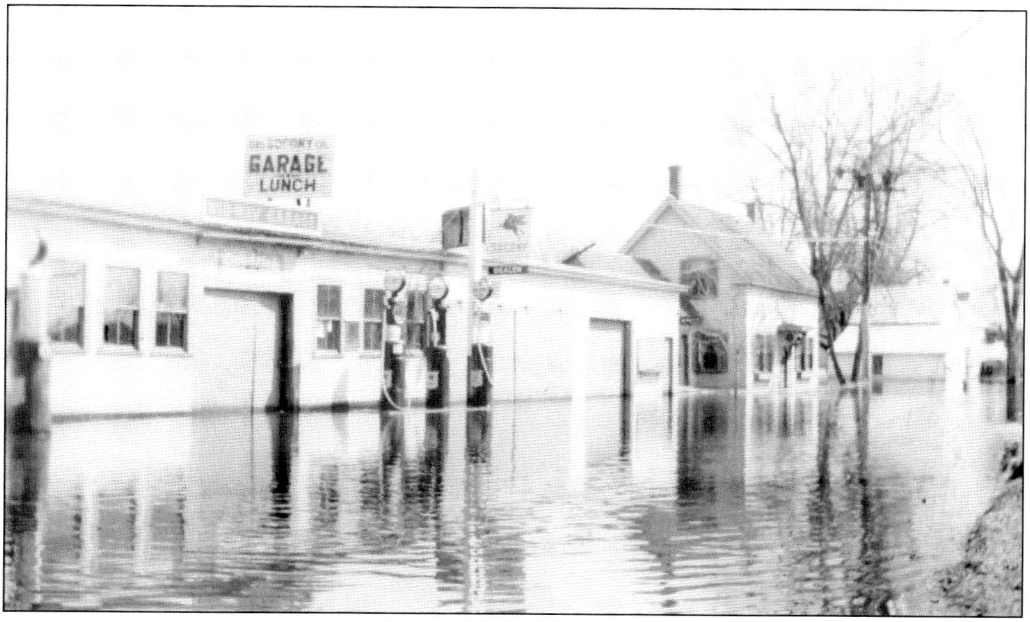

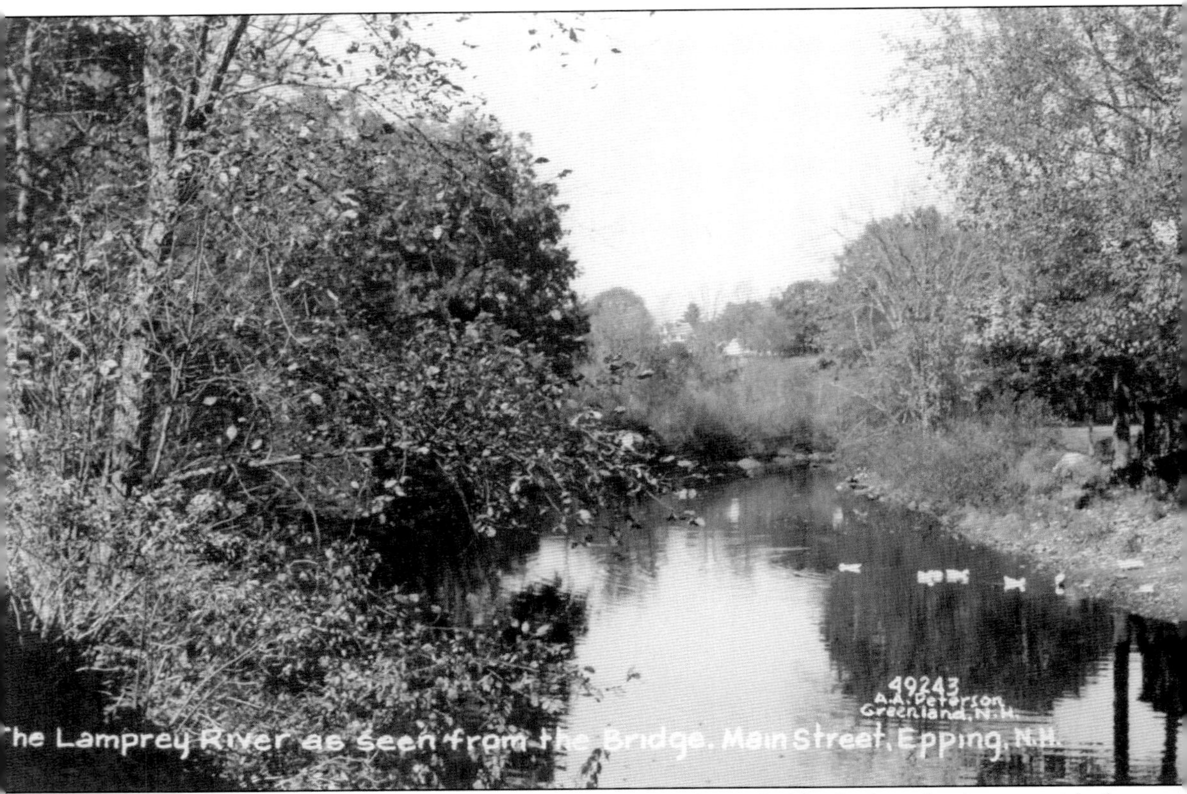


Even with all the damaging potential that the Lamprey River holds, the benefits far outweigh the costs. The Lamprey River has come to be an important part of the image and culture of Epping. As long as the Lamprey winds its way through the town, it will provide Epping with beautiful scenes like this one. Taken from the Main Street bridge about 1900, this image could easily have been photographed today.

# Six

# INDUSTRY

While the Lamprey River provided the water to power all sorts of mills, the ground beneath the residents of Epping provided yet another natural resource. It was discovered very early in the town's development that large deposits of clay lay beneath Epping's topsoil. For decades, Epping residents would dig up this clay, mold it into bricks, and let them bake in the sun for use as building material. This small-scale brickmaking among Epping's residents lasted until 1822. Seizing on the opportunity that the plentiful clay beds provided, Levi Thompson founded the first commercial brickyard in Epping on Main Street. Brickmaking would become Epping's most influential industry. More yards were established, and in 1882 eight million bricks were produced in Epping. By 1887, Levi Thompson's yard had five other brickyards in Epping with which to compete. In that year, the Levi Thompson yard produced 500,000 bricks, the John Leddy Yard produced 1 million, the Goodrich Brickyard produced 1.5 million, the George Rundlett yard produced 3 million, the Brown & Bunker yard produced 4 million, and the Fellows Brick Yard produced 5 million. Epping's six brickyards produced a grand total of 15 million bricks in 1887, and the Granite State Brickyard was built that year and would add to production for the next year.

Epping produced both water-struck (where the mold is dipped in water before the clay is put in) and sand-struck (where the mold is likewise lined with sand) bricks of a superior quality. These bricks were sent by rail to help build large mill and factory buildings in Manchester, New Hampshire; Nashua, New Hampshire; Lowell, Massachusetts; and Lawrence, Massachusetts. Epping bricks helped build the mills and factories that fueled industrialization in 19th-century New England.

While brickmaking was Epping's largest and most successful industry, shoe factories, box factories, a canning factory, woolen mills, a plaster factory, and an ax-handle factory further bolstered Epping's economy and influence.

All of these industries benefited from the fact that Epping was a crossroads of two bustling and important rail lines. One rail line ran east-west and the other north-south, and both were sold and acquired by multiple railroad companies. No matter the rail line owner, Epping's businesses prospered at the intersection.

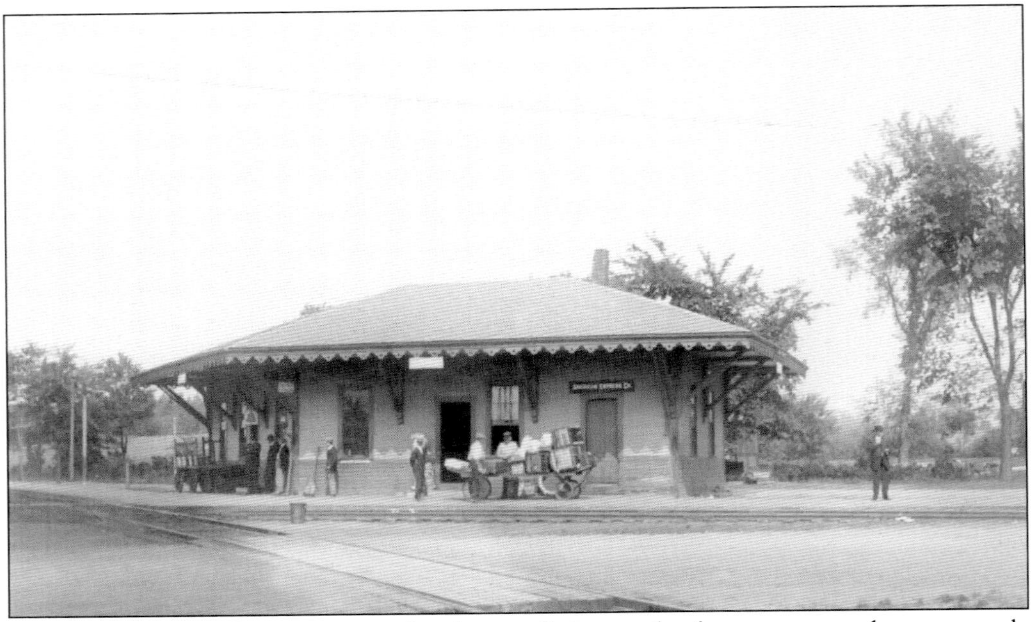

The Epping Railroad Depot received and sent off thousands of passengers, and one can only guess at how many tons of cargo. The view above shows the depot as it appeared in 1905 when Fred Knox was the stationmaster. Passengers wait patiently and exchange casual conversation as their trunks are readied to be loaded on board a train on the Portsmouth & Manchester line. Perhaps one of them has just sent a telegraph or used the new telephone in the station. The line that can be seen running perpendicular to the Portsmouth & Manchester line was the Worcester, Nashua & Portland line. Below, the depot can be seen five years later, in 1910. Not much has changed in the intervening years, but in this view are the milk station to the far left, the W.C. Brown Box Factory in the center, and the freight house to the right. A man stands on the freight house platform, perhaps waiting to take in cargo or to make sure his freight makes it safely onto the next train.

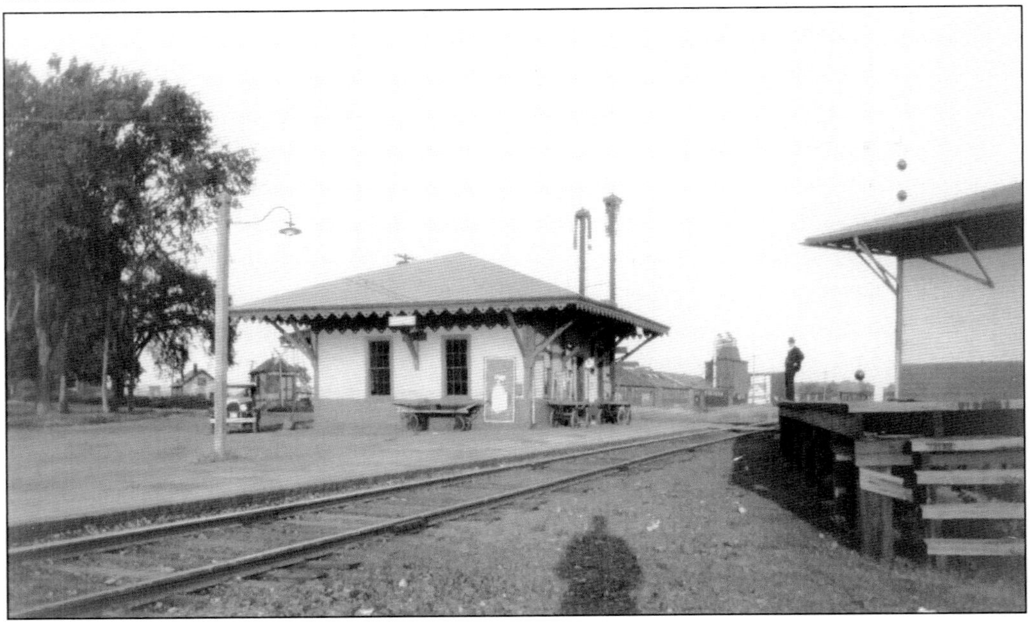

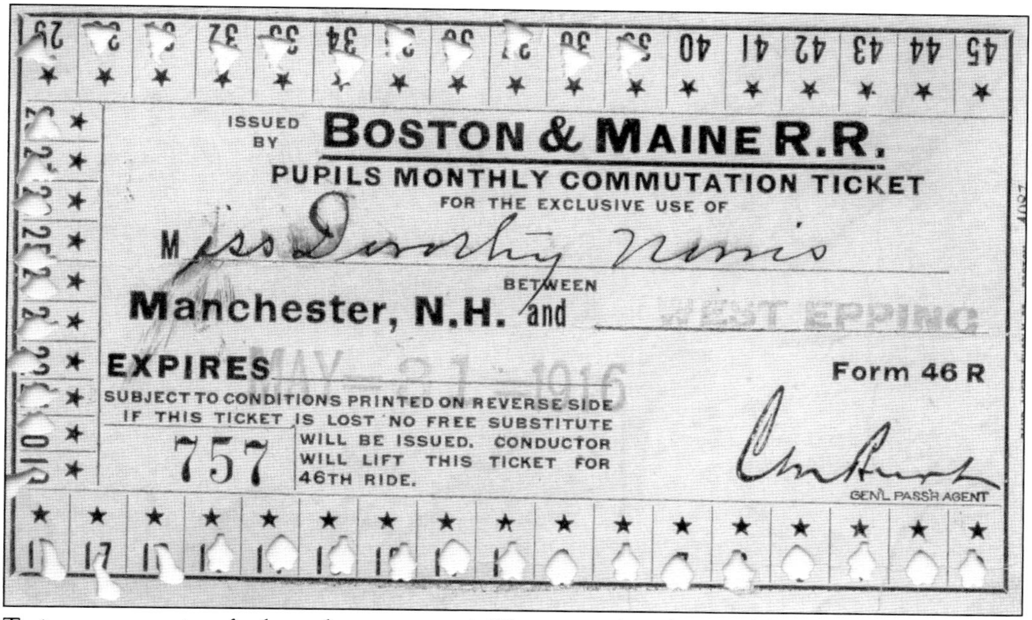


Trains were not just for long-distance travel. This is a ticket that could be bought monthly for a commuting student who traveled daily. The ticket is for Dorothy Norris, a student from West Epping who had to make her way to Manchester on the Boston & Maine Railroad line. Purchased for the month of May 1916, it can be seen from the punches in the ticket that Norris did not miss a day of school that month.

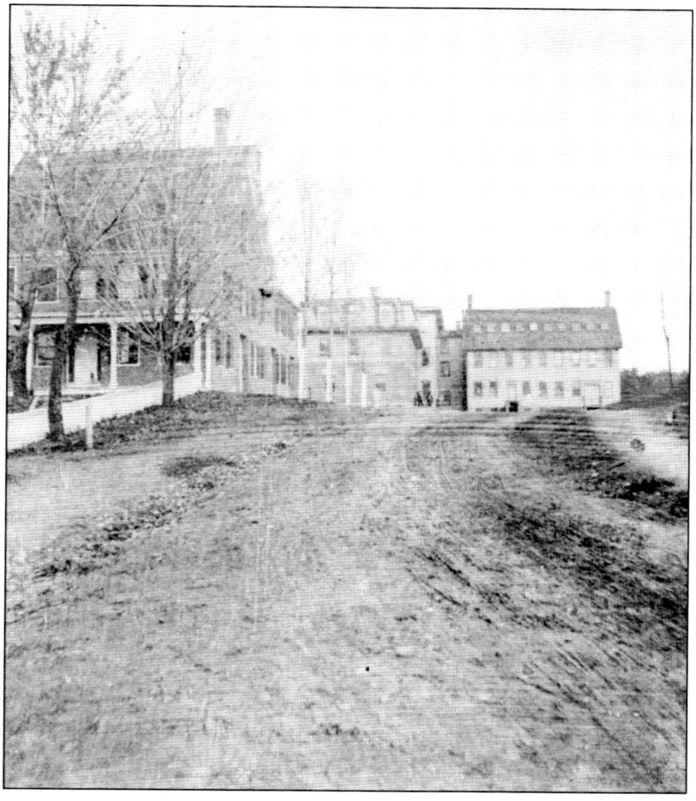

The shoe factories of B.W. Hoyt, built in 1870 and 1876, can be seen behind the brick Prospect House on Main Street atop Boar's Head Hill. These shoe factories manufactured more than 7,000 cases of women's shoes annually.

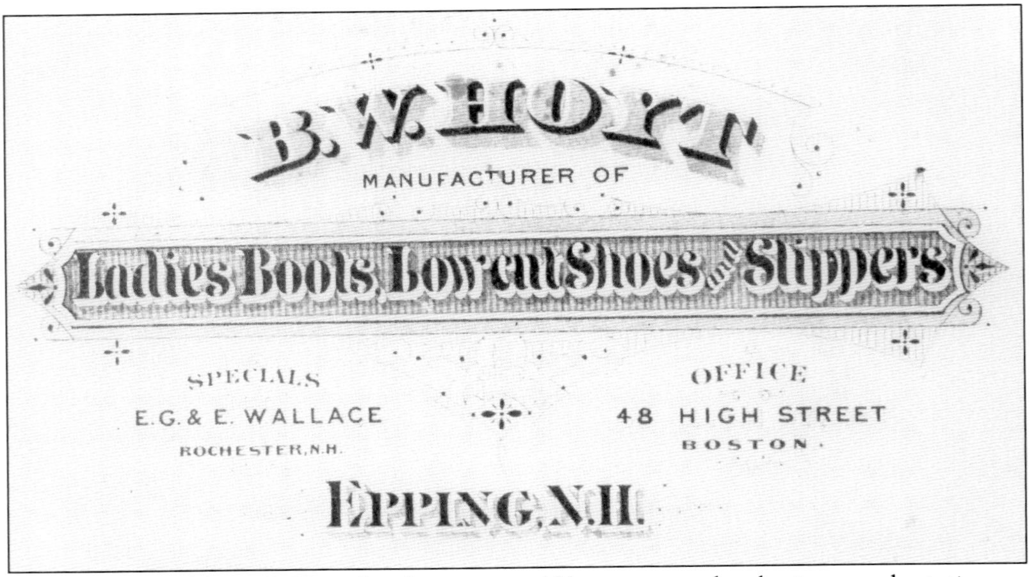


The letterhead of the B.W. Hoyt shoe factories would have appeared on business cards, stationery, shoeboxes, and cases of shoes. The shoes that B.W. Hoyt produced could easily be transported on the rail lines that ran through Epping.

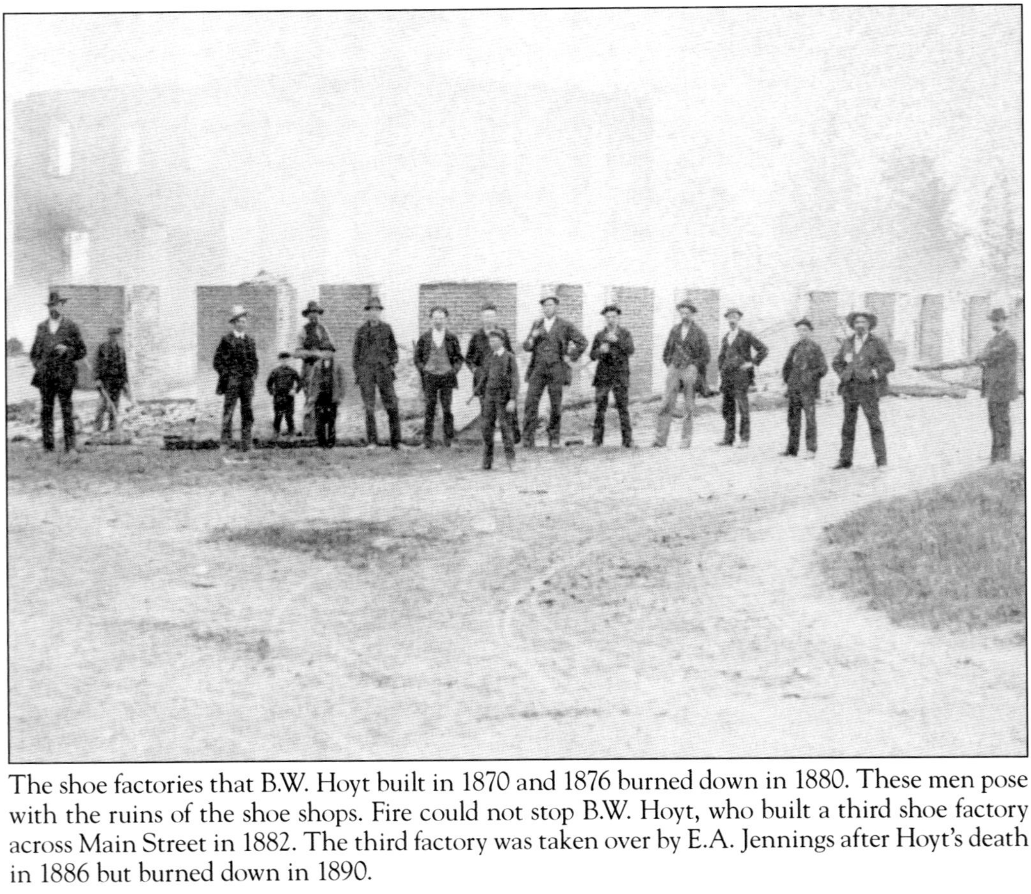

The shoe factories that B.W. Hoyt built in 1870 and 1876 burned down in 1880. These men pose with the ruins of the shoe shops. Fire could not stop B.W. Hoyt, who built a third shoe factory across Main Street in 1882. The third factory was taken over by E.A. Jennings after Hoyt's death in 1886 but burned down in 1890.

This shoe factory was built in 1881 by John T. Bartlett and his brother on Bartlett Street. The large shoe factory was successful but burned down in 1891. In the foreground, Main Street is unpaved and the Main Street bridge over the Lamprey River is constructed of wood, as are the guardrails. To the left of the factory is the Boar's Head Hill community.

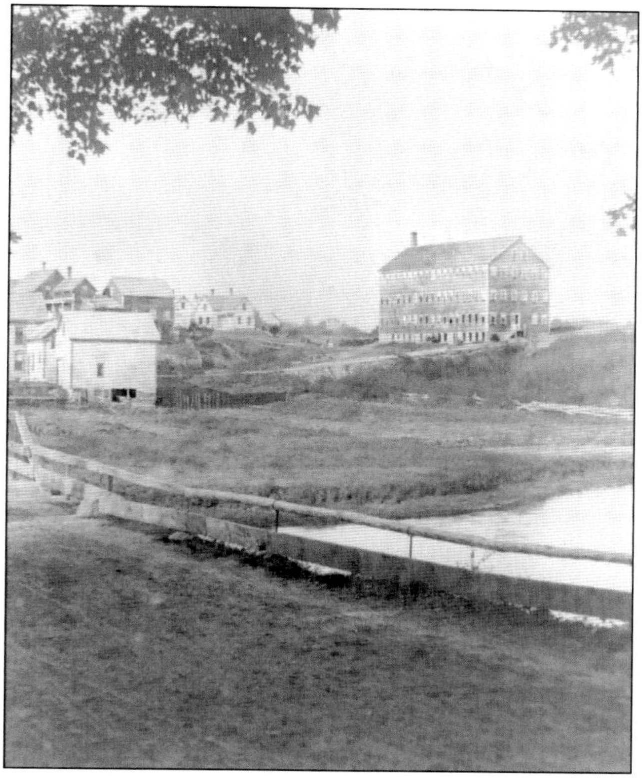

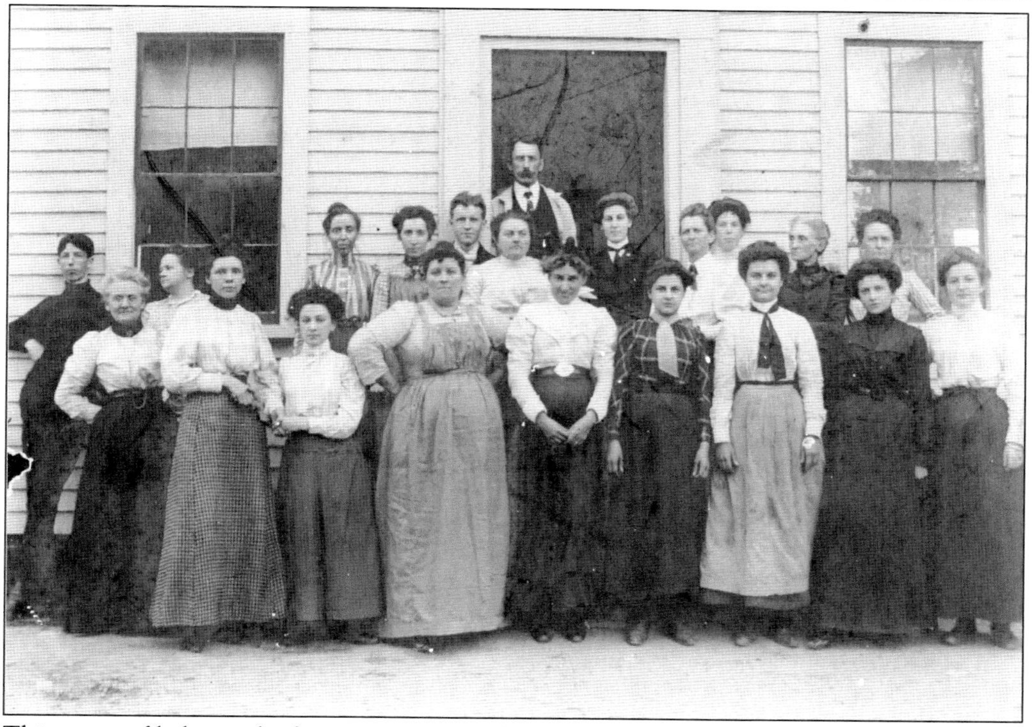

This group of ladies and a few men pose outside the Bartlett shoe shop. Large factories like the shoe shops in Epping provided many employment opportunities to women at a decent wage.

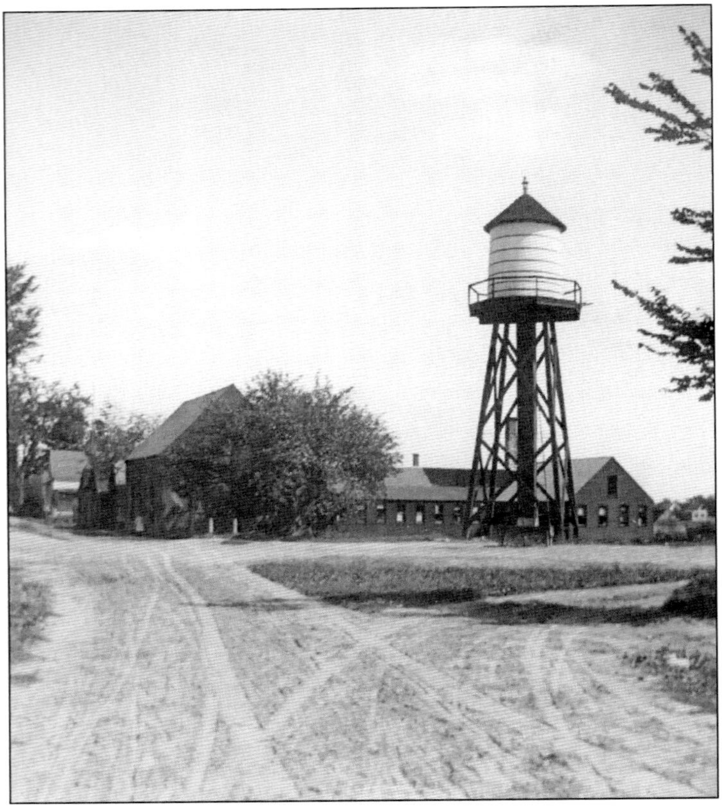

In 1880, William C. Brown built a factory on the corner of Main and Cate Streets. The W.C. Brown Box Factory manufactured paper boxes for shoes and built the wooden crates that they were packed in. Additions were made to the factory atop Boar's Head Hill until the building was finally deemed too small for the growing business in 1904. The W.H. Champlin Company of Rochester used the building as a shook mill for a number of years. Later, the building was used as a shoe factory by Louis Shapiro until 1921. The building was destroyed by fire in 1934 after lying vacant for a few years.

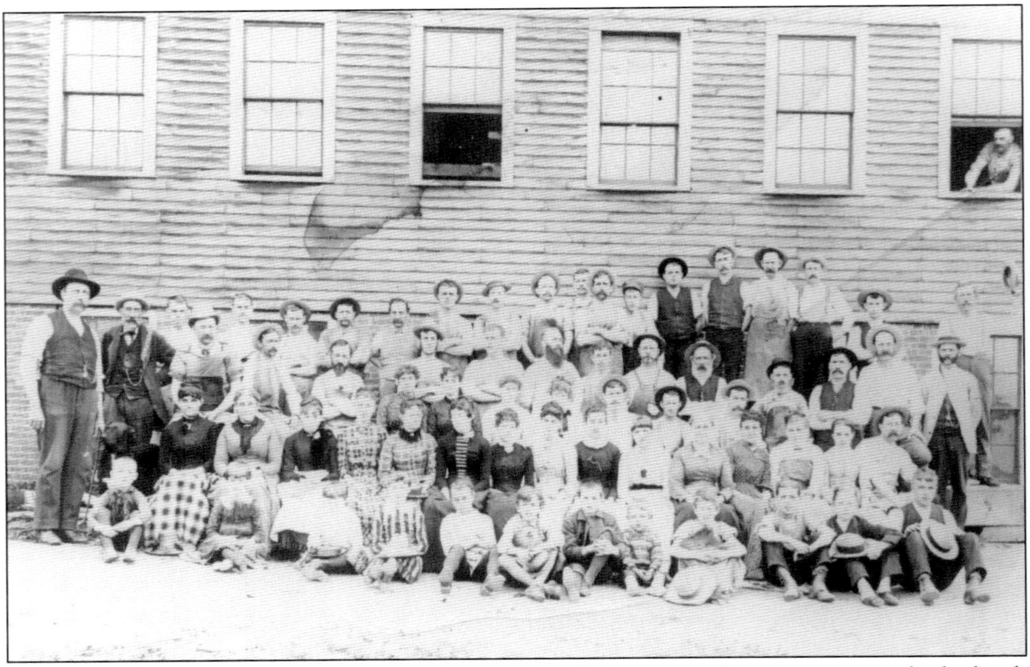

The workers of the Boar's Head Hill W.C. Brown Box Factory pose for a picture outside the brick and wood structure of the main building of the factory. This factory employed men and women of varying ages. One man, perhaps the supervisor, poses in one of the factory's windows.

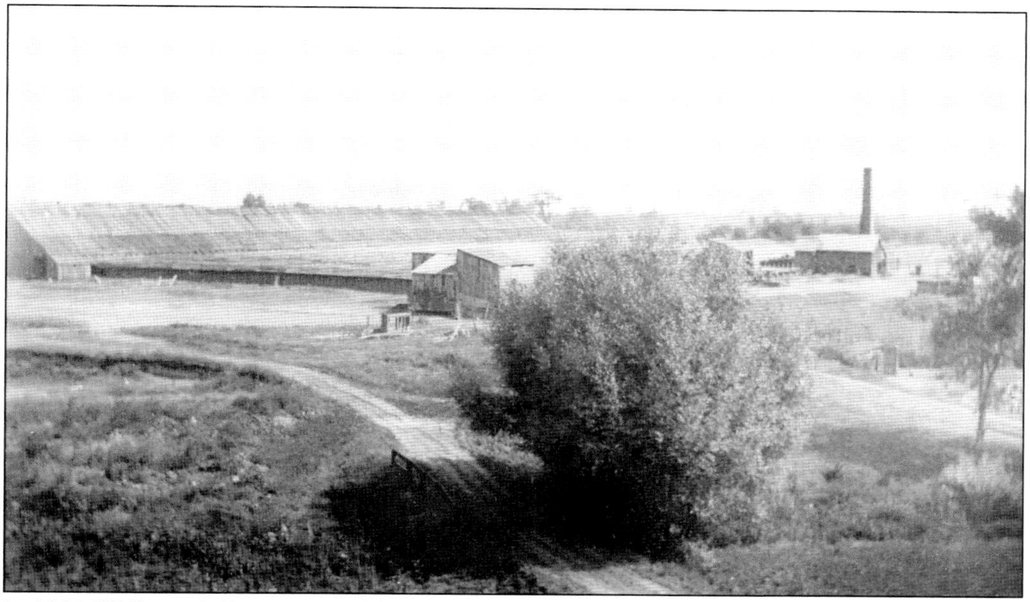

In 1904, William C. Brown moved his box manufacturing business into a larger factory near the railroad depot on Main Street. The W.C. Brown Box Factory continued to produce the paper boxes and wooden crates that had been produced at the Boar's Head Hill factory. The box factory is to the right while the Goodrich Brickyard's drying racks and long wooden building are to the left.

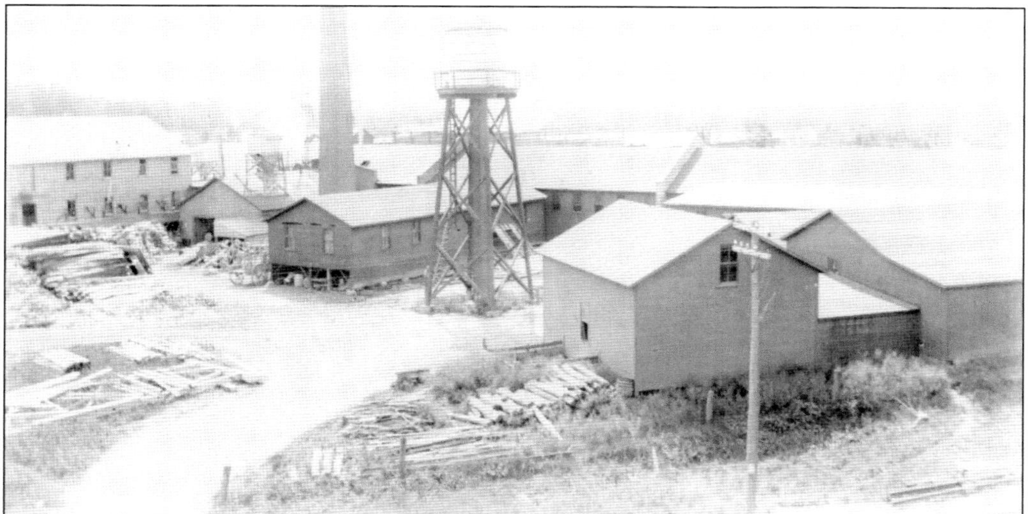

The yard of the W.C. Brown Box Factory shows the many materials and building sections used in the production of the paper shoeboxes and wooden crates. A man can be seen ascending the ladder to the water tower, which was 50 feet high and held 10,000 gallons of water.

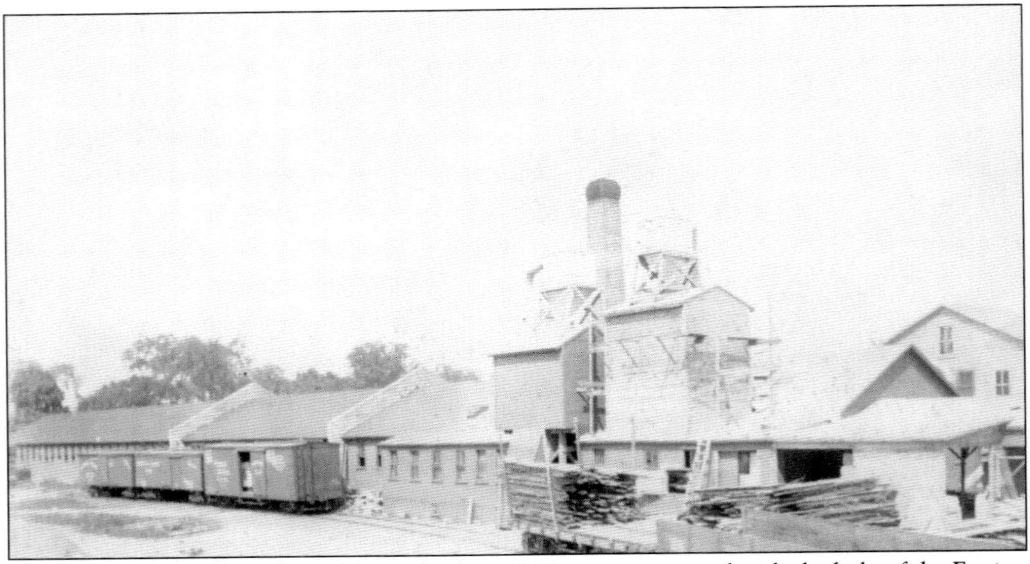

The W.C. Brown Box Factory that was built in 1904 was constructed with the help of the Epping Board of Trade. In 1904, this board consisted of Abram Mitchell, John Leddy, George Macauley, and John Ladd. This image shows how the factory was built alongside the train tracks so that cargo could be loaded directly onto the trains.

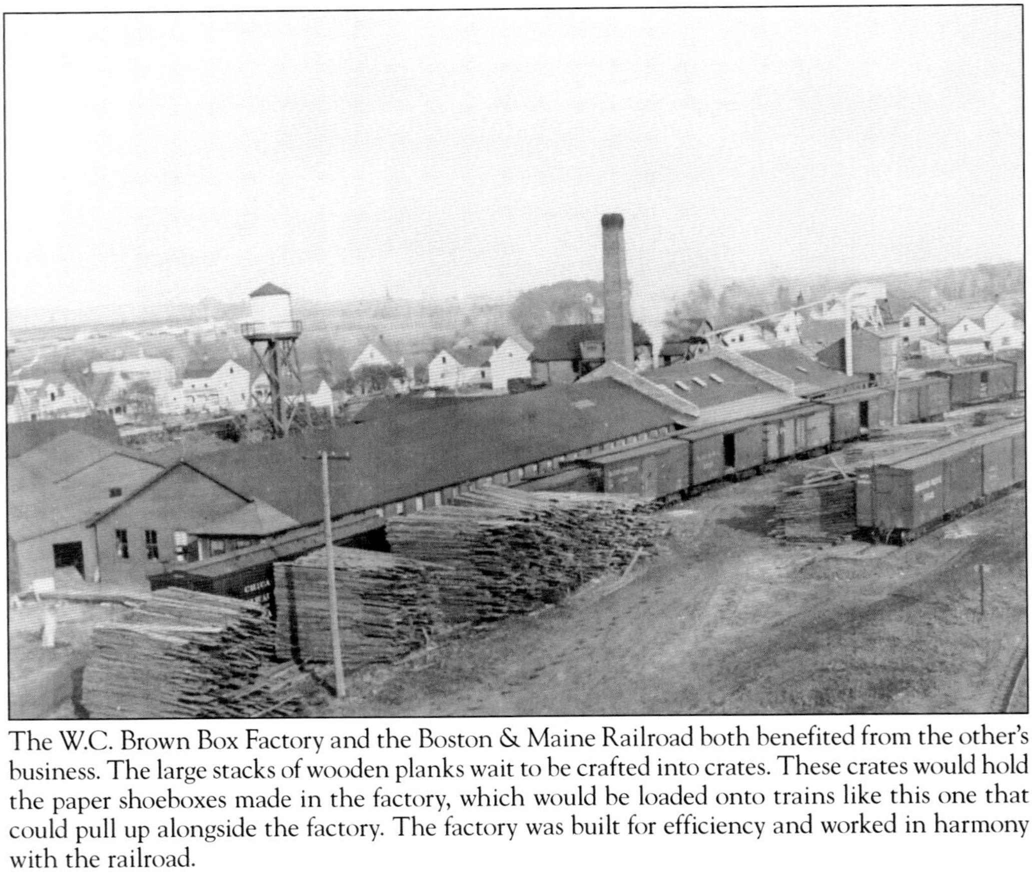

The W.C. Brown Box Factory and the Boston & Maine Railroad both benefited from the other's business. The large stacks of wooden planks wait to be crafted into crates. These crates would hold the paper shoeboxes made in the factory, which would be loaded onto trains like this one that could pull up alongside the factory. The factory was built for efficiency and worked in harmony with the railroad.

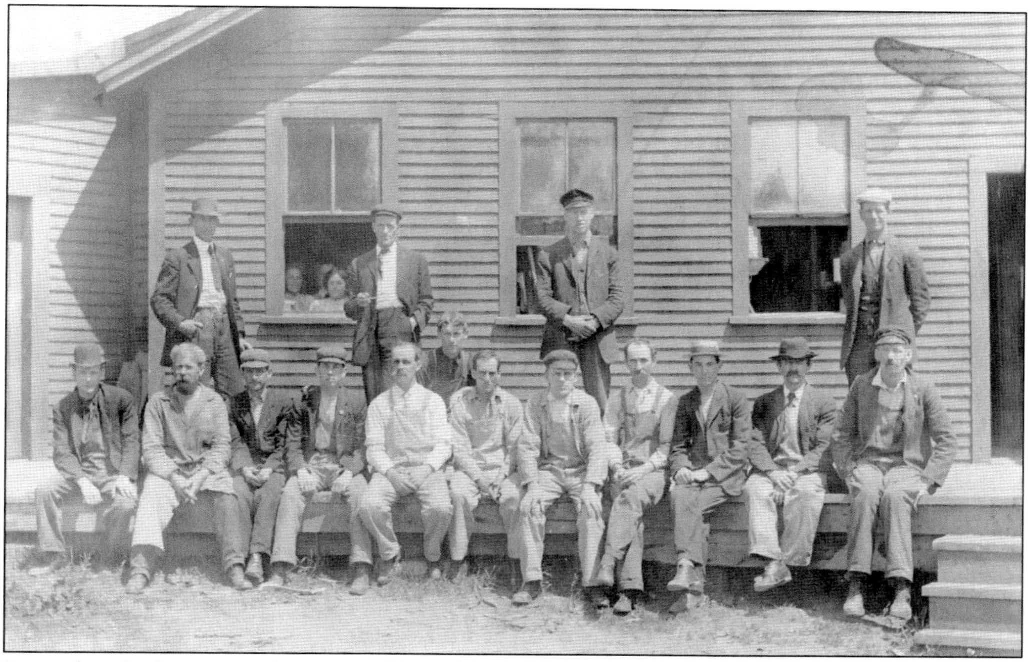

Several male factory workers sit and stand outside the W.C. Brown Box Factory. Some female employees can be seen peeking through the windows behind the men. The box factory would have provided long, tiring hours for these men and women, but Epping residents were proud their town was home to these factories and thankful for the number of jobs they provided.

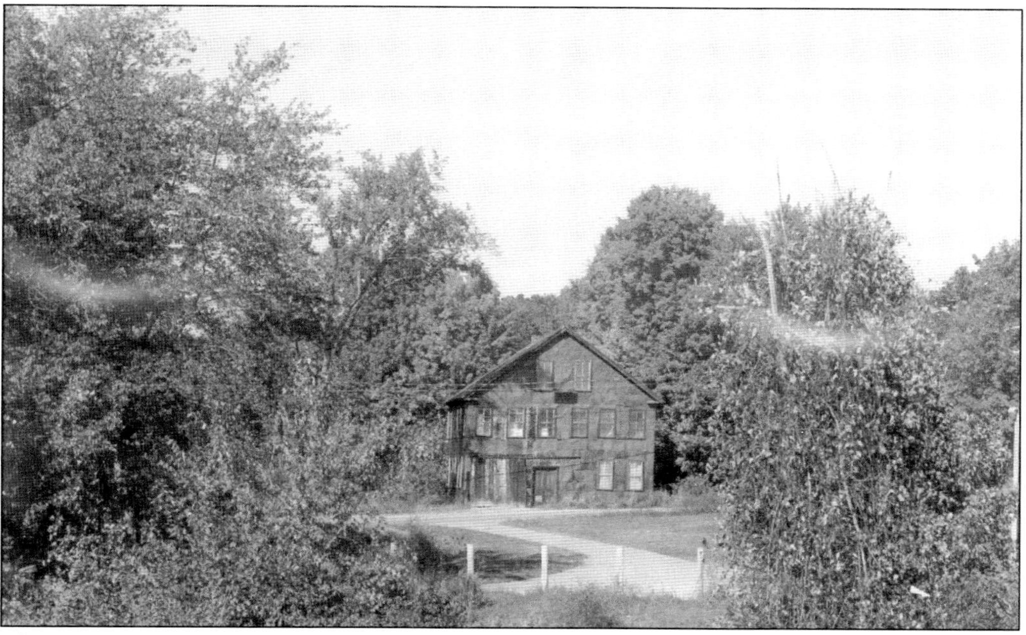

This building on Mill Street used to be surrounded by the icehouse and Howard Mile's sawmill, but now it stands alone. This building was a factory for the production of ax handles, and the machinery inside was run by water power from the Lamprey River, which sits just behind it. After the factory shut down, the building housed a steam laundry. The building burned down in 1980.

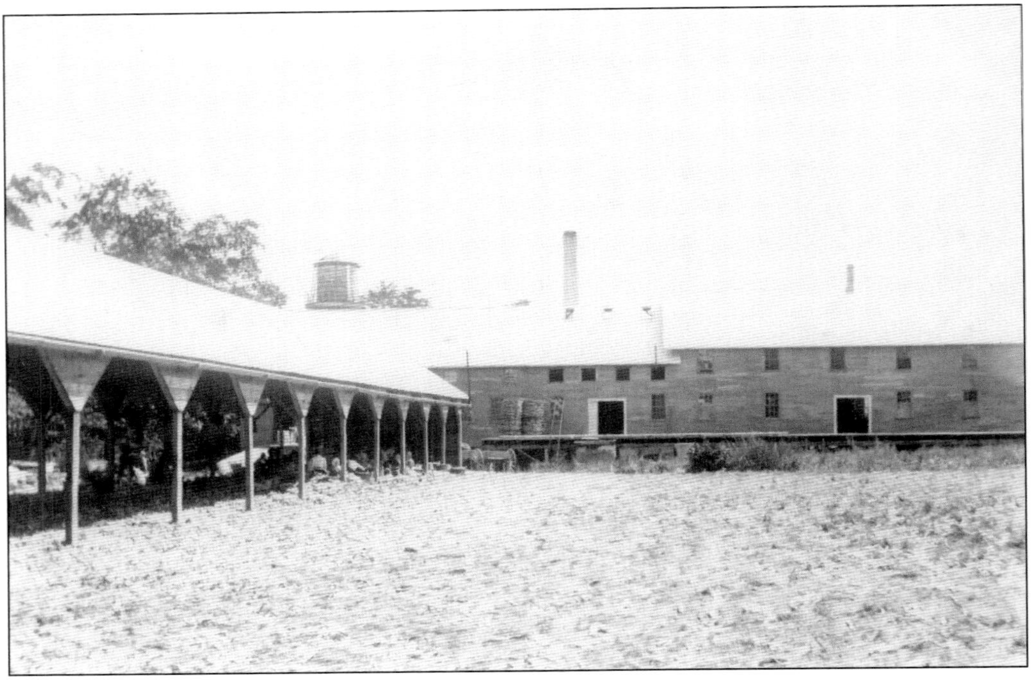

The canning factory of the Saco Valley Canning Company sat on Water Street. This factory canned corn. The corn was processed under the verandah to the left before being canned inside the main building. Above, workers can be seen processing the corn under the verandah. Below, workers pose for the photographer while standing next to a few large piles of husks that they have removed from the corn.

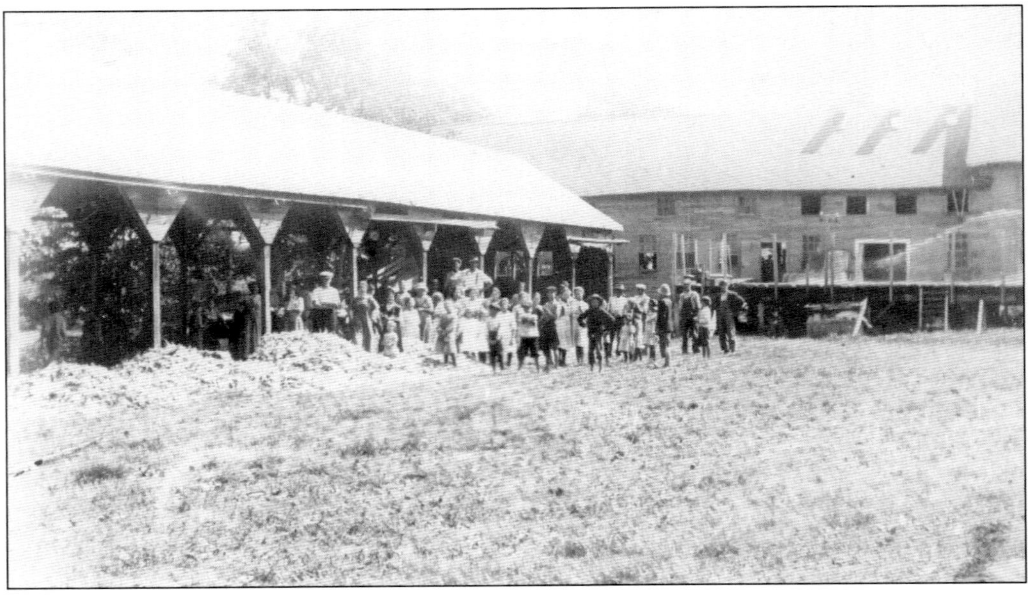

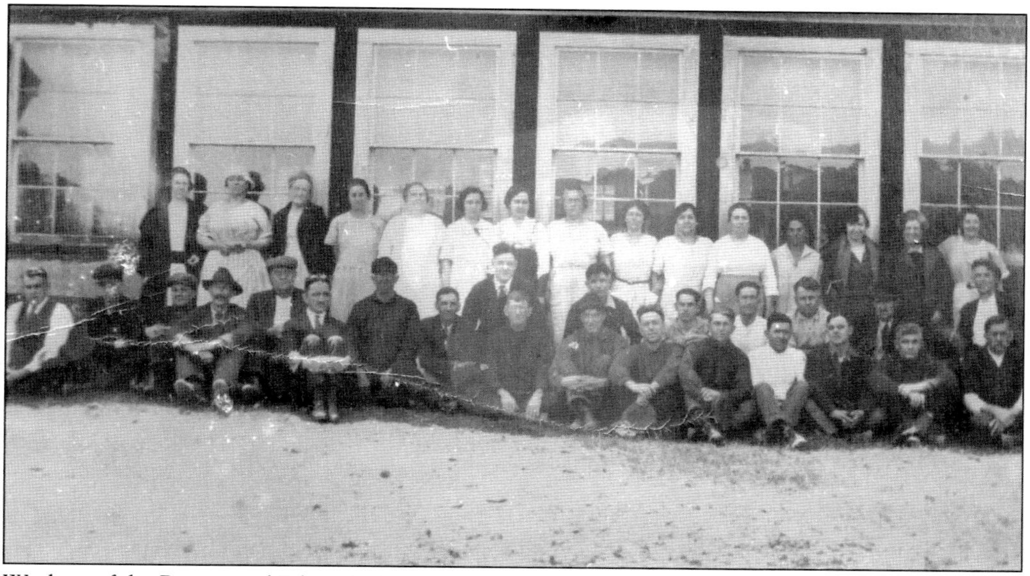

Workers of the Brown and Edwards shoe shop in West Epping take a break to pose for a photograph. Brown and Edwards purchased the building in 1919 from the C.O. Timson Shoe Factory, which opened in 1911. The Brown and Edwards Shoe Factory operated in the West Epping factory until it closed in 1930.

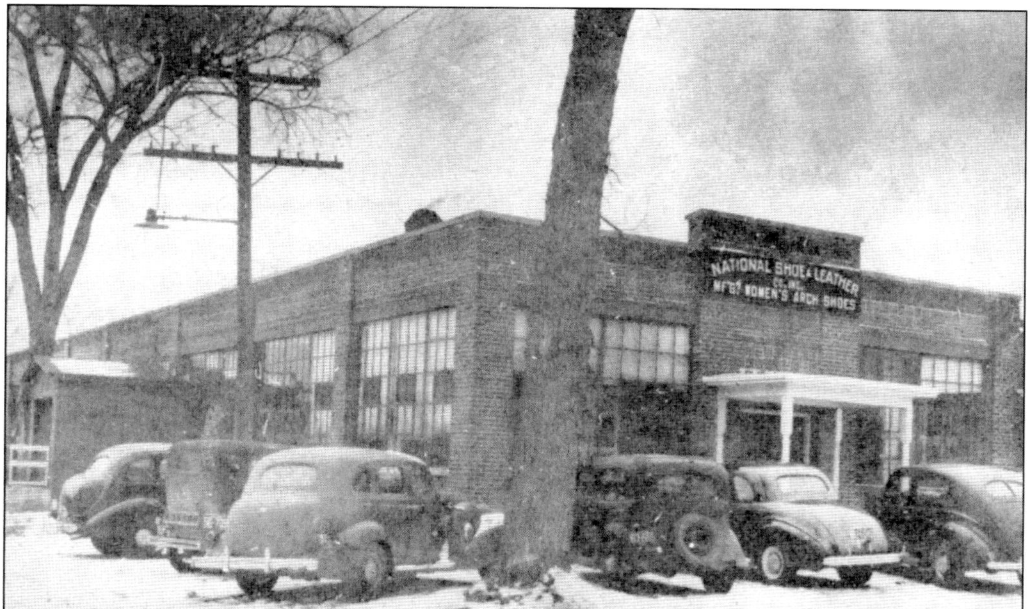


The National Shoe & Leather Co., Inc., manufactured women's shoes on Railroad Avenue. The building was originally constructed by Shapiro and Wagman for the same purpose in 1921 but was sold to National Shoe & Leather in 1933.

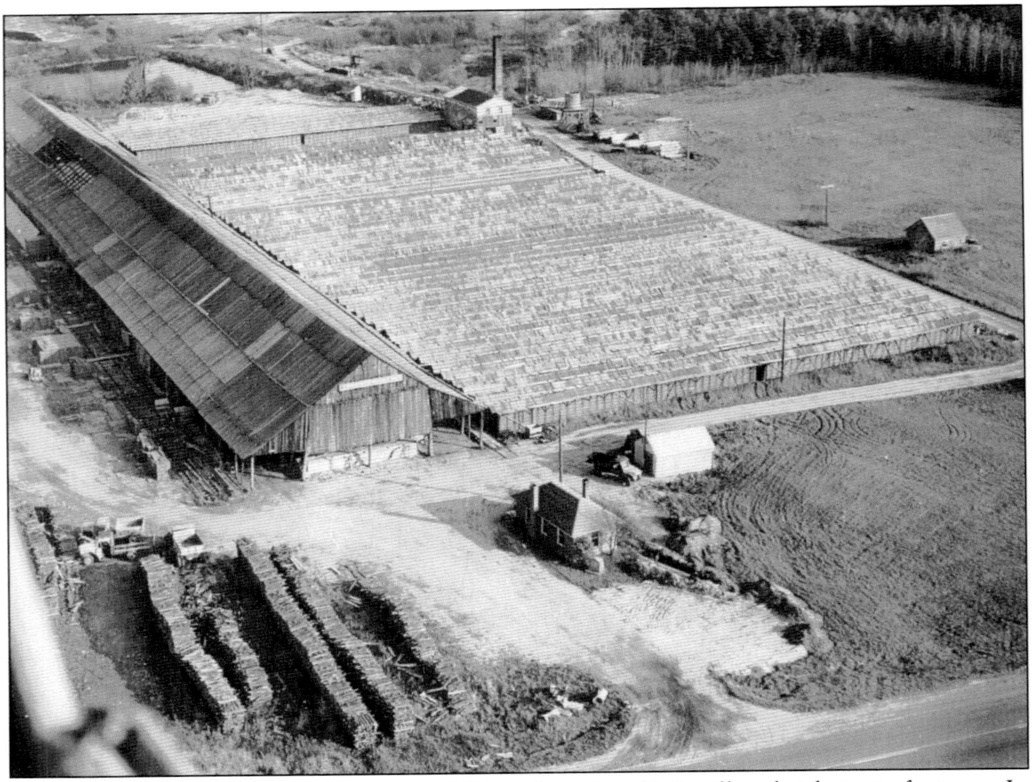

The Goodrich Brickyard was founded in 1887 and produced 1.5 million bricks in its first year. In 1926, the brickyard was incorporated as W.S. Goodrich, Inc., Brick Manufacturers. This bird's-eye view of W.S. Goodrich is a good example of how extensive Epping's brickyards were. Epping had as many as 20 brickyards operating at one time. (Courtesy of Robert Goodrich.)

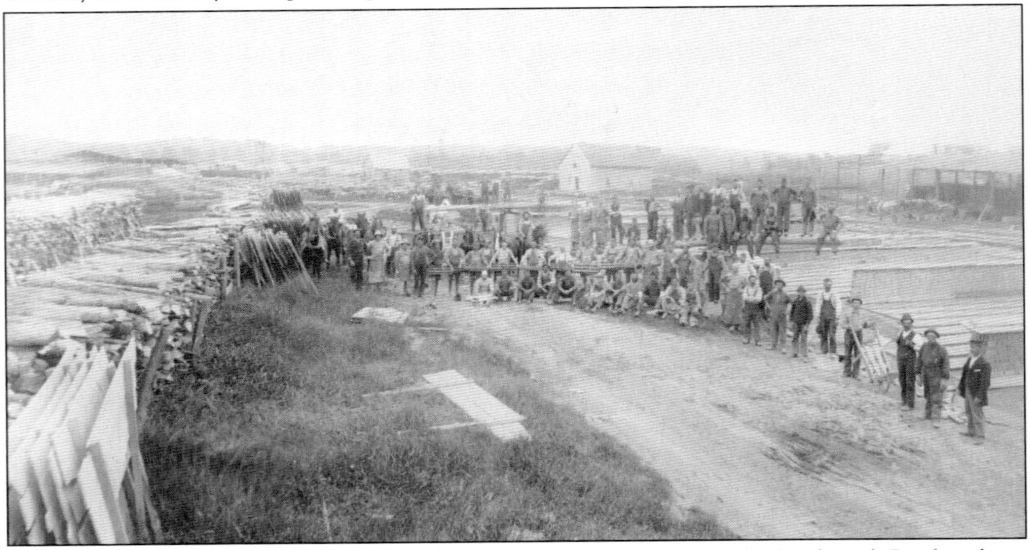

Employees of W.S. Goodrich pose for a photograph in the middle of the brickyard. Brickmaking was seasonal work because the cold air of the winter would freeze and crack the bricks as they lay out to dry before being fired in the kiln. Many of these men were likely loggers in the off-season. (Courtesy of Robert Goodrich.)

At right, a team of horses helps move the steam shovel into position to scoop clay out of the pits. Residents would simply dig up clay by hand in the early days of Epping brick production, but as brickmaking became commercialized, steam shovels like this one were required to dig more clay and deeper pits to keep up with production. The rail system that could be levered into different positions by a team of men maneuvering the steam shovel into the proper position can be seen in the image below. Men watch the shovel dig into the rich clay bed at the W.S. Goodrich Brickyard. (Both, courtesy of Robert Goodrich.)

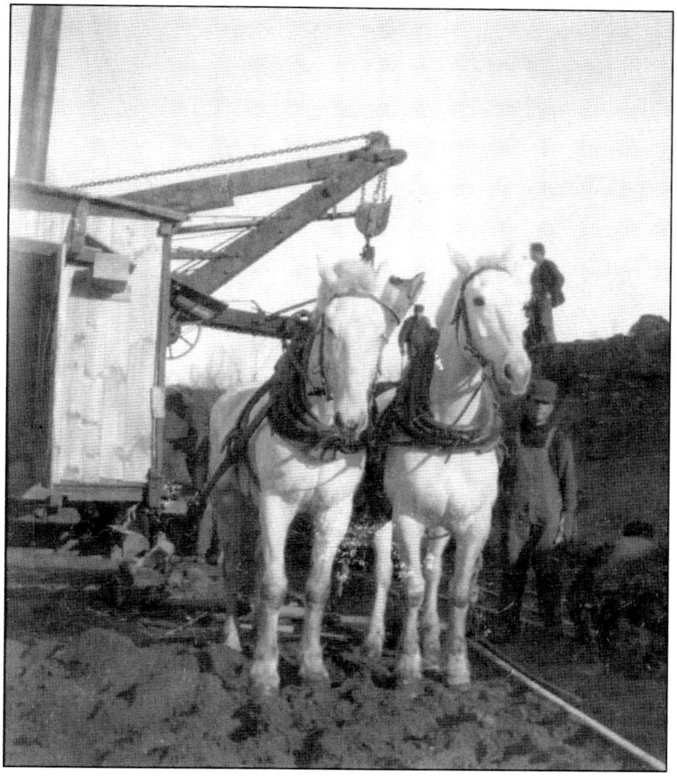

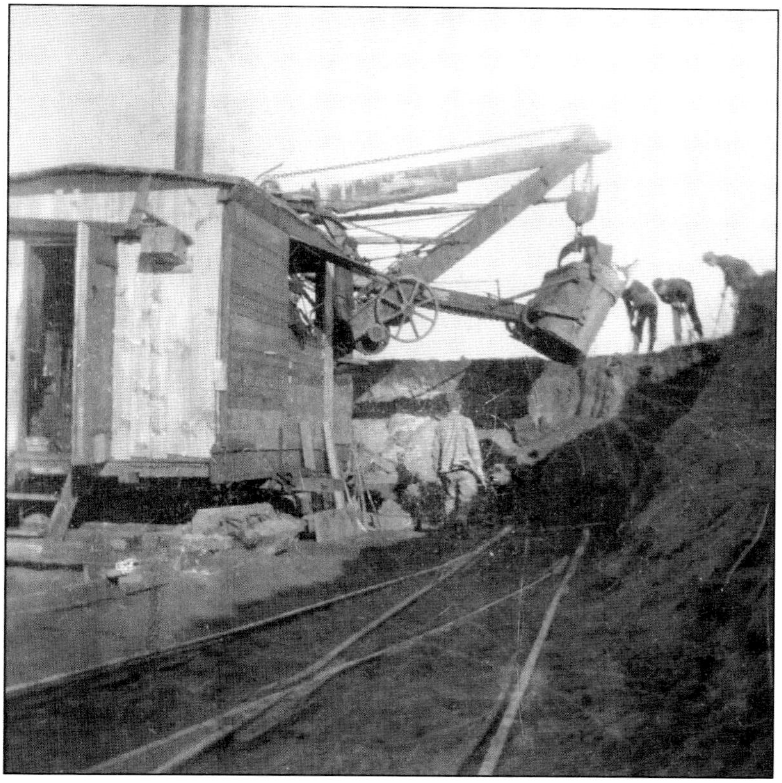

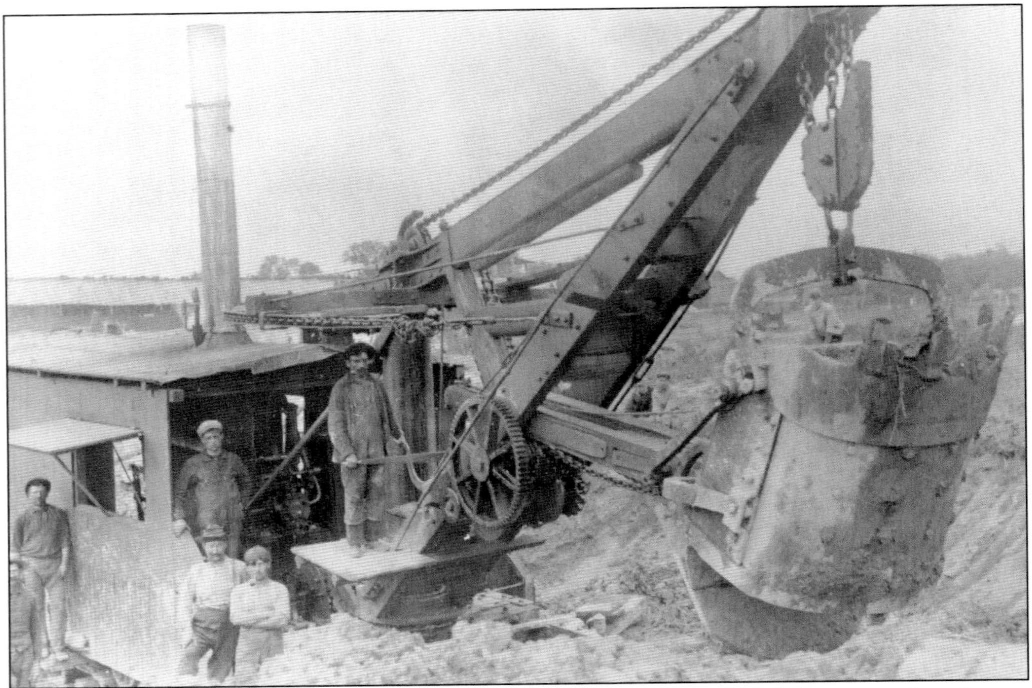

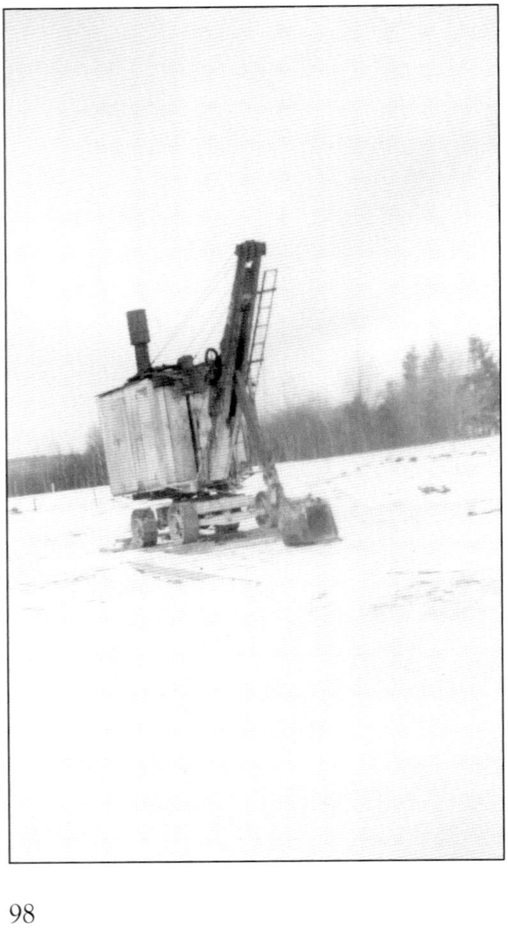

This is another view of the steam shovel, this one from Star Brickyard, as it collects clay for brickmaking. This steam shovel is almost identical to the one from W.S. Goodrich, which can be seen at left. Some of the men casually smoke their pipes as the team supervises the digging of the clay. (Both, courtesy of Robert Goodrich.)

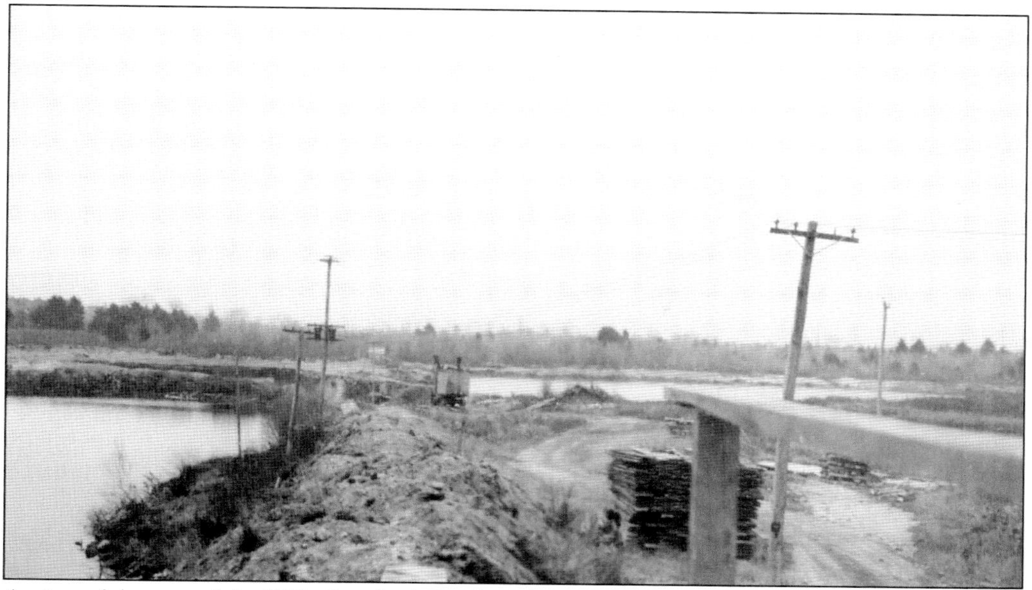

A view of the rear of the W.S. Goodrich Brickyard. Epping is strewn with clay ponds like the two in this image. As the steam shovels dug deeper and deeper, they would often hit natural springs and ground water that would fill up the clay pits. These clay ponds stand as proud markers of Epping's brickmaking past and provide habitat for a variety of wildlife and a welcome source of recreation. A steam shovel can be seen at center. (Courtesy of Robert Goodrich.)

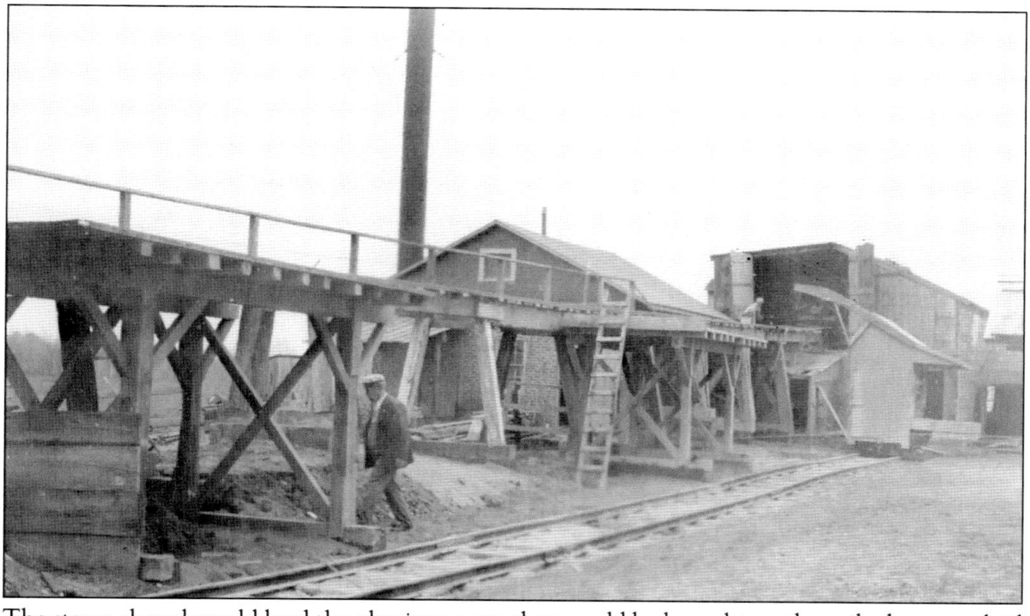

The steam shovel would load the clay into carts that would be brought up the rails that were laid down into the clay pits. The carts would be rolled away from the pit and back to the yard to be moved along the track that traveled atop the wooden structure that led into the wooden building at right. (Courtesy of Robert Goodrich.)

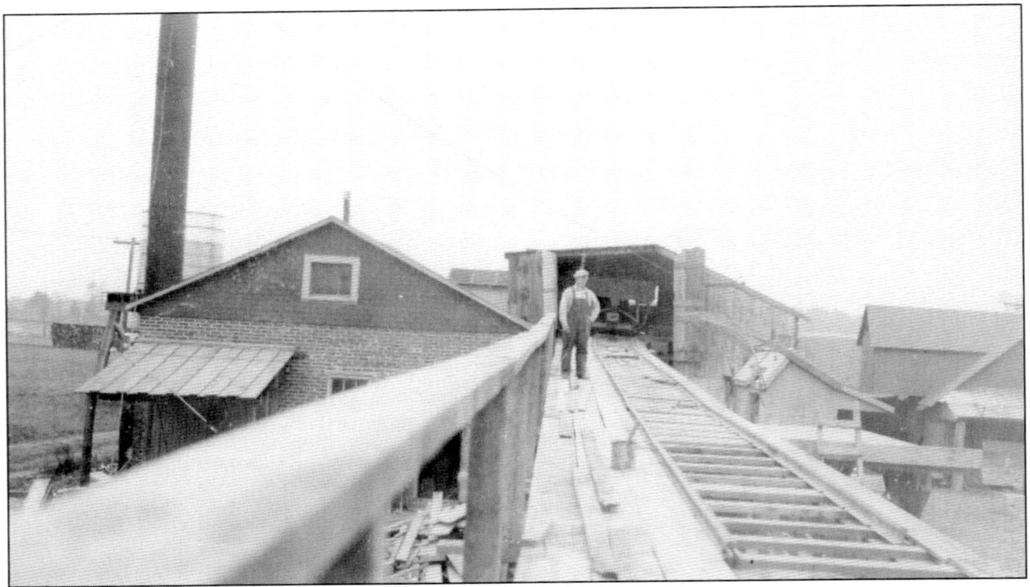

The track that carried the clay from the pit can be seen leading into the wooden building where the cart is now positioned. The cart would turn to the right, dumping the clay into the "pug mill," which churned the clay over and over. Water was added to the clay at this point, and the pug mill would churn the clay until it reached a consistency suitable for molding. A steam engine that ran the pug mill was located in the brick building to the left. Below, Ernest Bernier feeds coal into the steam engine that powered the pug mill. (Both, courtesy of Robert Goodrich.)

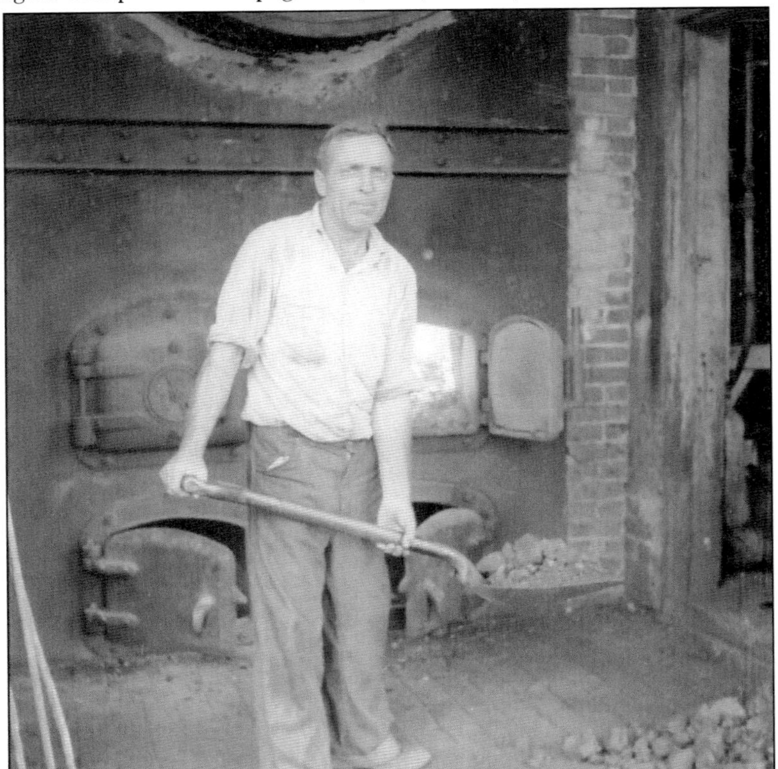

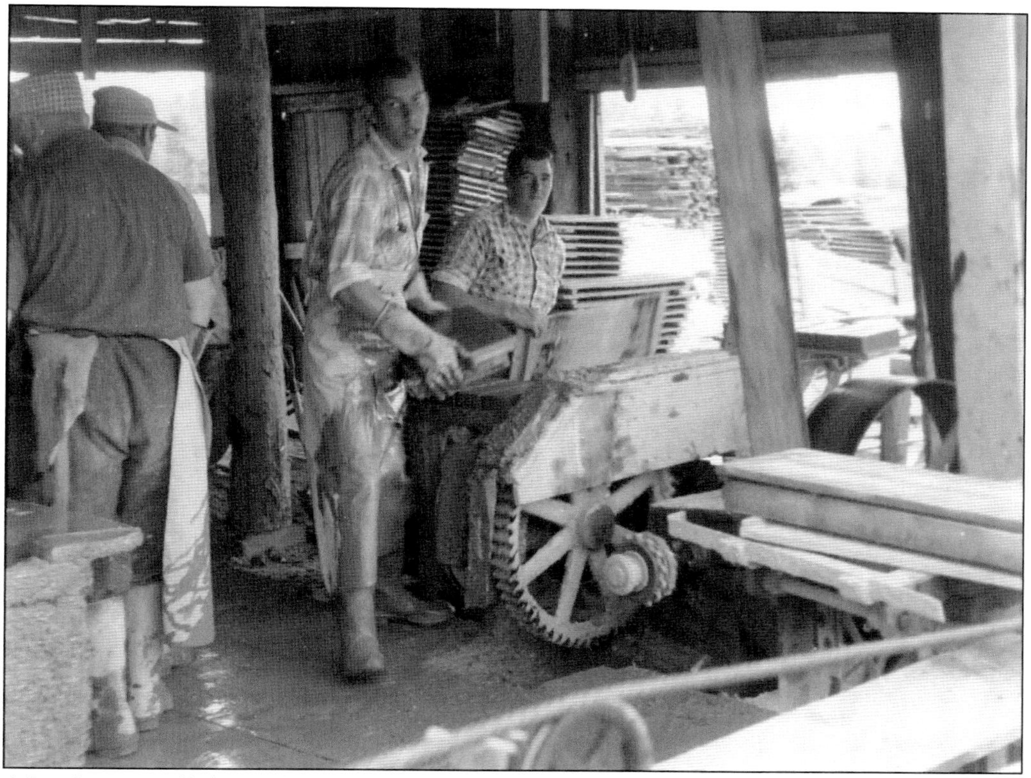

After the pug mill churned the clay into a proper consistency, the clay was set into molds. At this point, the bricks became either water struck, when the molds were lined with water before the clay was put in, or sand struck, when the molds were lined with sand. Sand-struck bricks were easier to get out of the molds because the water in the water-struck bricks created suction. Both methods produced bricks of high quality, and both types were produced in large quantities in Epping. Below, from left to right, Arthur Desjardin, Frank Camp, and Fred Drew set the clay in molds of six bricks each. Both images show how messy this job could be. (Both, courtesy of Robert Goodrich.)

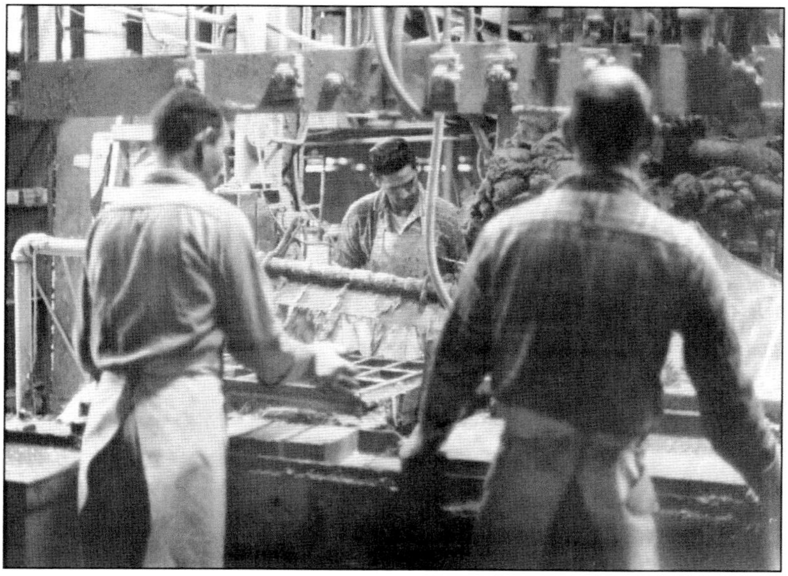

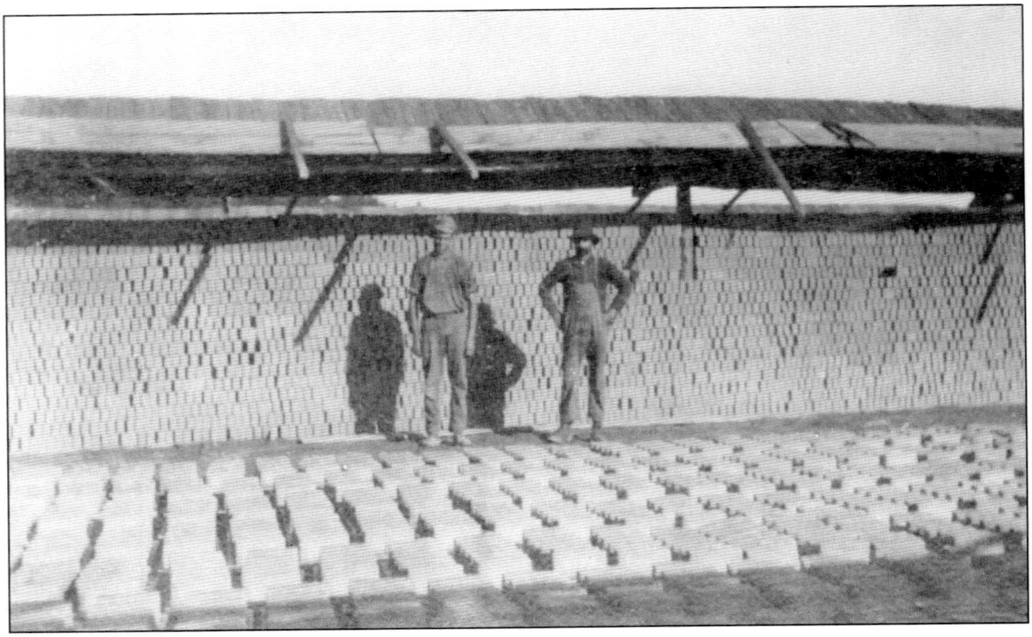

After the bricks were removed from the molds, which occurred almost immediately after the clay was formed, the bricks were laid out in rows to air dry. After about two days, the bricks could be rotated onto their sides to continue drying. Drying bricks often were laid out in the open, and a hard rain could ruin thousands of bricks. Some brickyards began to build roofed structures to dry the bricks under to offer some protection from damage. (Both, courtesy of Robert Goodrich.)

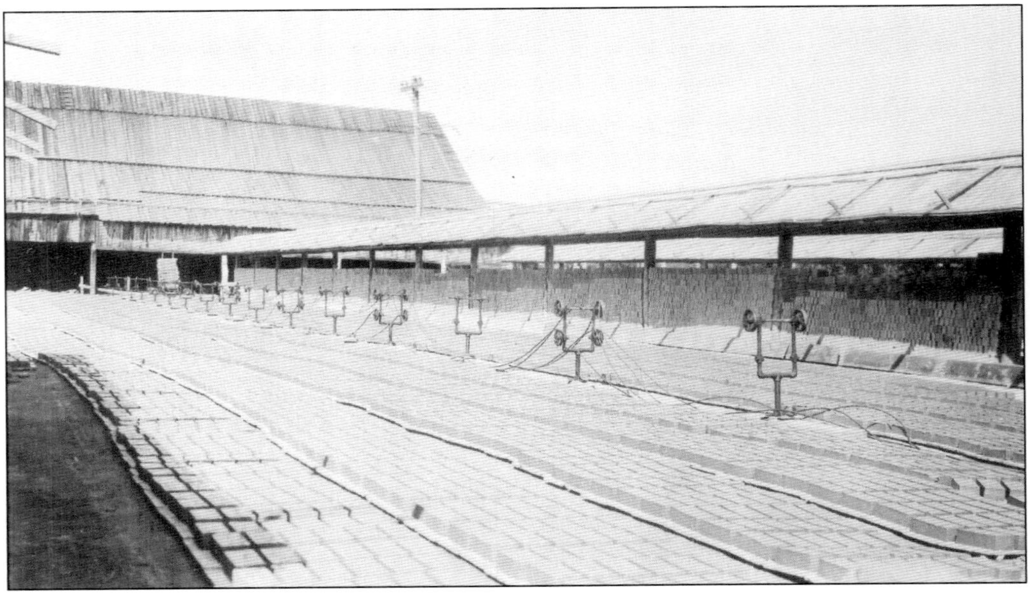

Roofed drying racks such as these allowed for the bricks to dry with much less chance of being damaged. A brickyard could also dry many more bricks at one time with drying racks that held more bricks vertically than they could simply place on the ground to dry. The men below work to empty a pallet of bricks onto the drying racks. The W.S. Goodrich Brickyard could produce up to 40,000 bricks a day, which meant the rotation to the drying racks needed to be constant to keep up with production. (Both, courtesy of Robert Goodrich.)

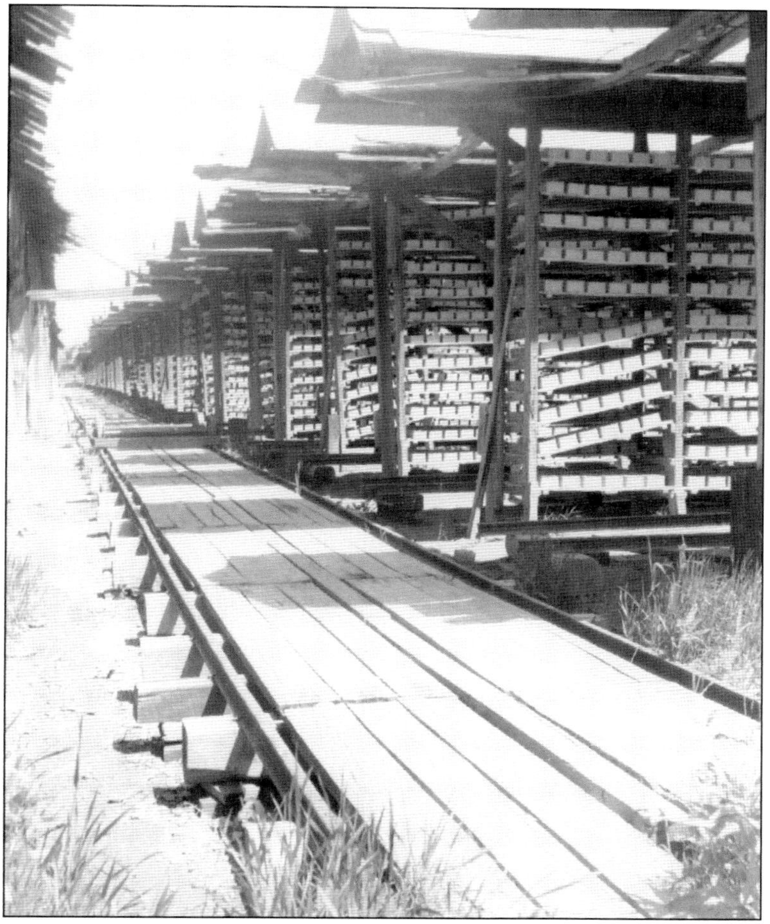

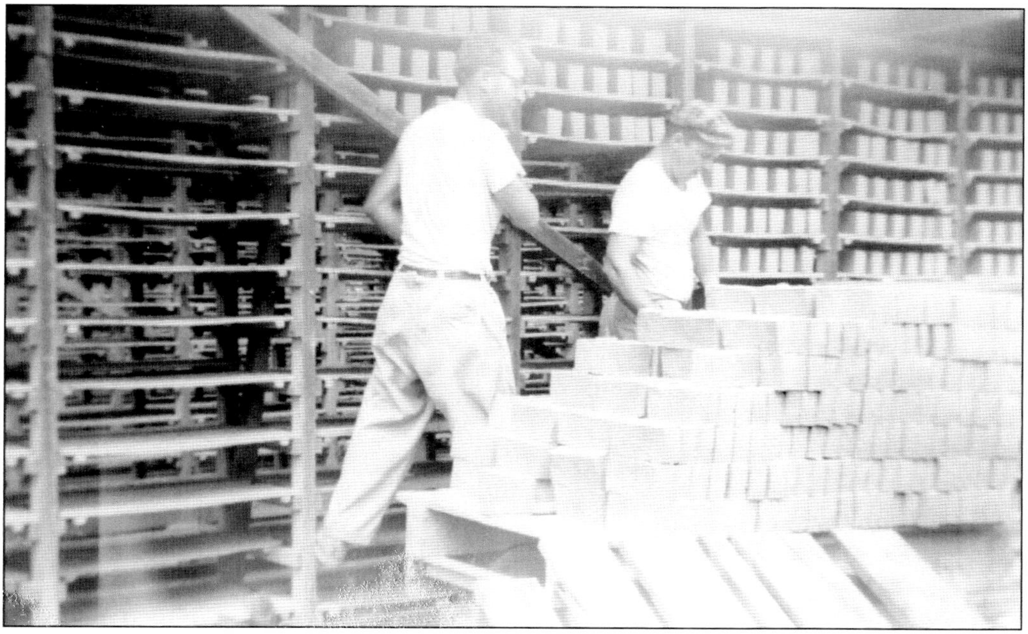

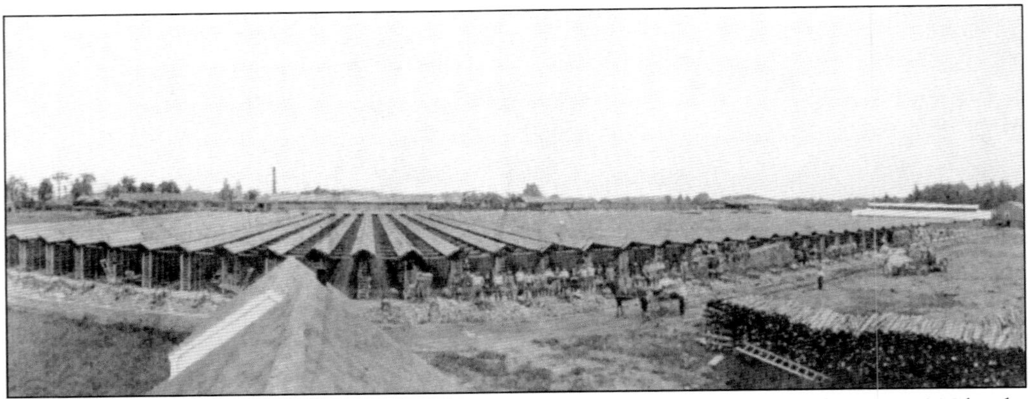

The drying racks of W.S. Goodrich Brickyard stretch the length of the yard. Producing 40,000 bricks a day required a crew of about 50 employees. Some of these men lodged in a company boarding house. Many of the workers were French Canadians and Italians who rotated between working the brickyards and then working as loggers in the winter. (Courtesy of Robert Goodrich.)

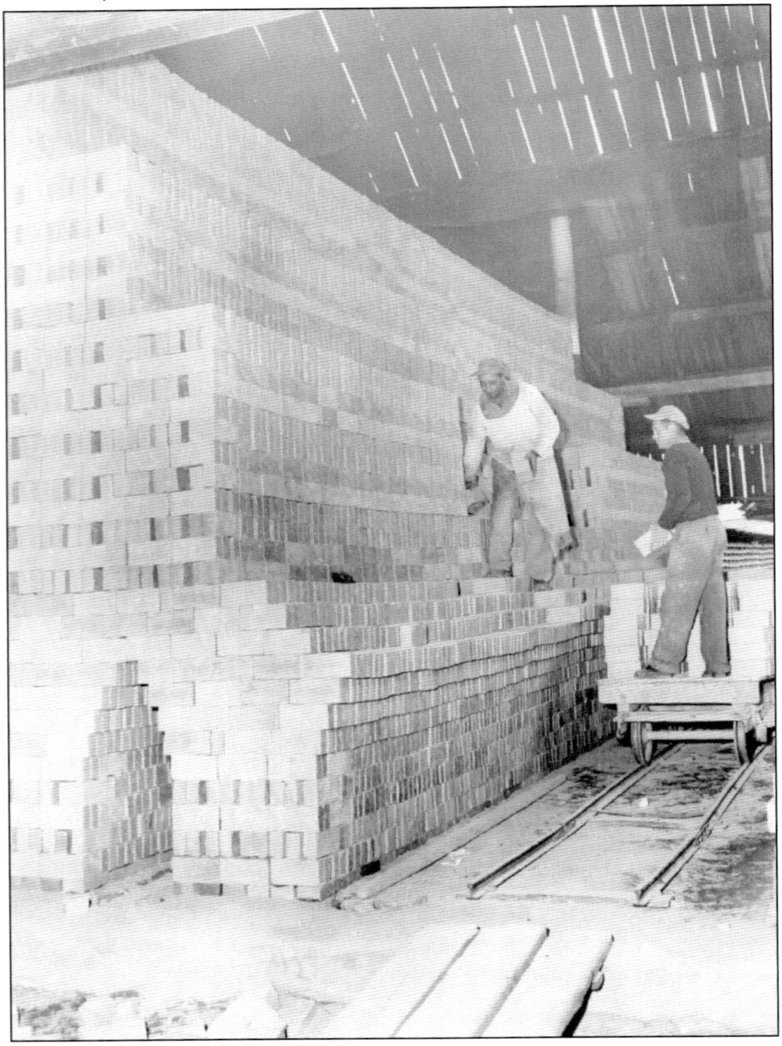

After the bricks dried for about a week, they were brought to the kiln area where a "scove kiln" was assembled by the brickmakers for each new set of bricks to be fired. Built of bricks itself, scove kilns required a particular pattern, which these men are assembling. The outer layer of the kiln was set with bricks that had already been fired, and then a layer of clay was added to make the kiln airtight to trap the heat inside. (Courtesy of Robert Goodrich.)

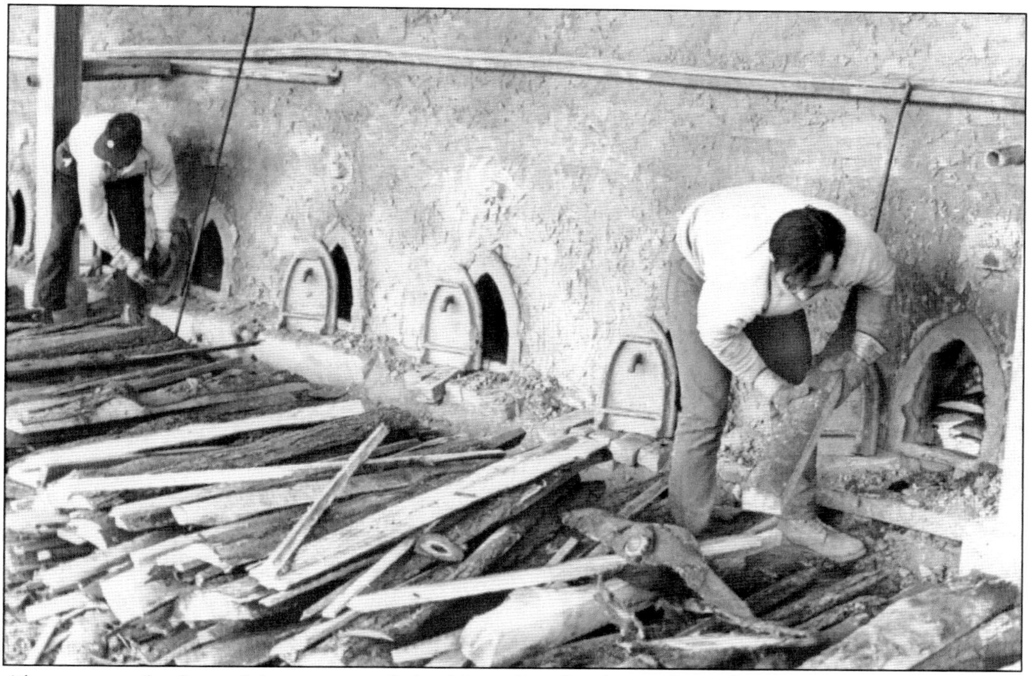

Above, men feed wood into a scove kiln. Note the clay layered on the outside to trap the heat. The kiln required constant supervision once it was fired. A "head burner" would monitor the kiln to assure that it was fired at the proper temperature. Hard and soft wood could be added at the head burner's discretion. Brickyards often bought woodlots and hired lumber crews in order to procure wood for the kilns. The felling of trees usually happened in the winter and was often done by the employees who worked the brickyards. W.S. Goodrich Brickyard consumed about 3,000 cords of wood every year. (Both, courtesy of Robert Goodrich.)

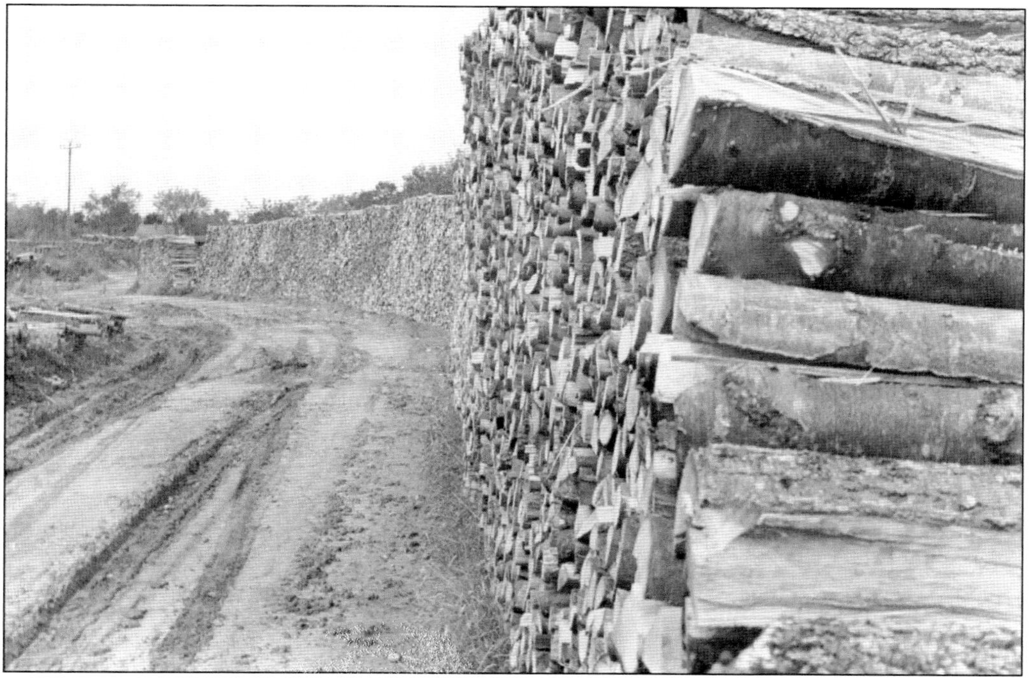

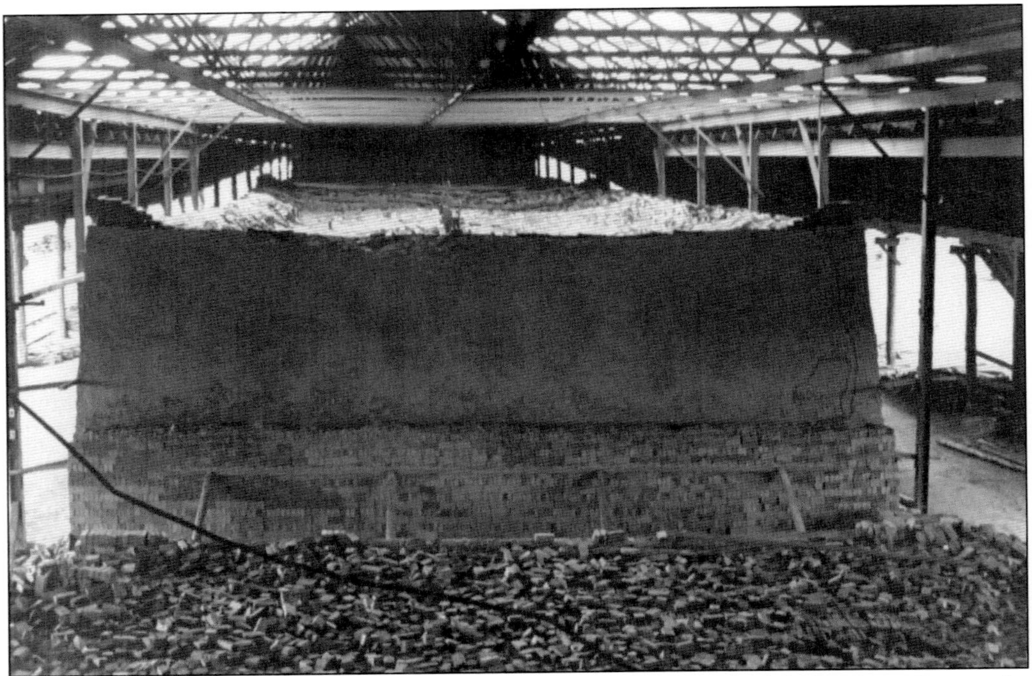

Above is a scove kiln after it has been fired. Note that the top of the kiln has bowed in as the moisture of the bricks has been fired out. Scove kilns could not disperse heat evenly throughout, which meant that bricks often came out with varying colors and textures. Below, men disassemble a scove kiln after it had been left to cool for several days. The men would stack these bricks onto pallets that could be loaded directly onto railcars. Most brickyards had spurs off the main rail line that ran through the yard so that bricks could be loaded onto the trains. (Both, courtesy of Robert Goodrich.)

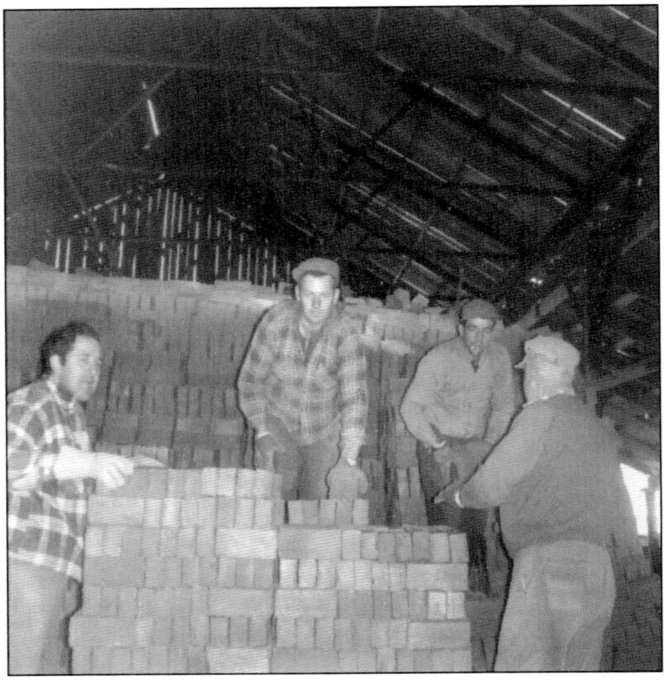

# *Seven*

# Eppinites

The term Epping residents use for themselves, and are referred to as by others, is Eppinites. Eppinites have moved on from Epping, stayed in Epping, or have moved to Epping from elsewhere. They have forged political careers, circled the globe, set records, and created businesses. But not all Eppinites rise to greatness. What makes Epping unique is the mixture of Eppinites who aspire to do great things and those who aspire to make Epping a great community.

Epping's nickname is the "Home of Three Governors." The town has produced three New Hampshire governors, and signs erected by the Garden Club at the town line let passersby know Epping's pride at this fact.

Epping was also the birthplace and home to the first man to circumnavigate the globe on a motorcycle. From 1912 to 1913, Carl Stearns Clancy rode 18,000 miles on his 934 cc seven horsepower 1912 Henderson Four motorcycle across Europe, Africa, Asia, and North America. Carl Stearns Clancy would later go on to produce a number of Will Rogers movies, starting with an adaptation of *The Headless Horseman* in 1922, the screenplay for which he also wrote. At the end of his career, he made documentaries for the US Forest Service. His book *The Gasoline Tramp or Around the World on a Motorcycle (1912–1913)* about his circumnavigation is still available for purchase.

Kerry Bascom is the most successful athlete Epping has ever produced. She left the Epping High School basketball team as the all-time leading scorer. Bascom then went on to the University of Connecticut, where she helped lead the UConn Huskies—who did not, at the time, have much of a reputation for basketball—to divisional and national success from 1987 to 1991, success that has come to define the school. She left the school as the leader for points scored while winning individual awards and remains near the top of a number of school records. Bascom also helped the United States team win the gold medal at the World University Games in 1991, played professionally in Spain and France, and was an assistant coach for the University of New Hampshire women's basketball team. Bascom's number remains the only one retired by Epping High School.

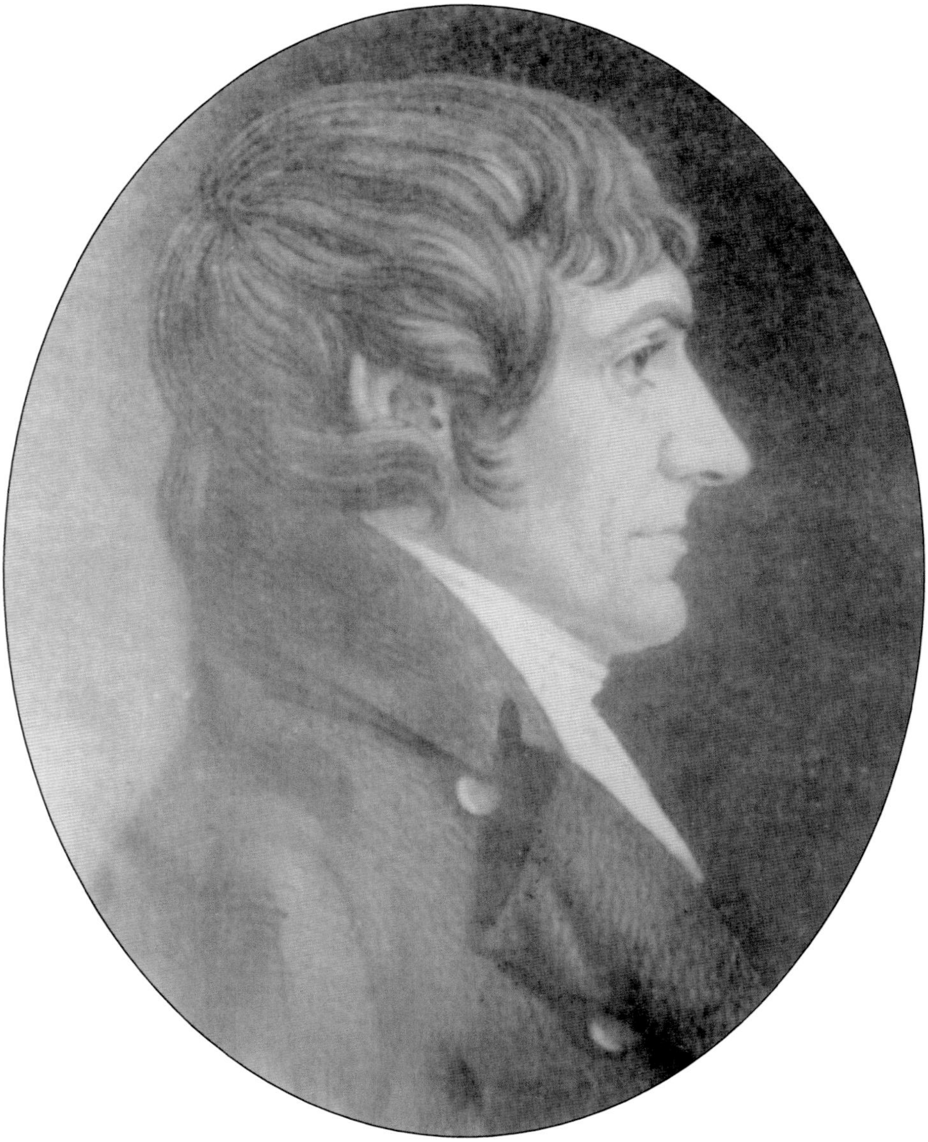

William Plumer grew up on his father's farm on Red Oak Hill and attended the Red Oak Hill School until he was 17. His father wanted him to become a farmer, but Plumer was a voracious reader who would sometimes walk miles to borrow a book from a neighbor. Plumer decided to become a Baptist preacher, to his father's stern disapproval, but soon soured of receiving no pay except that of room and board. At the age of 27, Plumer began studying law and was admitted to the New Hampshire Bar in 1787. He went on to become a selectman for the town of Epping; an eight-term representative to the New Hampshire General Court, holding the post of Speaker of the House for two of those terms; one of the developers of the state constitution in 1792; US senator from 1802 to 1807; and governor of New Hampshire in 1812 and from 1816 to 1819. Plumer was an influential Federalist who corresponded with Thomas Jefferson and John Adams, among others. As a presidential elector in 1820, Governor Plumer cast the sole vote against James Monroe for president of the United States in the Electoral College, an act that was widely believed to have been done to preserve George Washington's status as the only president ever unanimously elected.

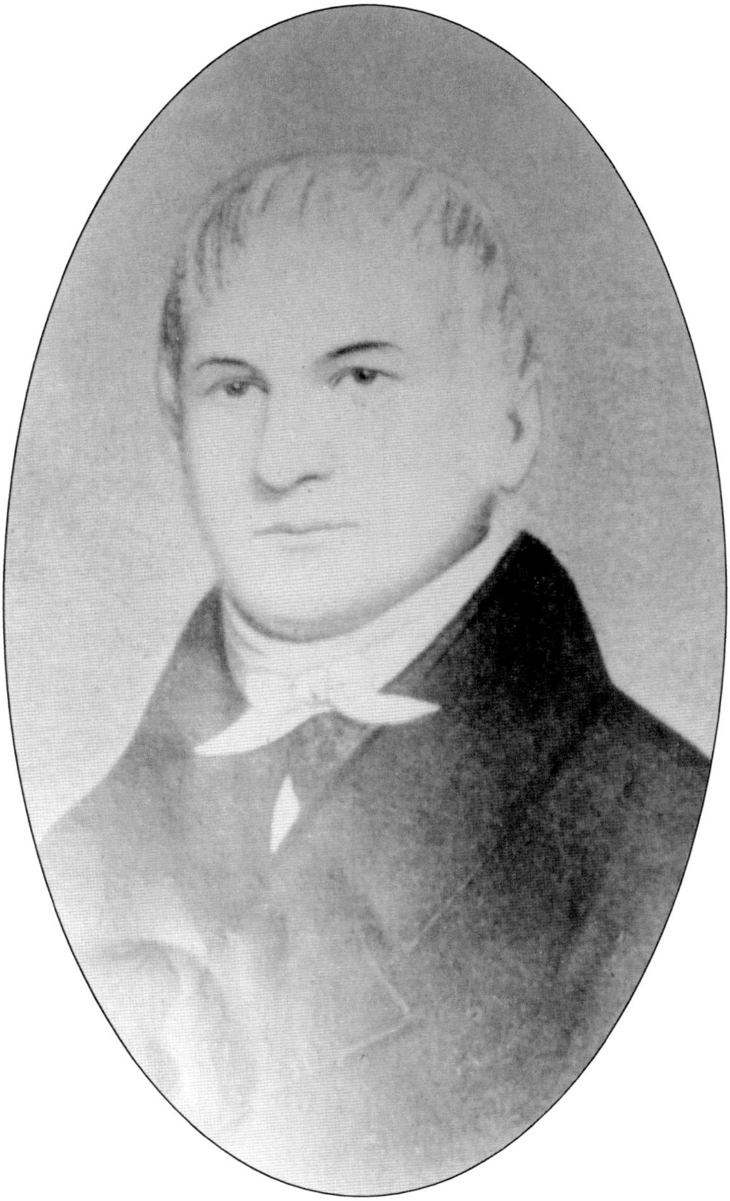

The second Eppinite to become the governor of New Hampshire, David Lawrence Morril was born in Epping on June 10, 1772. His father was the Congregational minister for the town, and he and Morril's grandfathers gave Morril a spiritual education. David Morril received a teaching certificate from Phillips Exeter Academy in 1790 and earned degrees at both Dartmouth College and the University of Vermont. Isaac Morril, his uncle, later gave him training in medicine. Morril began a practice in medicine that lasted from 1790 to 1800. In 1802, he became a minister in the Congregational Presbyterian Church. In 1808, Morril was elected to the New Hampshire House of Representatives and served until 1816, the last year of which he served as Speaker of the House. Morril then served as a US senator from 1817 to 1823 and governor of New Hampshire from 1824 to 1827. Governor Morril pushed for improvements in the condition of New Hampshire roads and schools, as well as the establishment of a state university, which did not come to fruition until much later. Governor Morril died on January 26, 1849, and is buried in Concord, New Hampshire.

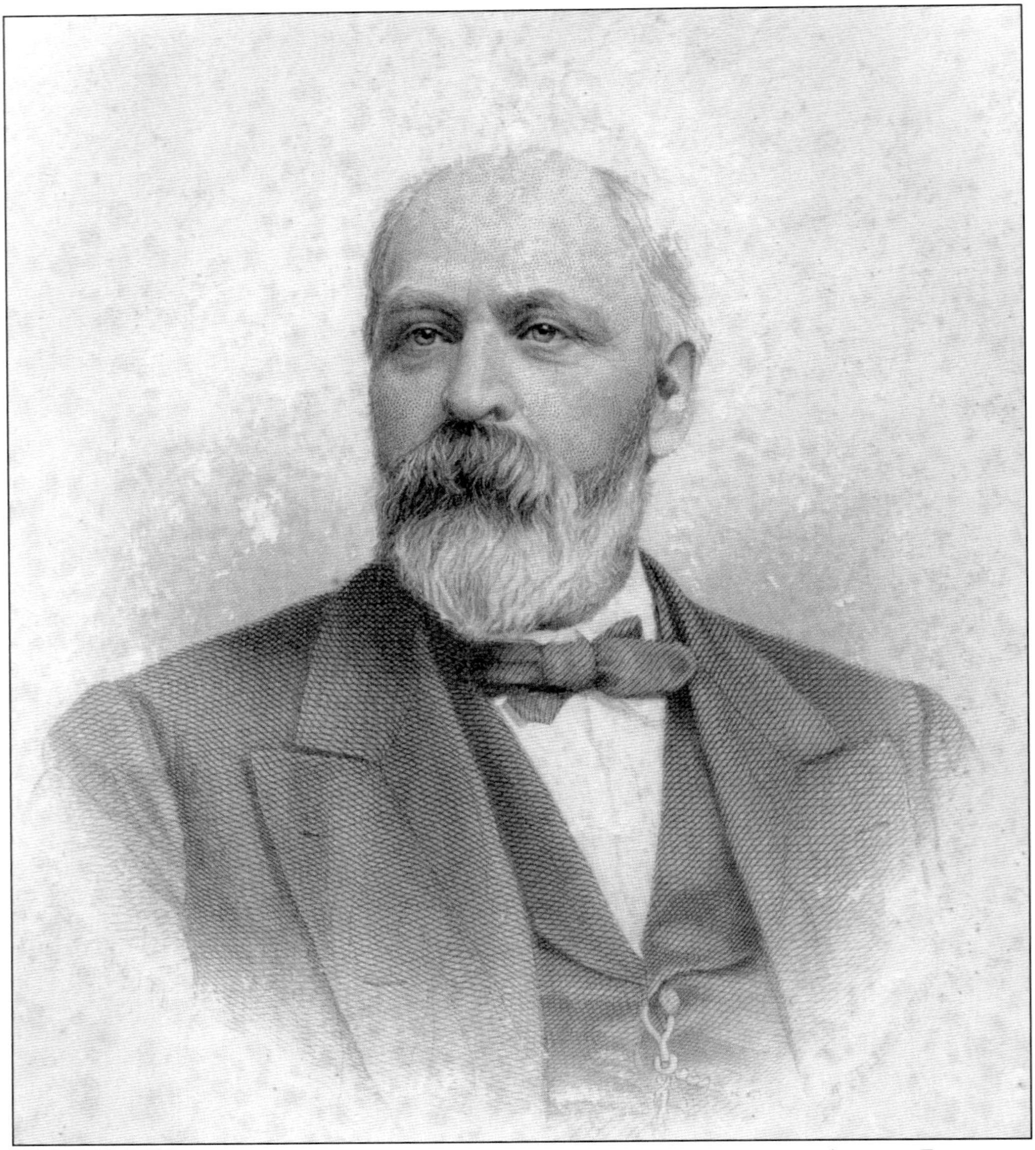

The third governor to call Epping home, Benjamin Franklin Prescott was born in Epping on February 26, 1833. The best educated Eppinite governor, Prescott attended Pembroke Academy from 1848 to 1849, Phillips Exeter Academy from 1850 to 1852, and Dartmouth College from 1853 to 1856. Prescott then studied law in Concord and was admitted to the New Hampshire Bar in 1859. In 1861, Prescott became the associate editor of the *Independent Democrat*, an antislavery newspaper that strongly supported the election and administration of Abraham Lincoln. From 1859 to 1864, Prescott served as the secretary of the Republican State Committee. From 1865 to 1869, he served as special agent to the US Treasury Department for New England. Prescott was New Hampshire's secretary of state from 1872 to 1873 and from 1875 to 1876. In every election from 1860 to 1880, Benjamin Prescott served as secretary of the New Hampshire Electoral College of president and vice president of the United States. Prescott was elected governor of New Hampshire from 1877 to 1879 and, in 1880, helped nominate James Garfield as the Republican candidate for president while serving as chairman of the New Hampshire delegation to the Republican National Convention in Chicago.

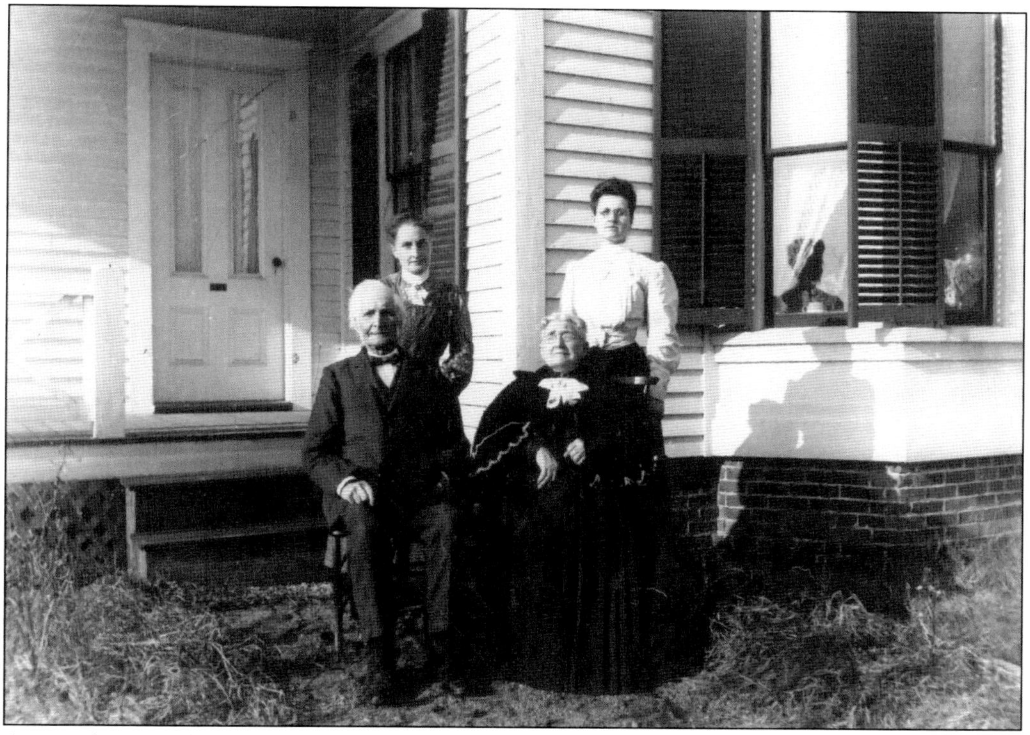

A very distinguished looking Mr. and Mrs. Dolliver sit while Mrs. Walter Hill and Annie Pike stand for a picture in front of the Dollivers' house on Bartlett Street in 1900.

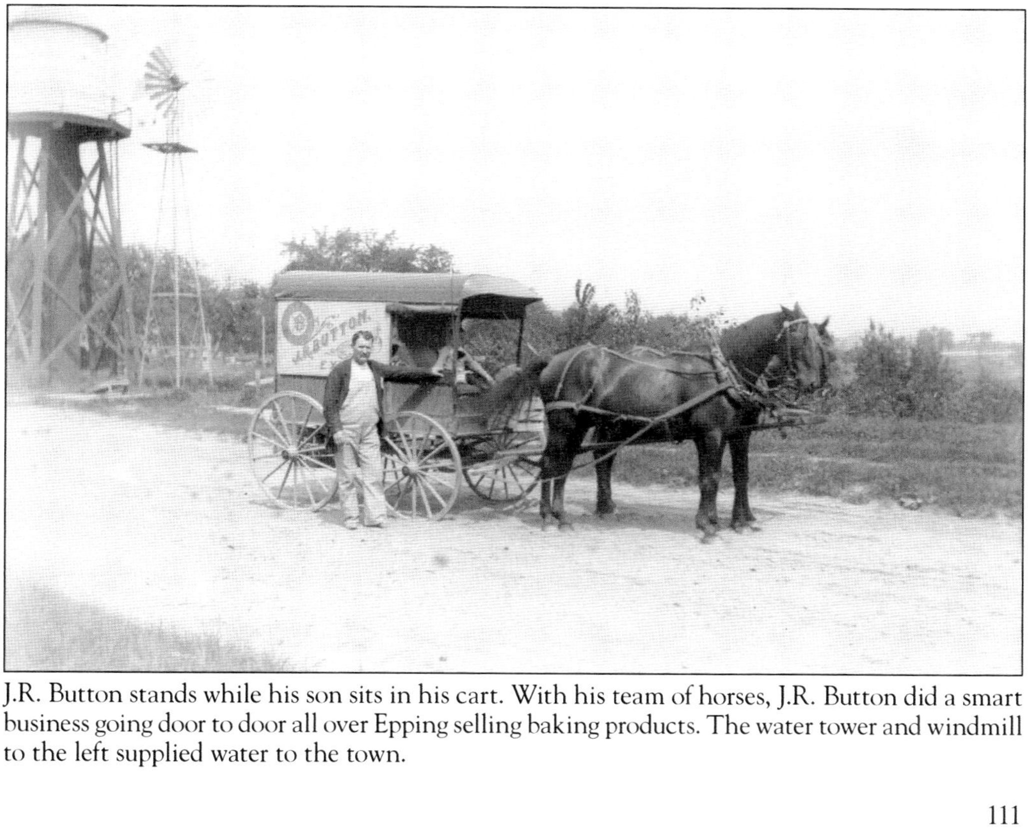


J.R. Button stands while his son sits in his cart. With his team of horses, J.R. Button did a smart business going door to door all over Epping selling baking products. The water tower and windmill to the left supplied water to the town.

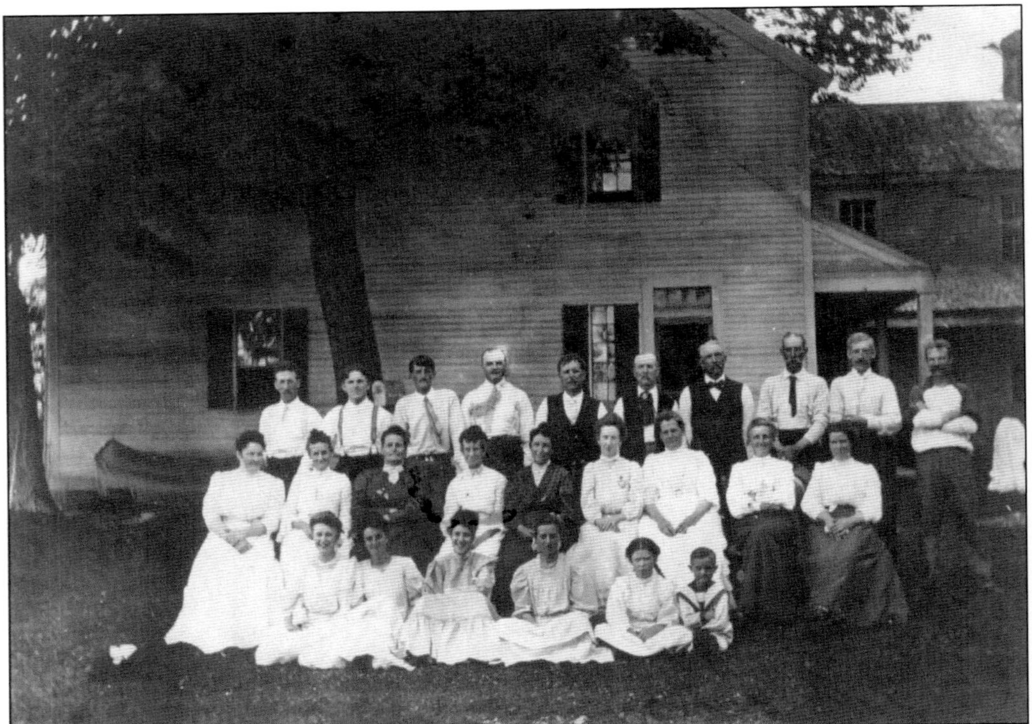

A group poses in front of the Folsom house. Group outings of all kinds help forge bonds of community. This one could be an outing of the millworkers of West Epping.

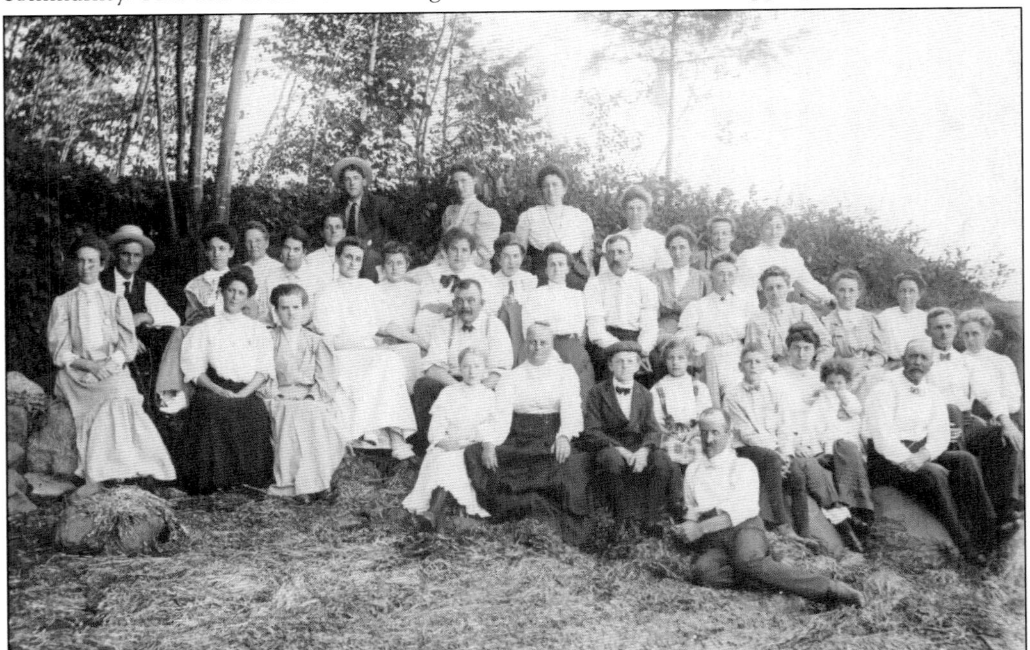

The members of Epping's Rockingham Grange take an outing to Great Bay in 1900. Aside from helping to disperse different views and practices in farming, the Grange served to form bonds between Epping's farming families.

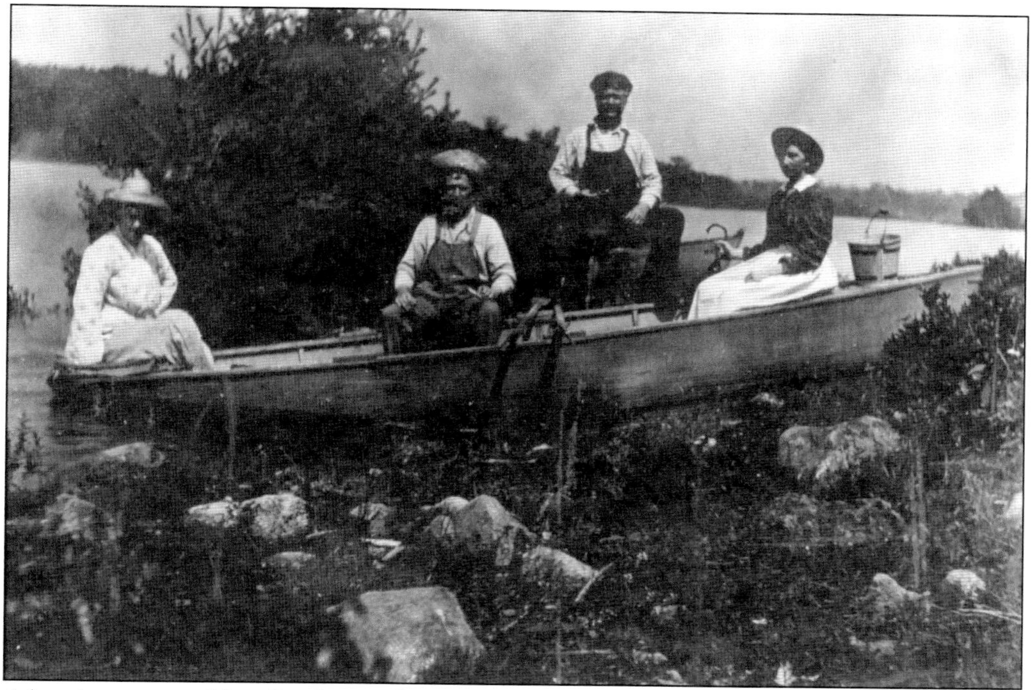

A boating party on Hoar Pond, one of Epping's largest bodies of water, includes, from left to right, an unidentified woman, Fred P. Dearborn Sr., Charles Pike, and Jennie Dearborn. Boating parties have long been a favorite of Eppinites and an opportunity for community gatherings. The Lamprey River Canoe Race, held every spring, is just one example of these pleasure trips.

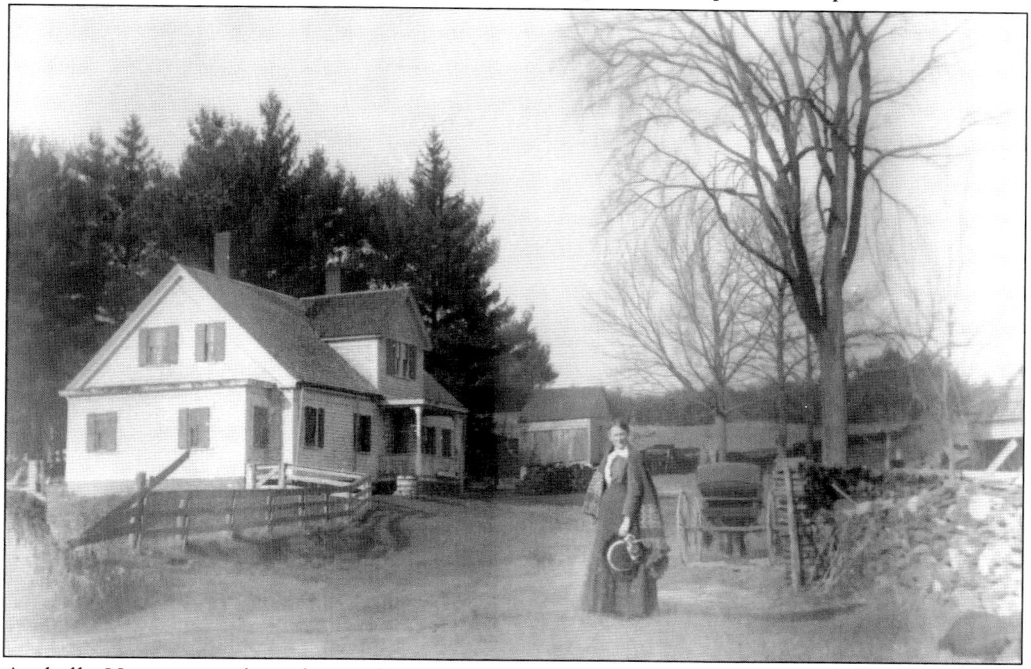

Arabella Harvey stands in front of her farmhouse on Red Oak Hill in 1900. Arabella Harvey raised sheep as well as produce. It appears that her carriage is hitched and ready to go, perhaps into town to buy some goods or to a meeting of the Grange.

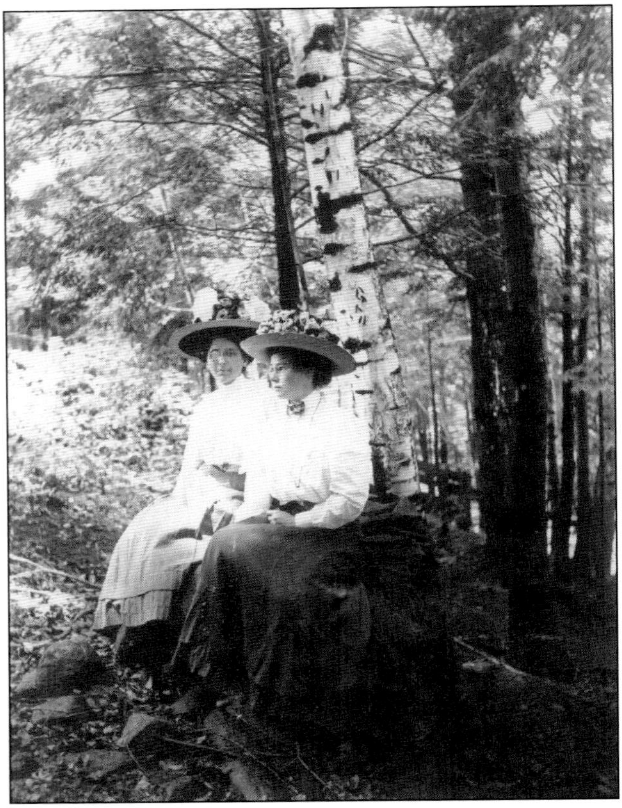

Mary Jenness (left) and Hannah Ahern (right) enjoy the shade of the trees along the banks of the Lamprey River in 1900. The ladies seem to be dressed for the best in their dark skirts, white blouses, and beautifully flowered bonnets.

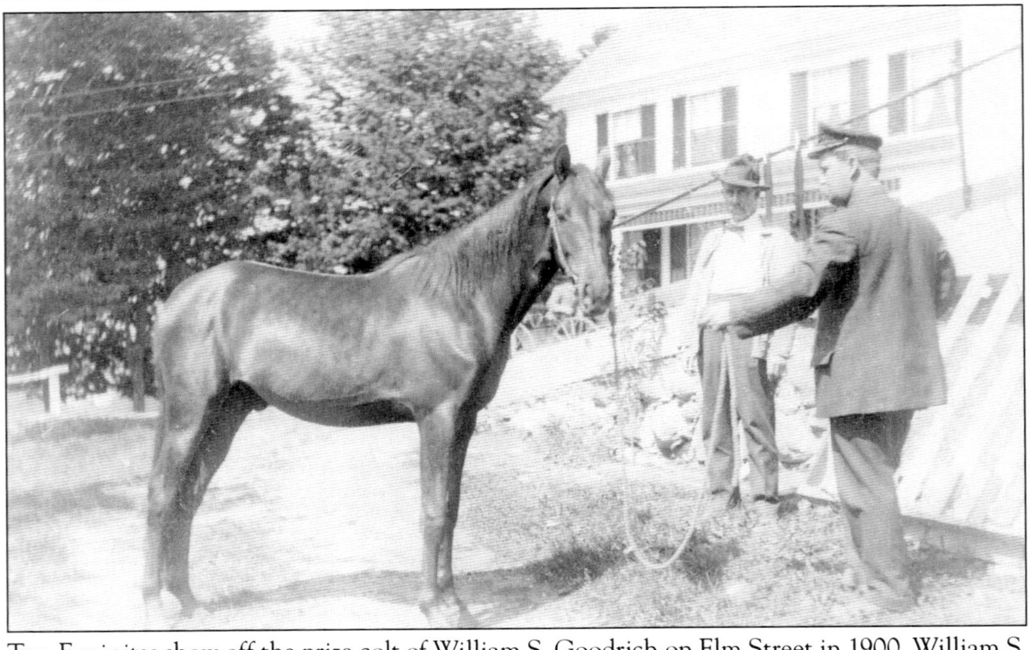

Two Eppinites show off the prize colt of William S. Goodrich on Elm Street in 1900. William S. Goodrich, the owner and founder of the W.S. Goodrich Brickyard, was a successful businessman who could afford horses for both work and pleasure. One of these men might have been Goodrich's groom, the man in charge of tending to the horses.

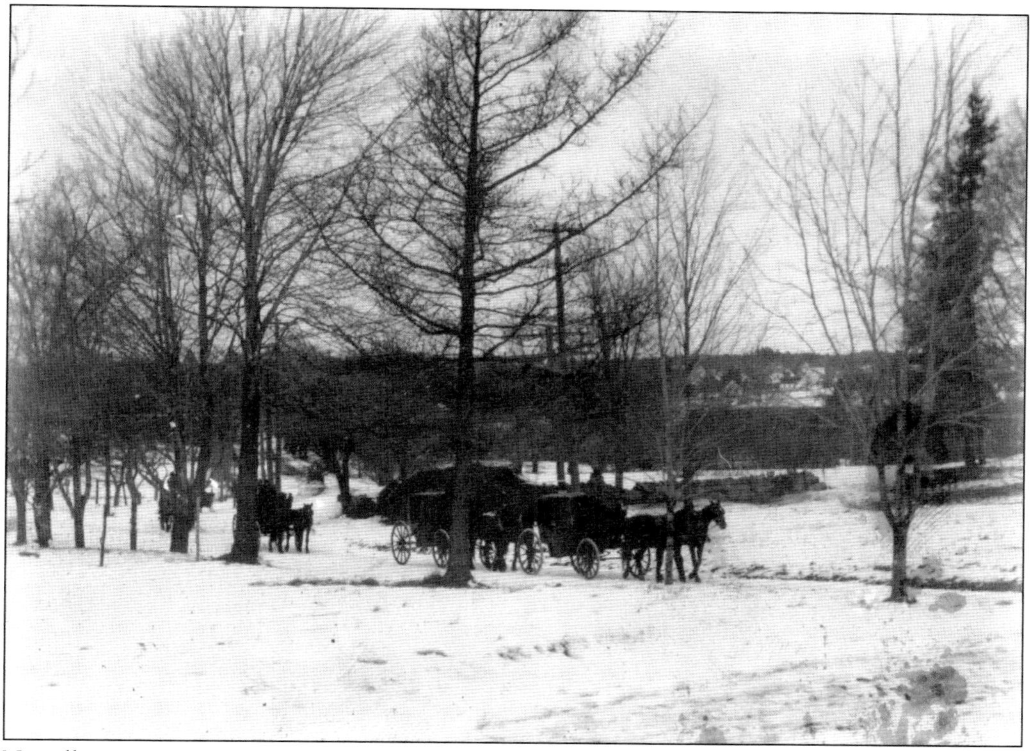

Not all community outings are as pleasant as a boating party or a trip to Great Bay. This funeral procession makes its way past the Chester Goodrich house. While not as joyful as other occasions, funerals have always been an opportunity to remember and appreciate connections in the community.

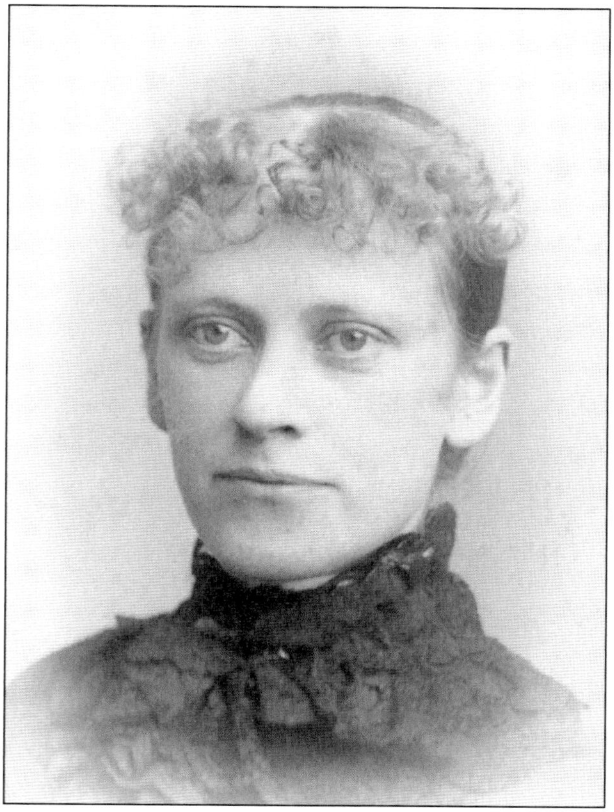

Hattie Chase was the longtime schoolteacher at Watson Academy. A kind and talented teacher, Chase was also a strict disciplinarian. She believed in the use of corporal punishment, and the strip of leather that she used to rap unruly students can be seen at the Epping Historical Society.

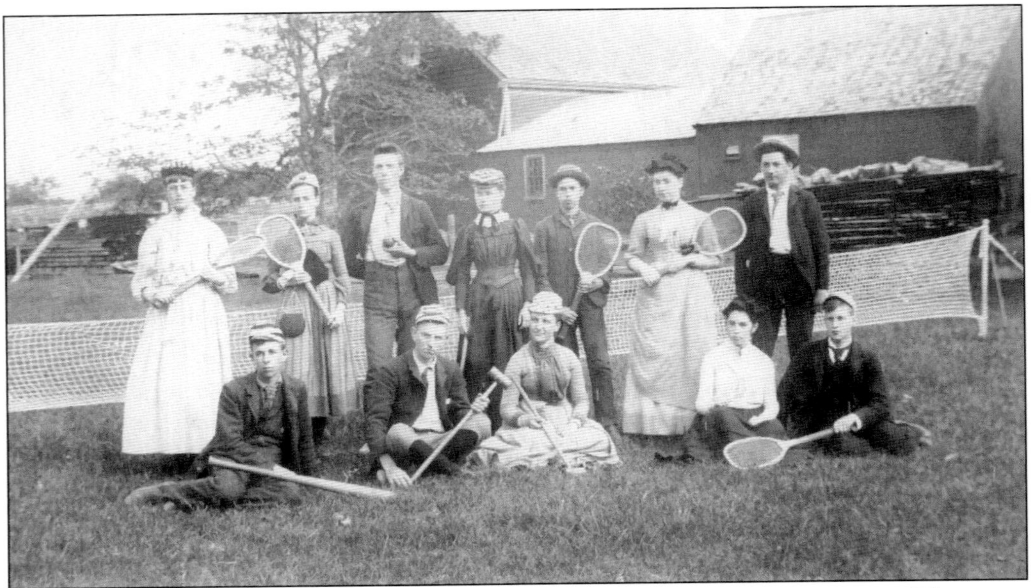

Like many American towns, Eppinites have always enjoyed sports as a favorite pastime. This group of young men and ladies are ready and equipped to play tennis, croquet, and baseball.

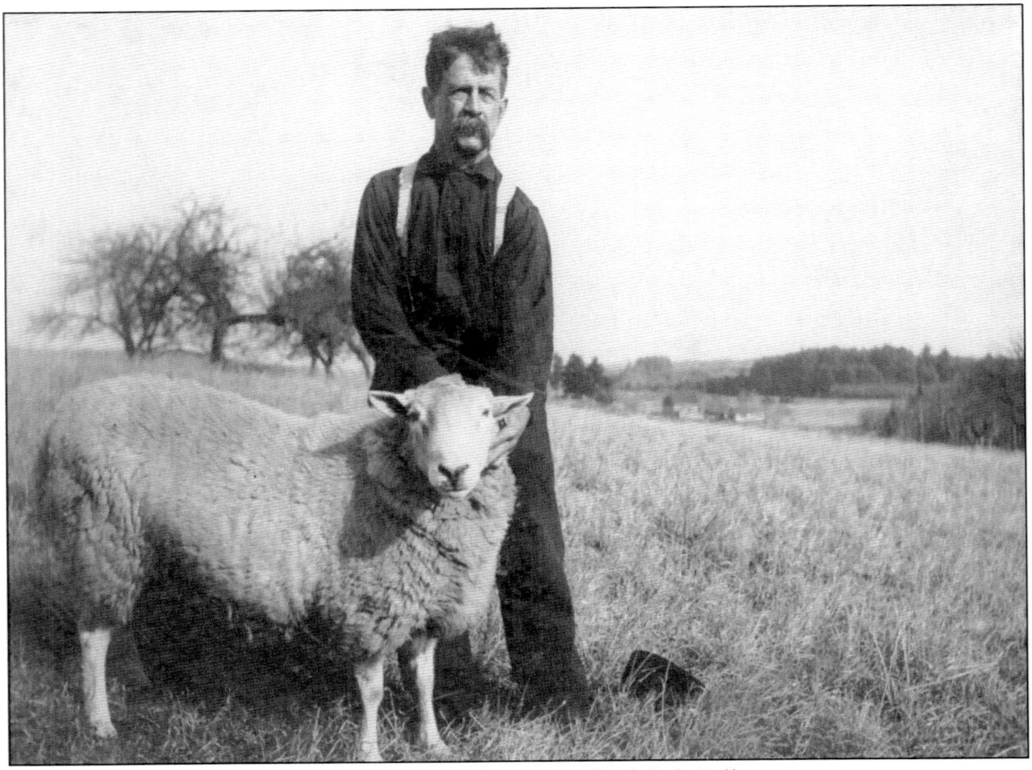

William Whitehouse poses with one of his sheep atop Red Oak Hill.

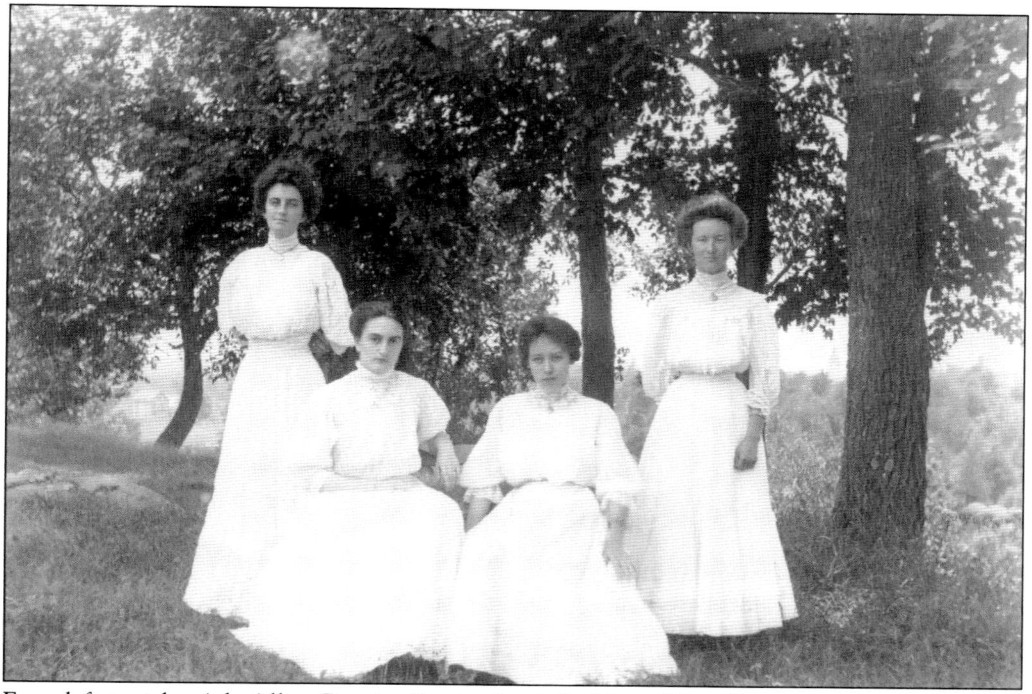

From left to right, Ada Allen, Bernice Swain, Sarah Ladd, and Tina Demerritt pose for a picture in their new white dresses in 1905.

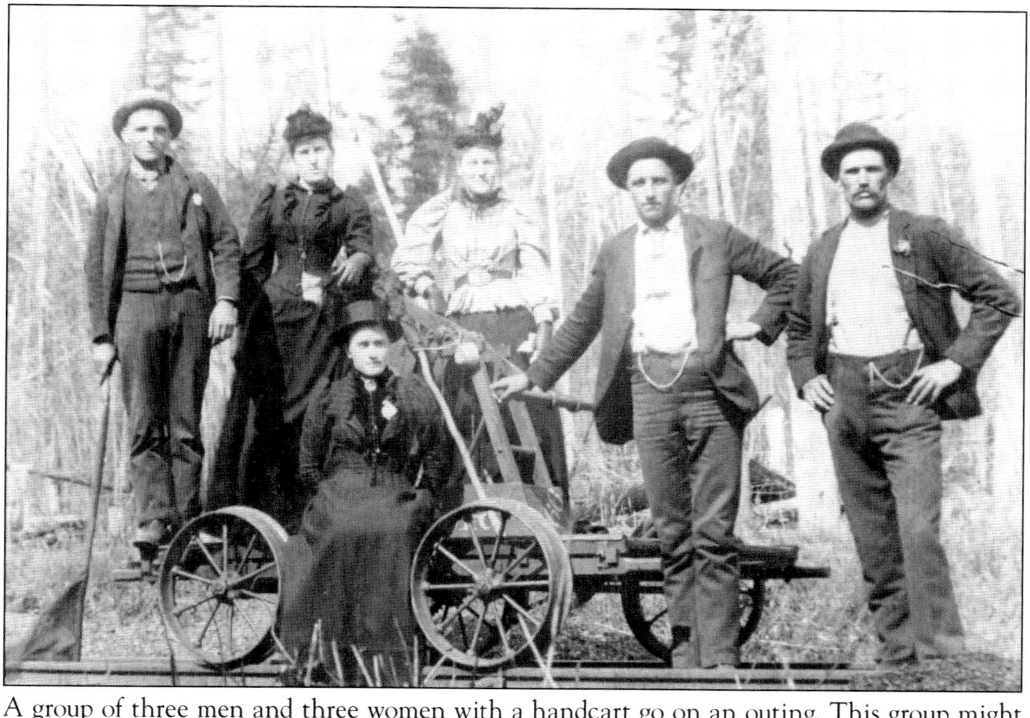

A group of three men and three women with a handcart go on an outing. This group might have been going down the rails for fun, or one or all of these men might have been employed by the rail company to inspect the Epping stretch of rail. The women might have come along as accompaniment for a good bit of fun.

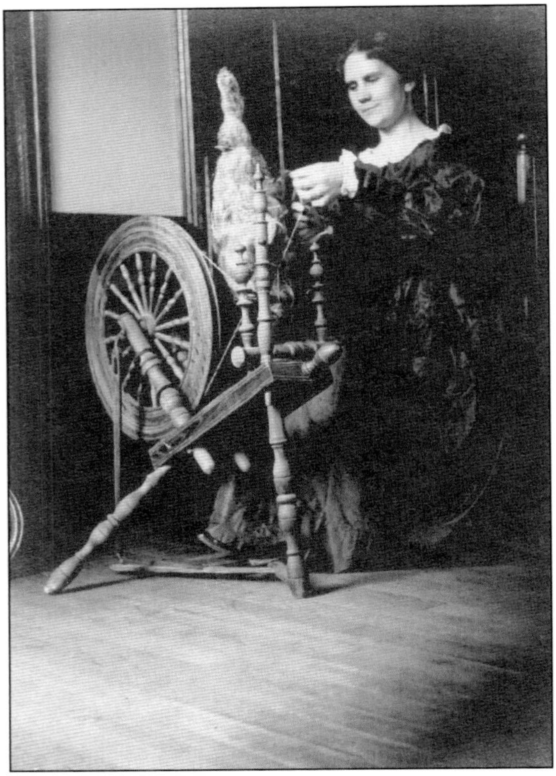

An Epping woman spins wool into yarn. The process of taking raw wool, washing it, carding it, and spinning it was a skill that was passed down from mother to daughter in early America. Before the Industrial Revolution, homespun yarn was the basis for textiles in America. The great woolen mills of New England eventually overcame the need for homespun yarn. Epping became home to a woolen mill in 1840.

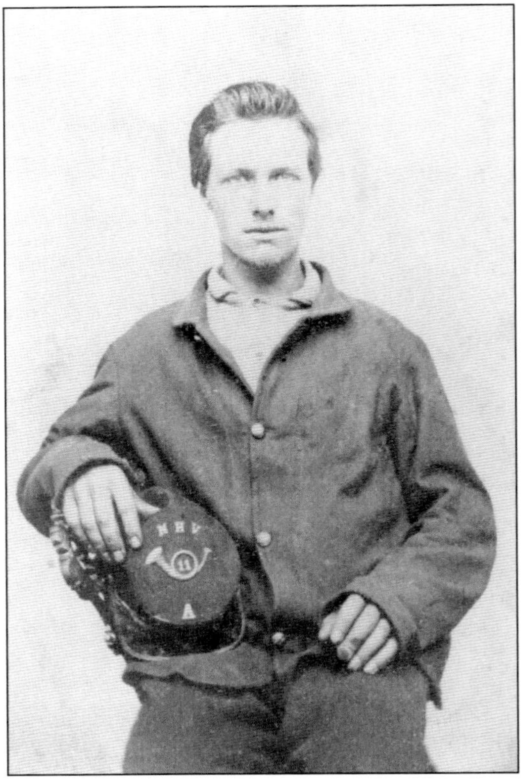

John Ham is pictured here wearing his Civil War uniform of the 11th New Hampshire Regiment, Company A. Company A was mustered into service from August 28, 1862, to June 4, 1865. John Ham was wounded and captured at the Wilderness on May 6, 1864. Ham became one of Epping's Civil War casualties when he died of his wounds on September 28, 1864, while imprisoned at the Confederate prison camp in Florence, South Carolina.

George A. Ham, also of the 11th New Hampshire Regiment, Company A, lived to see the end of the war. Many Civil War veterans had portraits like George Ham's made, marched in parades in their uniforms, and met at large reunions.

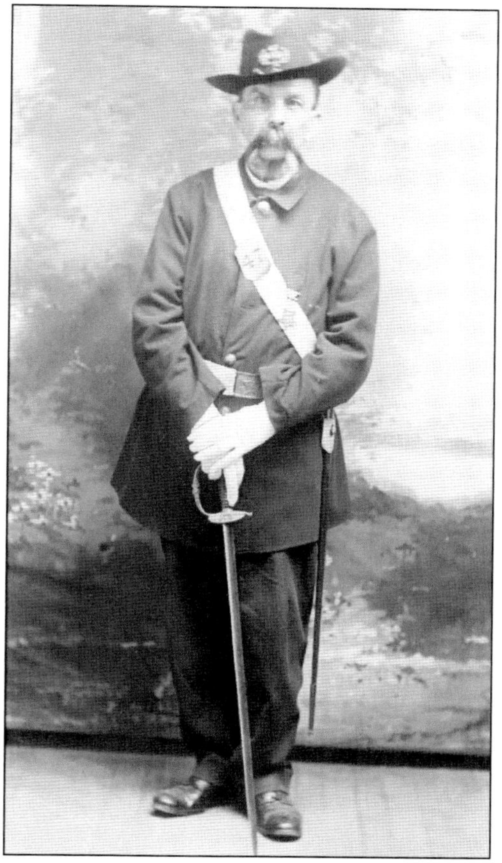

A group of men and ladies gather around one of Epping's Civil War veterans. As Civil War veterans grew into old age, they became romantic figures and revered heroes of the violent past. Civil War veterans were cheered on in parades and often met at reunions, where sometimes Union and Confederate soldiers mixed.

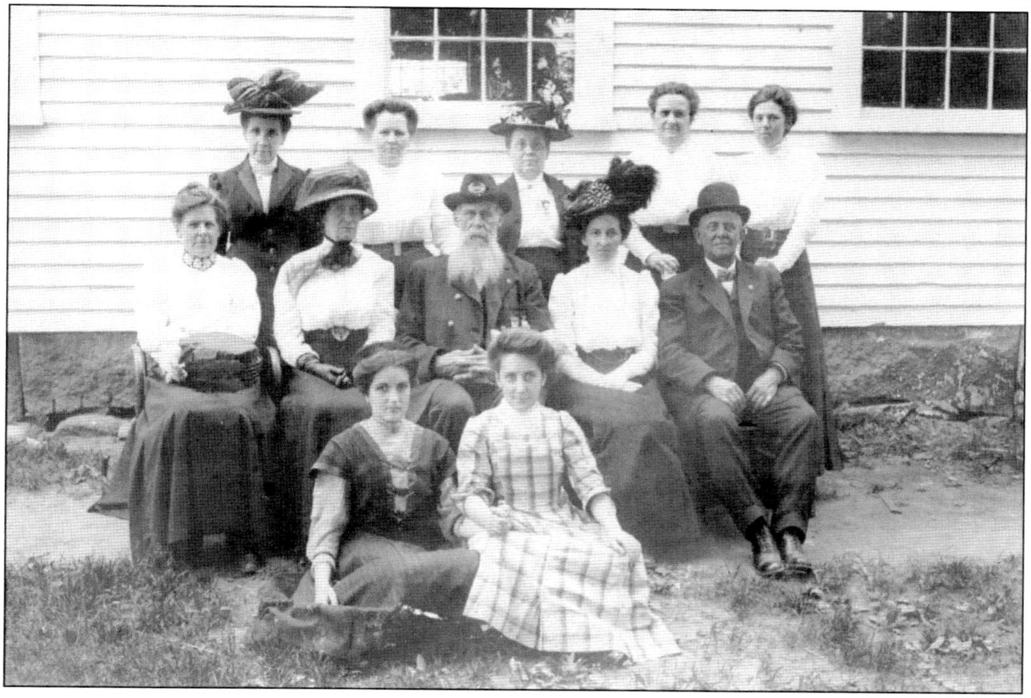

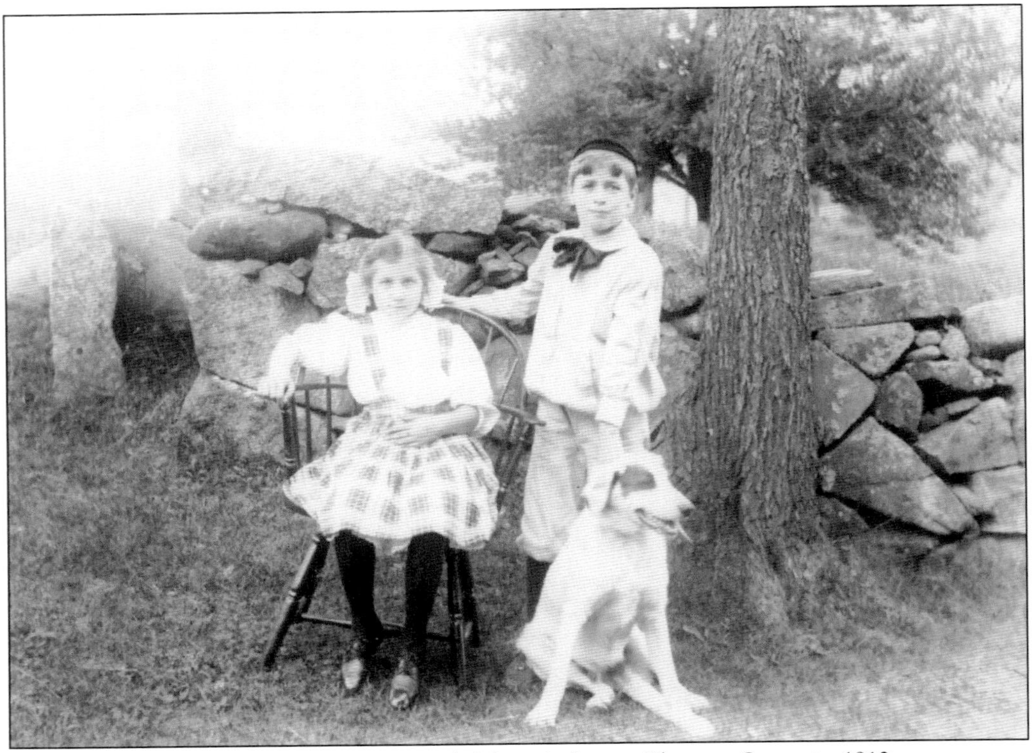

Helen Forgan and Myron Bagley pose with Myron's dog on Pleasant Street in 1910.

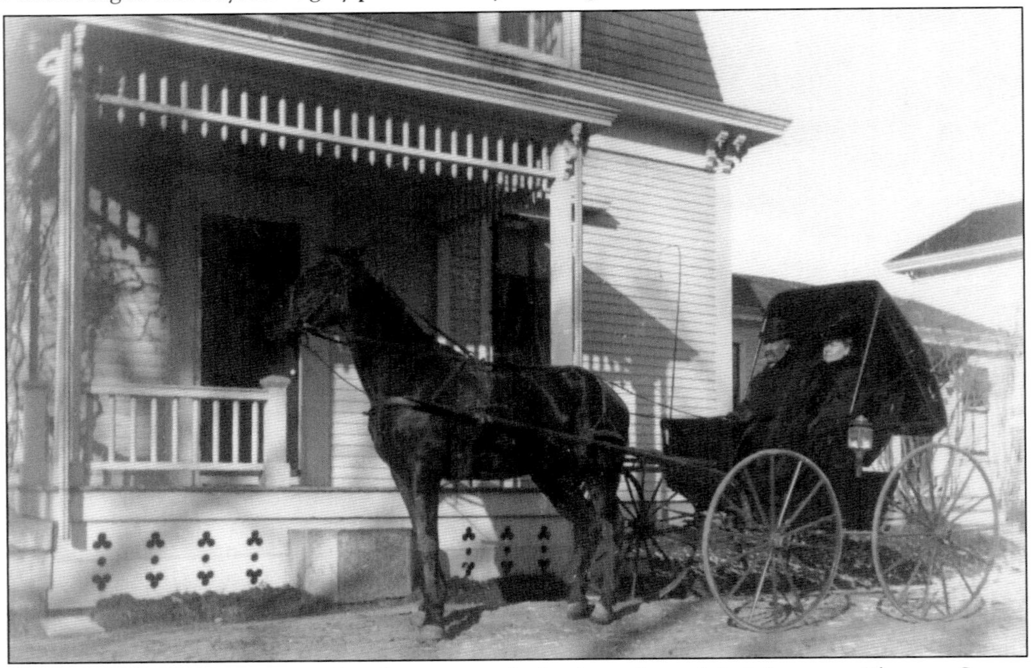

Richard and Ada Morris sit in their buggy outside the front door of their home on Pleasant Street. Richard and Ada were born in England but moved to Epping, where their son was later born. Their son William married another Eppinite, Bernice Ladd, in 1905. The square of granite in front of the horse served as a step to get into and out of the buggy or to get on a horse's back.

Mae Prescott and George Aiken Gilmore take a photograph on their wedding day on August 12, 1903. Weddings at this time were often held in the parlor of a home, as this one seems to have been.

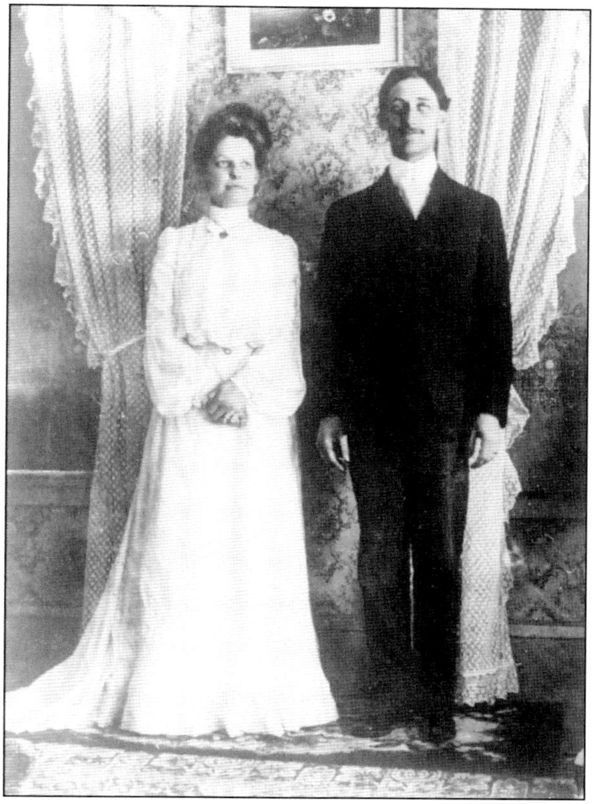

A grandmother and granddaughter pose at the corner of Main and High Streets in 1900.

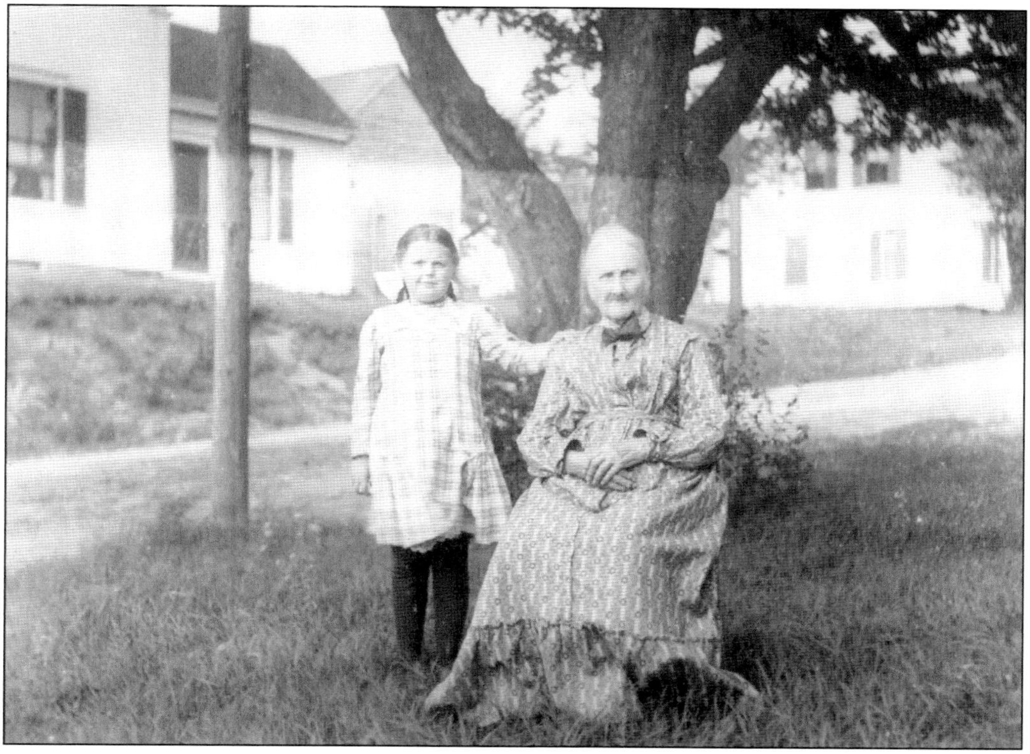

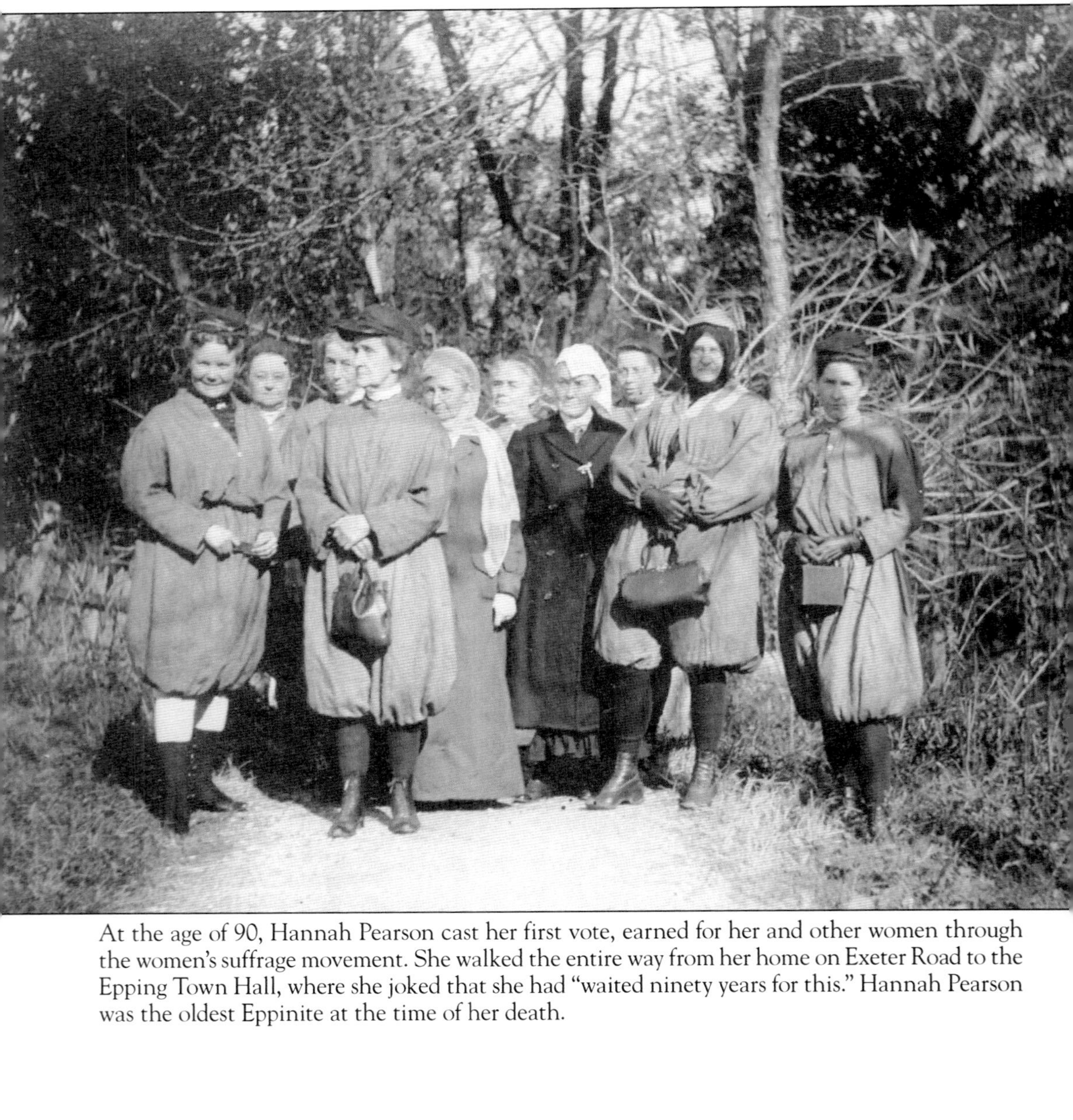

At the age of 90, Hannah Pearson cast her first vote, earned for her and other women through the women's suffrage movement. She walked the entire way from her home on Exeter Road to the Epping Town Hall, where she joked that she had "waited ninety years for this." Hannah Pearson was the oldest Eppinite at the time of her death.

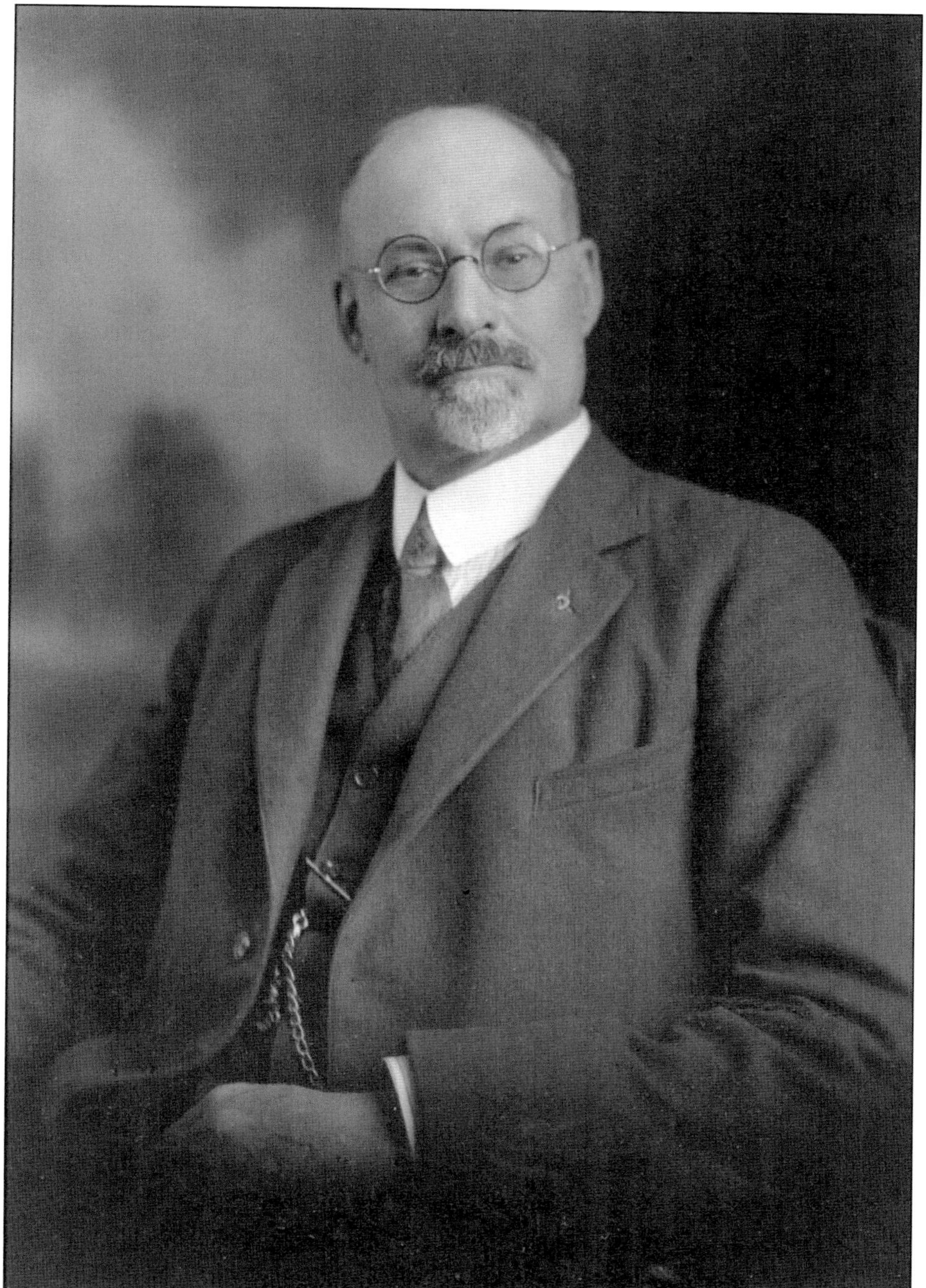

Dr. Abram Mitchell began a medical practice in 1888 that would serve the town of Epping for 47 years. Dr. Mitchell became a beloved figure in the Epping community as he served multiple generations of Eppinites of all ages. He, along with the Harvey family, donated money to help fund the public library, which was later named the Harvey-Mitchell Memorial Library, partly in his honor. The entire community poured into the Methodist Church on August 2, 1935, to attend the respected doctor's funeral. He did not live to see the opening in Brentwood of the county hospital, of which he had been a key supporter. In August 1937, the county hospital opened and was named the Mitchell Memorial Hospital in his honor.

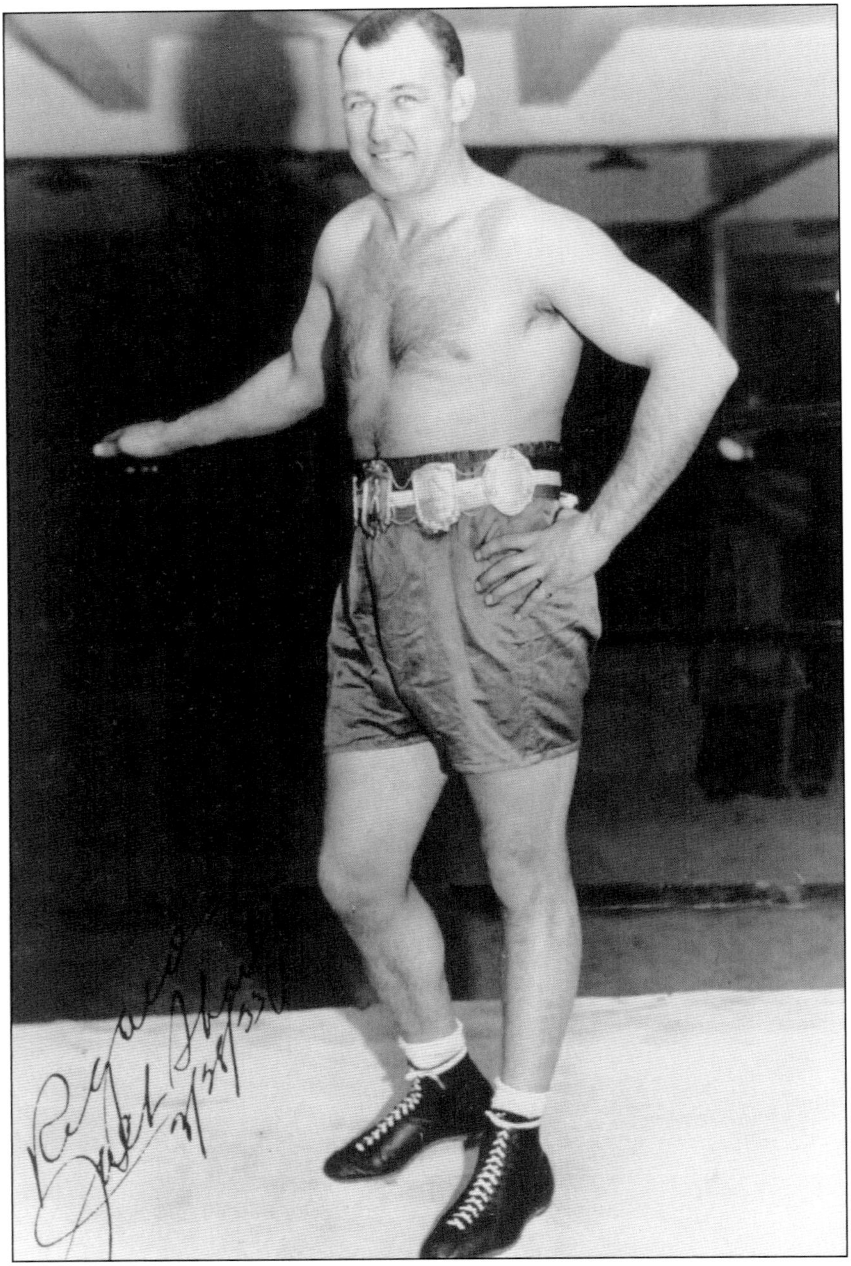

Jack Sharkey, born Joseph Paul Zukauskas on October 26, 1902, grew up in Boston and began boxing as a young man in the Navy. Taking his ring name from Tom Sharkey and Jack Dempsey, two of his boxing idols, Jack Sharkey had a breakout year in 1927. Sharkey won some important fights that year and ended up in the ring with his idol, Jack Dempsey. Sharkey lost that fight but went on to beat Tommy Loughran to win the US heavyweight title in 1929 at Yankee Stadium. On June 21, 1932, Jack Sharkey defeated Max Schmeling by split decision to become the World Heavyweight Champion at the Madison Square Garden Bowl. Jack Sharkey moved to Epping in his retirement, purchasing a house on Pleasant Street near downtown. He spent time in New Hampshire fishing with fellow fly fisherman Ted Williams. Sharkey could be seen every morning running for miles all over Epping as he tried to maintain his boxing fitness.

A parade marches down Main Street in 1932. Taken from in front of the town hall, looking north on Main Street, the photograph shows the parade stopped on the Main Street bridge. The selectmen are probably performing a wreath-laying ceremony in the Lamprey River, as they still do during Epping's annual Memorial Day Parade.

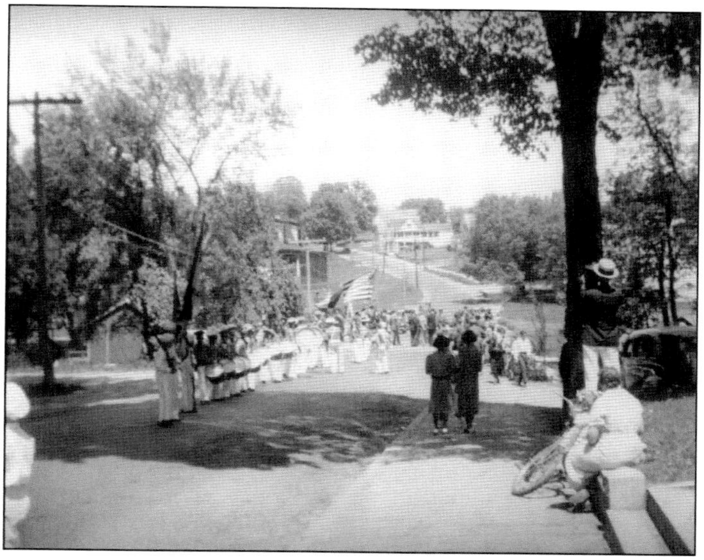

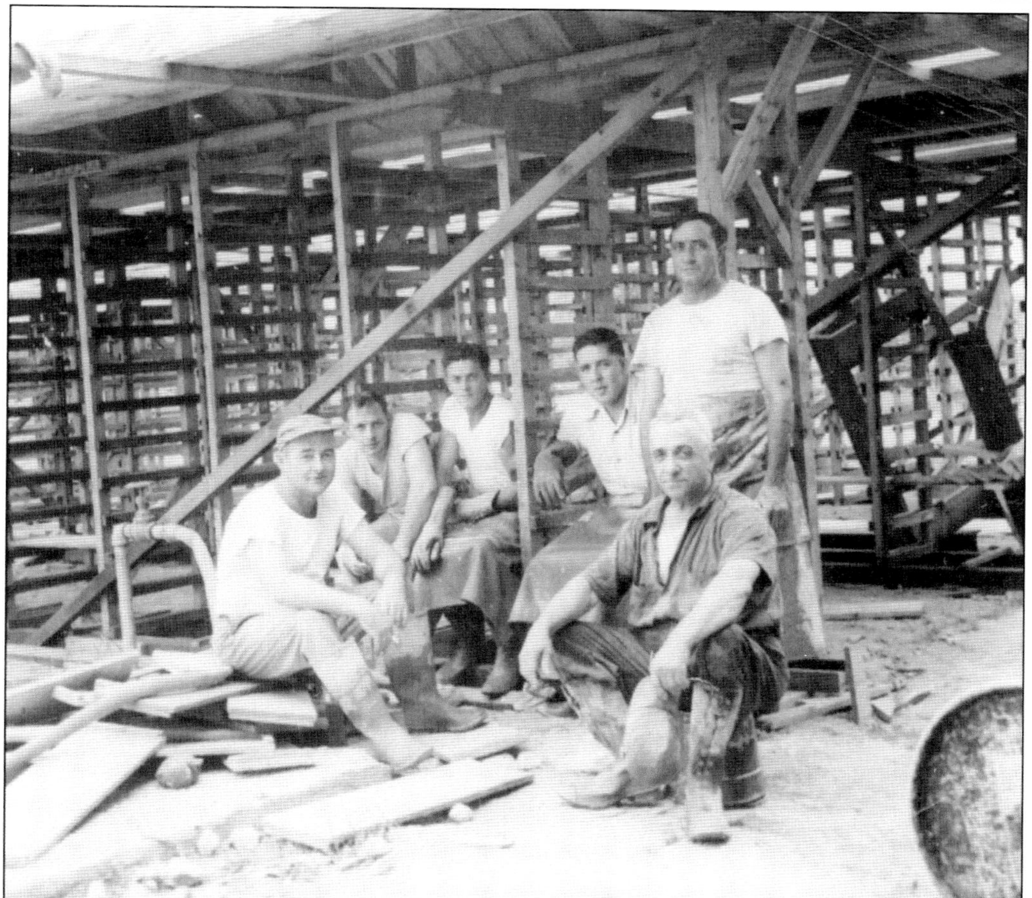

From left to right, Henry Dionne, unidentified, Tommy Jean, George Levesque, Armand Gagnon, and Dante Burgoune take a break from the long, hot day as they sit among the drying racks at the W.S. Goodrich Brickyard. (Courtesy of Robert Goodrich.)

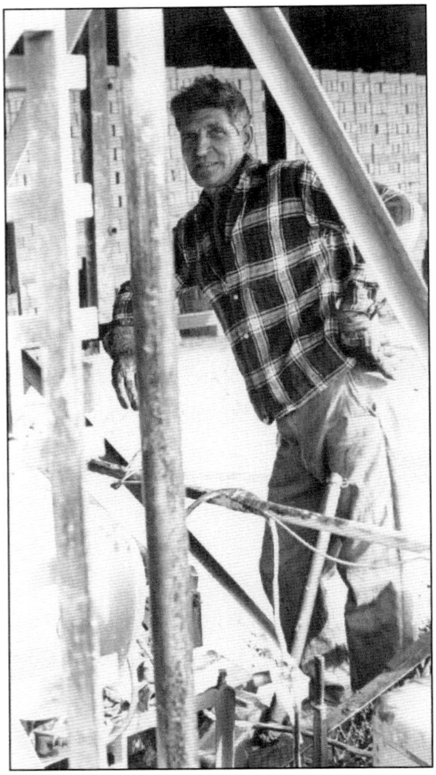

A longtime Eppinite, Chester "Chet" Kinnart leans against the "mule," a piece of equipment used for moving bricks to the drying racks, at W.S. Goodrich Brickyard. Before working at the brickyard, Chet Kinnart owned and operated a sawmill in the neighboring town of Fremont. After retiring from the brickyard, Chet opened a garage next to his home on Railroad Avenue that serviced Epping's automobiles. (Courtesy of Robert Goodrich.)

Judge Kendall Chase served as the judge for the Epping Municipal Court for 25 years. Kendall Chase was appointed to preside over the court by Gov. Wesley Powell in 1958, having no legal training. In 1963, the State of New Hampshire formed district courts, eliminating the municipal courts that had been established in 1915. Any town with a population greater than 2,000 was required to have a municipal court. Judge Chase was grandfathered in when the municipal courts were ended in 1963, keeping the Epping Municipal Court going every Saturday morning in the town hall until his retirement. Judge Chase was considered an honest and fair judge, and when he retired, he received letters of congratulations and appreciation from the governor of New Hampshire, US senators, the director of the Federal Bureau of Investigation, and Pres. George H.W. Bush.

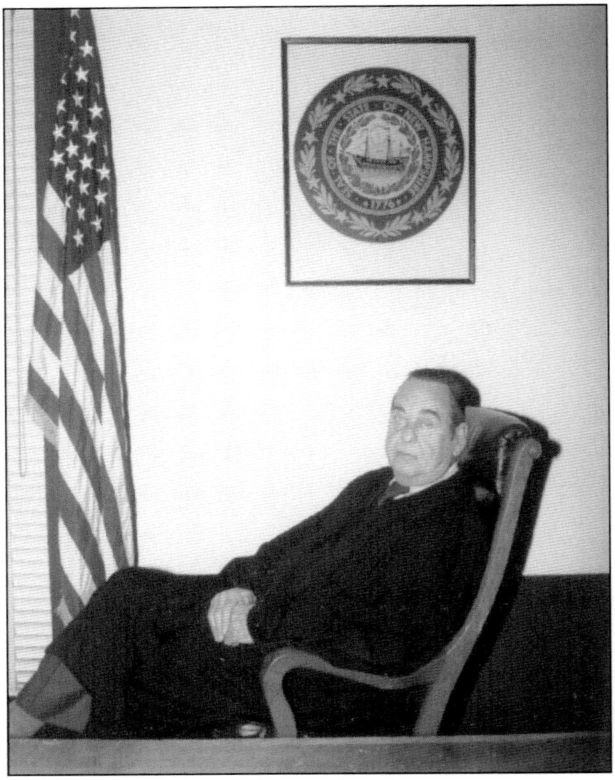

# Bibliography


Robertson, James A. *Hedding Among the Pines: A History of the Hedding Meeting Grounds Epping, New Hampshire*. Exeter, NH: Publishing Works, 2008.

Sanborn, Richard B. *A Bicentennial History of Epping New Hampshire*. Seabrook, NH: Withey Press Inc., 1976.

Consistent with our mission to preserve history on a local level, this book was printed in South Carolina on American-made paper and manufactured entirely in the United States. Products carrying the accredited Forest Stewardship Council (FSC) label are printed on 100 percent FSC-certified paper.

MADE IN THE USA